Windows 10 Simplified Vol 2

Guides to Fix Advanced Windows 10 Problems

By Victor ASHIEDU

Sign up to my Windows 10 mailing list

Want more useful Windows 10 guides? Visit this link to sign up to Itechguides' Windows 10 mailing list:

Itechguides.com/subscribe-windows-10/

Table of Contents

How to fix "The Active Directory Domain Services is Currently Unavailable"

The error message "The Active Directory Domain Services is Currently Unavailable" could be received in any of the following situations:

1. When you try to add a printer from an application like Microsoft Word or Excel.
2. Sometimes when you try to print.

The following could cause this error message:

1. When you try adding a printer from an application like excel or word
2. The Printer spooler service stopped or needs to be restarted.
3. The Printer driver is out of date and needs to be updated

Based on the possible causes of the error message, below are your options to resolve this annoying error message:

Method 1: Add a Printer Using the Printer Wizard

The most common cause of this error message occurs when you try to add a printer from an application like Microsoft Word or Excel. The solution is to add your printer using the add printer wizard instead of trying to add the printer directly from the application.

Info
If your printer was shipped to you with a CD, the driver will likely be on the CD. Otherwise, you may need to download your printer driver from the internet. The easiest way to find your printer driver is to search "<replace this and the brackets with the name of your-printer> driver" on Google.

Here is how you add a printer in Windows 10

- Type **Control Panel** in the Windows 10 search bar. Then click it in the search result.

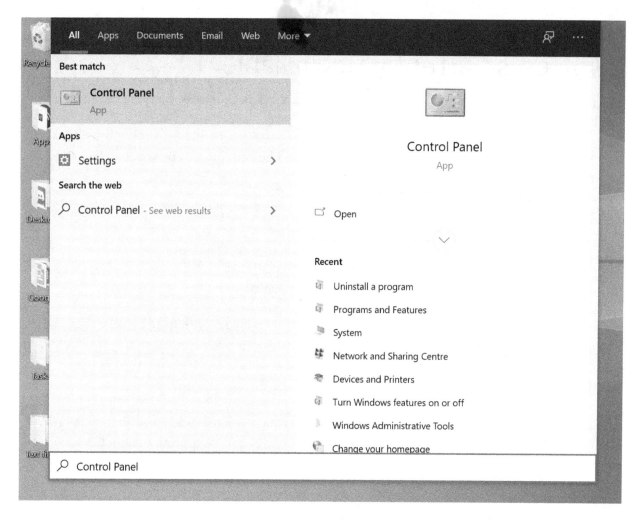

- When Control Panel opens, at the **Hardware and Sound** category, click **View devices and printers**.

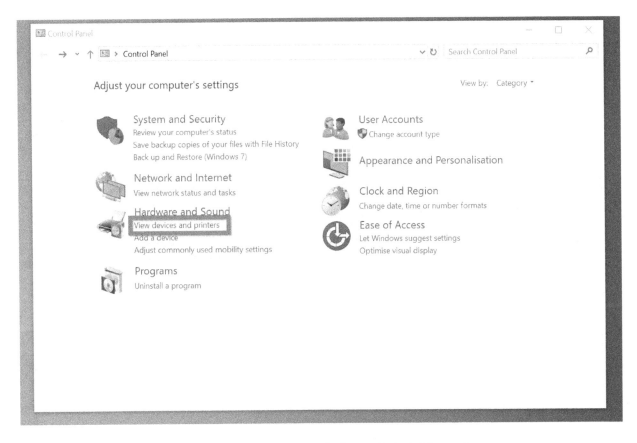

- On the top left of **Devices and Printers** window, click **Add a printer**.

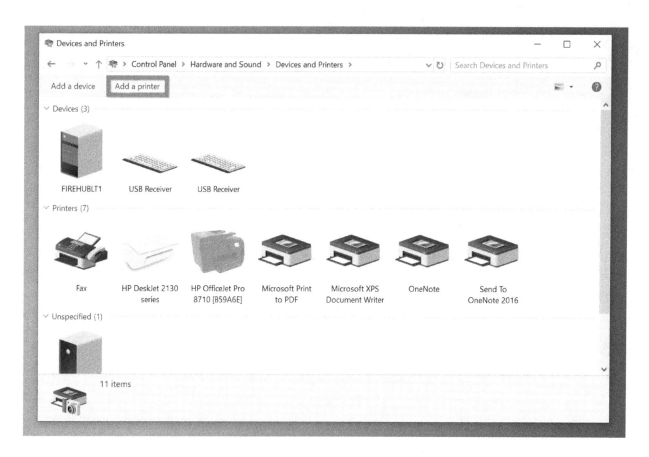

- If your printer is not listed (as shown below), click **The printer that I want isn't listed**. This will load the add printer wizard. The Add printer wizard will open.

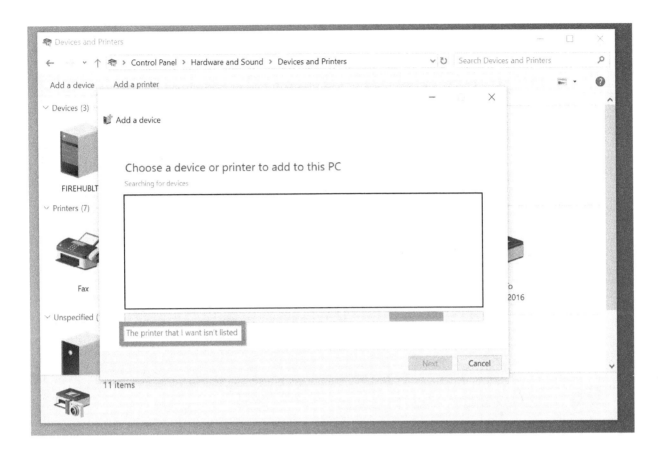

- Select the option that applies to you then click Next to install your printer.

Important Tip

If you are installing a printer on your home computer, you are likely to select the last 2 options. Otherwise, if you are adding a printer in a corporate office, options 2 and 3 will most likely suite your needs.

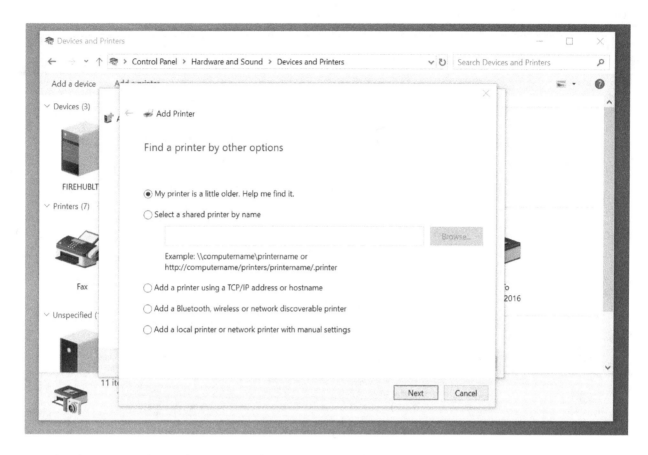

Method 2: Start the Printer Spooler Service and set it to Automatic.

The second potential cause of the "The Active Directory Domain Services is Currently Unavailable" Error message is spooler service.

To see the status of your printer spooler service and restart or start it, follow the steps below:

- Right-click the Windows logo on the left corner of your taskbar and select **Computer Management**.

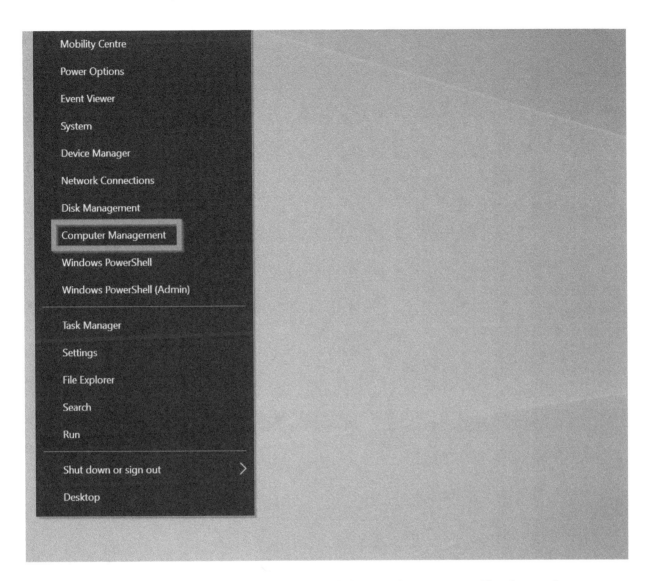

- On **Computer Management** console, expand the **Services and Application** node.

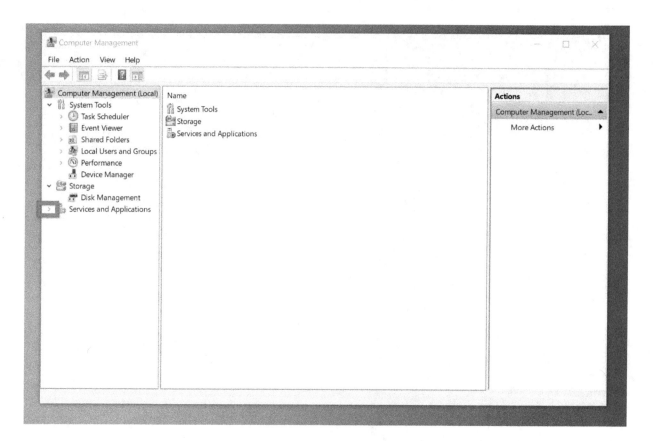

- Then click the **Services** node.

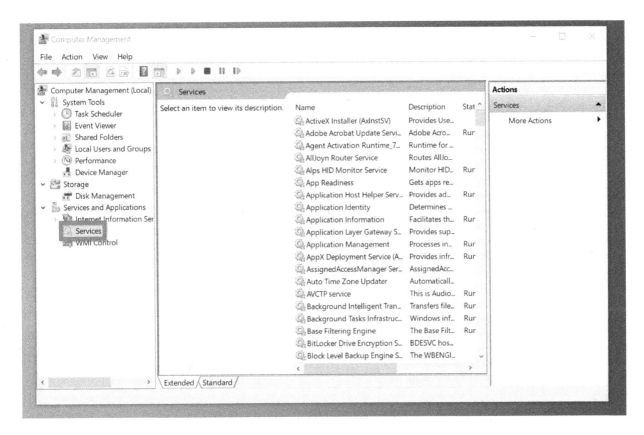

- Finally, on the right pane of the services node, locate and double-click the **Printer Spooler** service. The properties of the Print Spooler service will open.

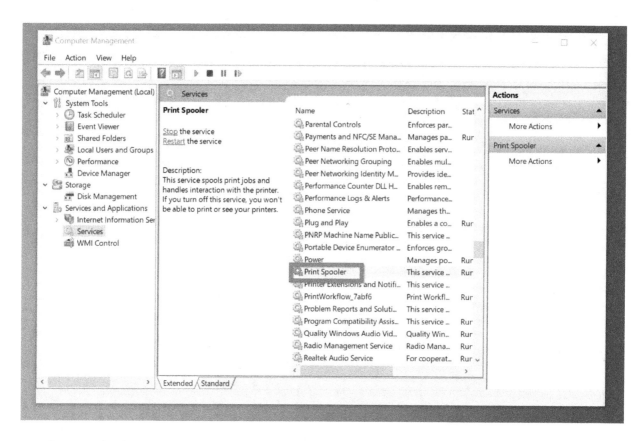

- Ensure the **Startup type** is *Automatic*. If the **Service status** is **Stopped**, click **Start** to restart the service. Finally, click OK to save your changes.

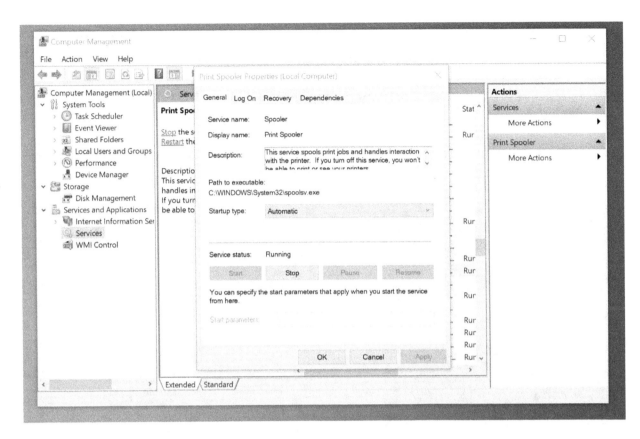

If the above methods do not resolve the "The Active Directory Domain Services is Currently Unavailable" Error for you then try the last method described next.

Method 3: To Resolve "The Active Directory Domain Services is Currently Unavailable" Error, Update the Printer Driver.

Here is my final recommended fix for "The Active Directory Domain Services is Currently Unavailable":

- **Right-click** Windows 10 Start Menu (Windows logo on the left of your taskbar). From the displayed menu options, click **Device Manager**.

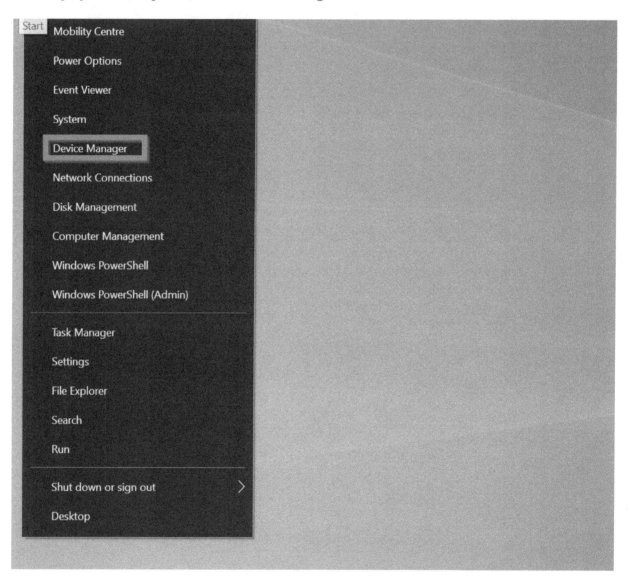

- When **Device Manager** opens, locate the **Printers** group and expand it.

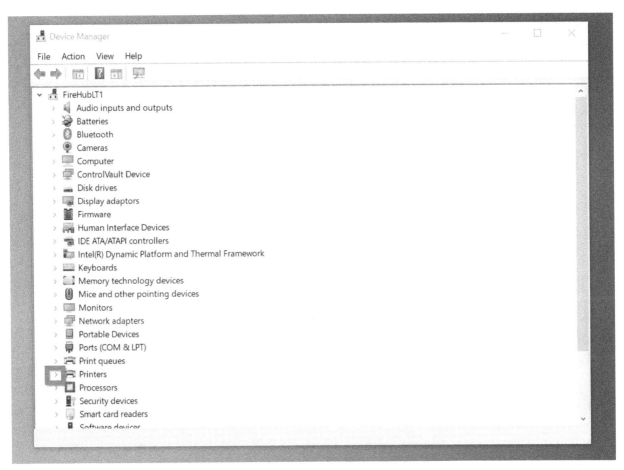

- **Right-click** your printer and click **Update Driver.**

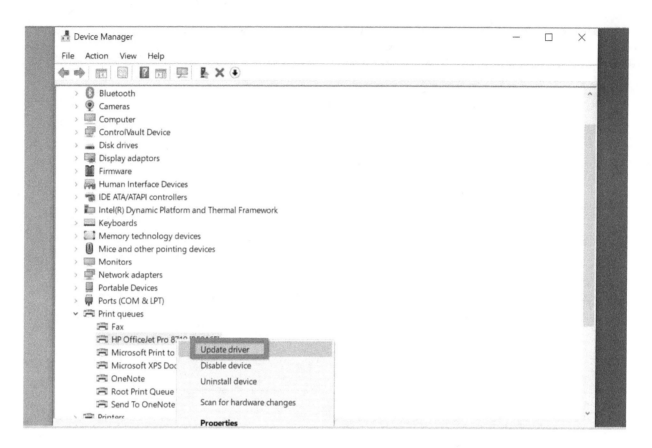

- Click the first option..."**search automatically for updated driver software**...". If that option does not update your printer driver, download the driver. Then use option 2 to update the driver manually.

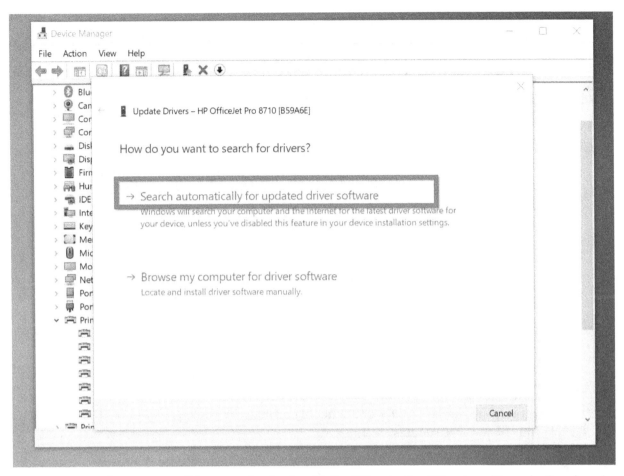

From my experience, one of these methods should fix "The Active Directory Domain Services is Currently Unavailable" Error message.

How to fix "DNS Server Not Responding" Windows 10 Error

What Could Cause "DNS Server Not Responding" Error Message?

The error messages "DNS Server Not Responding" or "DNS server is unavailable" may be caused by the following:

1. You are not connected to your wireless router or your network cable is disconnected.
2. Your DNS Server IP address may be wrong.
3. You may not have picked an IP address
4. Your network card driver may be out of date

Below, I have listed the high-level solutions that will resolve the error message "DNS Server Not Responding" or "DNS server is unavailable"

1. Run the "Identify and Fix Network problem" wizard
2. Reconnect to your wireless router or connect your network cable
3. Check your IP and DNS address settings
4. Disable and Enable your network card
5. Restart your router
6. Update your network card driver
7. Temporarily Turn off firewalls
8. Turn off Antivirus
9. Check that Flight mode is off
10. Restart your computer

First Solution: Run the "Identify and Fix Network problem" Wizard

Performing the steps in this method may help resolve most network-related problems including "DNS Server Not Responding" or "DNS server is unavailable" Error Messages.

Here is how you use this method in Windows 10:

- Type *Network problems* in the Windows 10 search bar. Then select either **Identify and Fix Network problems or Find and Fix Network problems.** The result depends on your Windows 10 version.

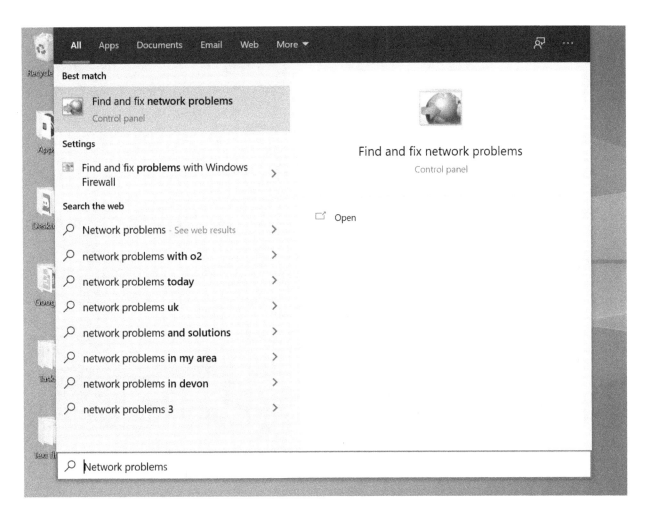

- When the "Troubleshoot and help prevent computer problems" wizard opens, click Next.

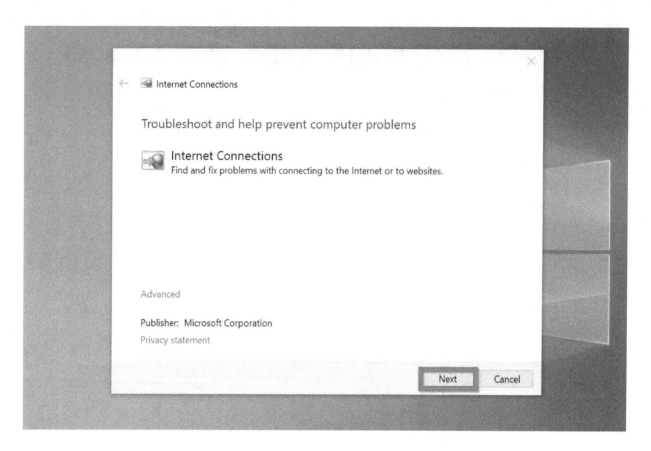

- Give the wizard time to complete initial diagnostics.

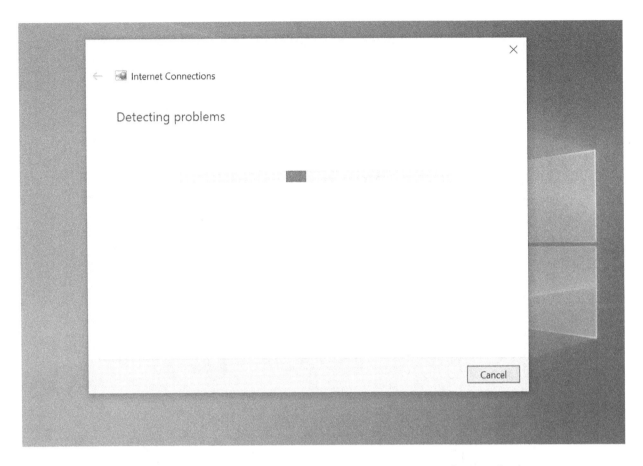

- On the next screen, select the first option, **Troubleshoot my connection to the internet**.

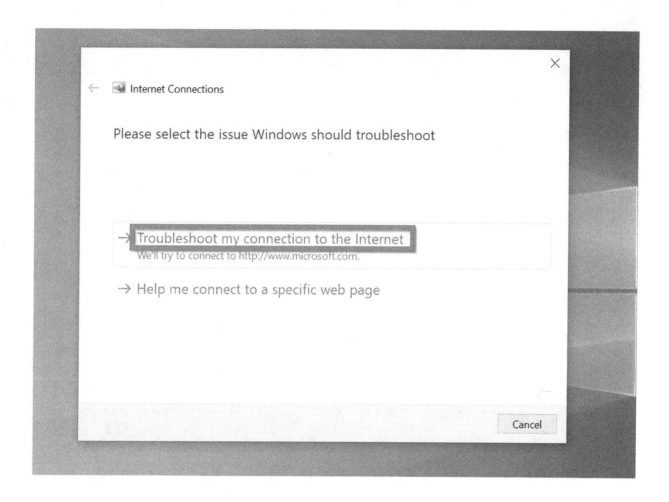

- The troubleshooter will attempt to detect problems with your internet connection.

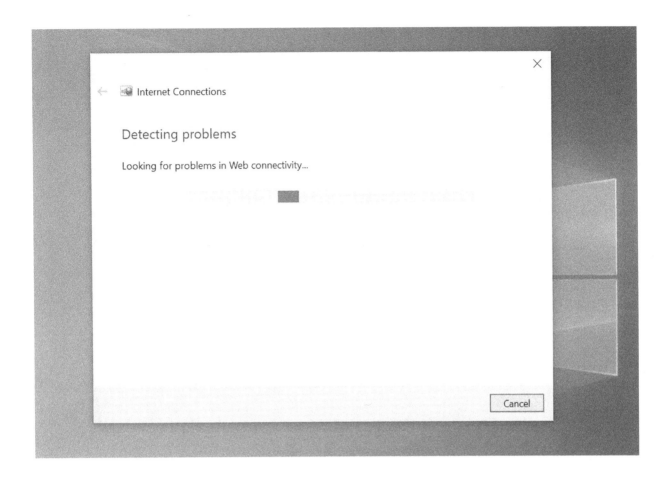

- When it finishes, it will return results. If it finds a problem, follow the wizard to fix it. Otherwise, if it returned a result like the image below, proceed to the next fix…

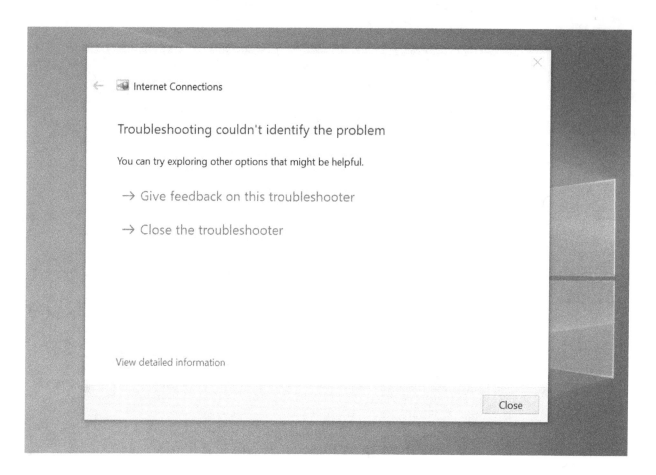

Second Solution: Reconnect to Your Wireless Router or Connect Your Network Cable.

The next possible cause of "DNS Server Not Responding" or "DNS server is unavailable" error messages could be that you are not connected to your wireless router. Also, if you use a physical cable, it may be disconnected.

Follow the steps below to check your network connection status:

- If you use a wireless router, check the connection status on the bottom right corner of your taskbar - close to your time. If you are not connected, the wireless status will be greyed out. See image below:

- If your Wifi is grayed out, ensure you are connected to your WiFi.
- When you successfully connect to your Wi-Fi, the Wi-Fi status will "lit up". See the image below.

- Alternatively, if you use a cable to connect your computer to the internet, and the status looks like the image below, then you have a problem with your connection. If this is your situation, check that your network cable is properly connected to your computer.

- On the other hand, if the status of your network card is as shown below, then you are connected to the internet.
- If your network card is as shown but you still can't connect to the internet, you may need to consult your Internet Service Provider (ISP) or your System Administrator.

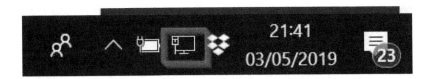

Third Solution: Check your IP and DNS address settings

The next possible cause of the error message "DNS Server Not Responding" or "DNS server is unavailable" could be the wrong settings in your TCP/IPv4 IP and DNS settings.

Here is how you can resolve this problem:

- Search for **Control Panel** and click to open it.

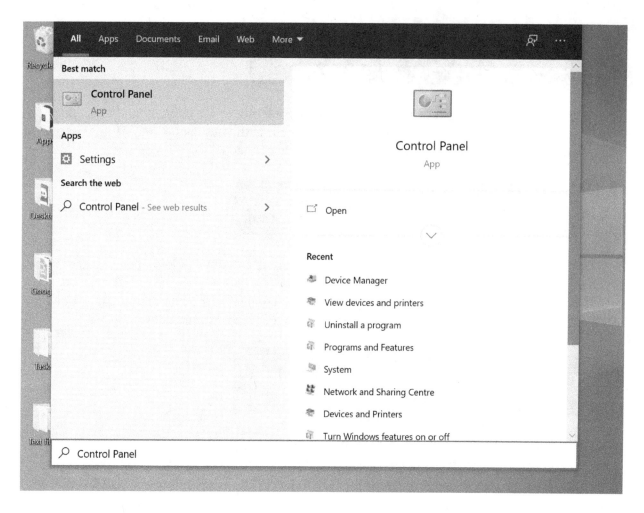

- When Control Panel opens, on the **Network and Internet** group, click **View network status and tasks**.

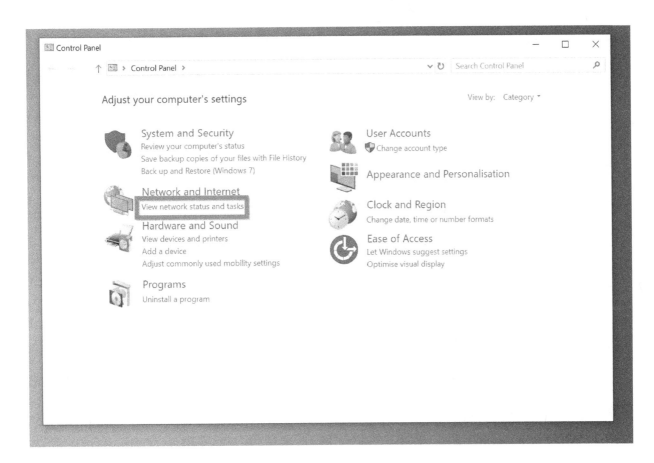

- Then, click **Change adapter settings**.

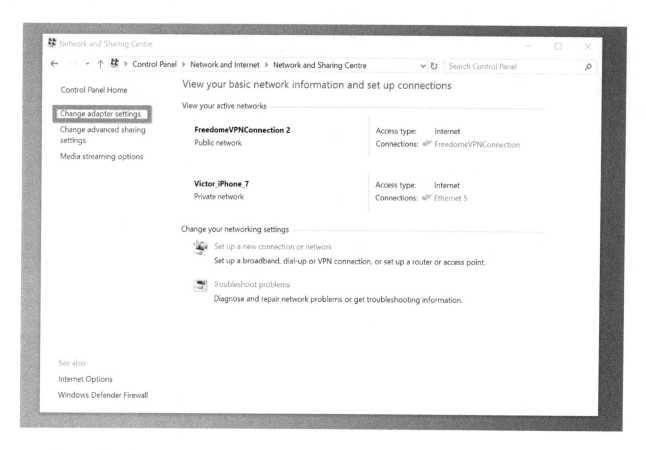

- **Right-click** the adapter you use to connect to the internet and select **Properties**.

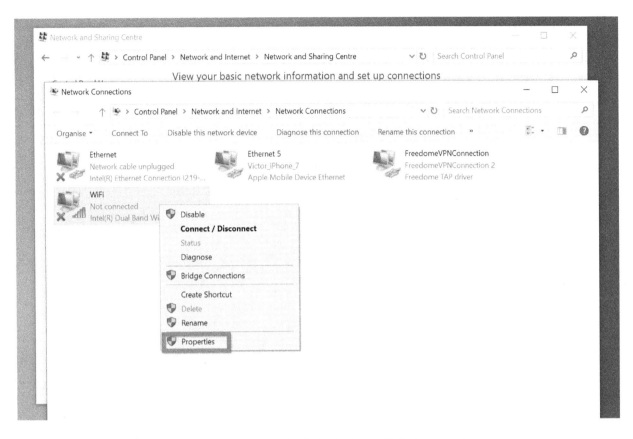

- Highlight **Internet Protocol Version 4 (TCP/IPv4)** then click **Properties**.

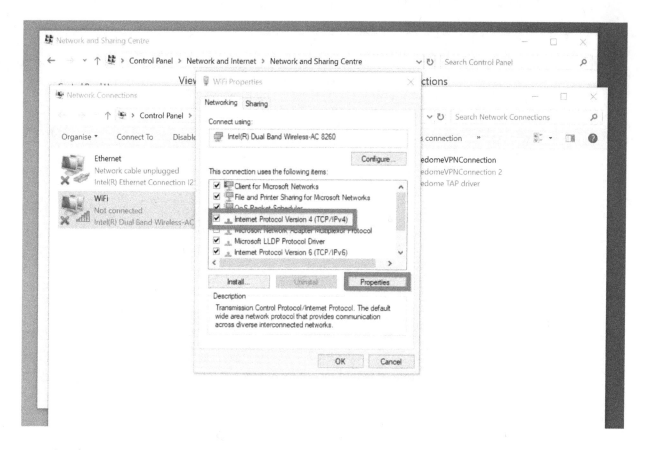

- On the **Internet Protocol Version 4 (TCP/IPv4)** Properties, confirm that yours is set up as shown below. If yours is different from the image below, modify it as shown. Then click OK to save your changes.

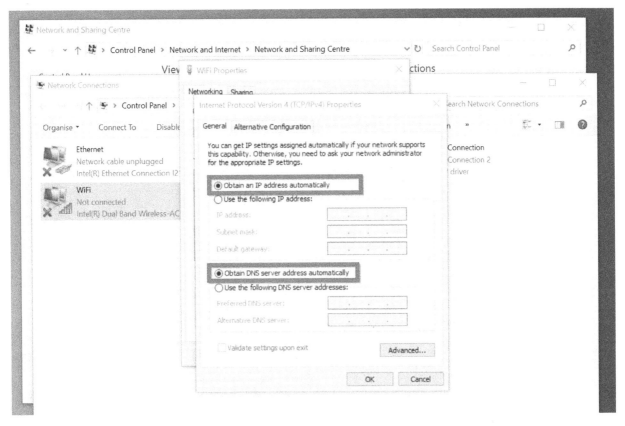

Important Note

By setting "Obtain an IP address automatically" and "Obtain DNS server address automatically" your router will issue the correct addresses.

Check whether the error is fixed. If not, try the next fix.

Fourth Solution: To Resolve "DNS Server Not Responding" error, Disable and Enable your network card

Resetting your network card settings may resolve the "DNS Server Not Responding" error message.

Here are the steps to help you perform this task:

- Search for **Control Panel** and click to open it.

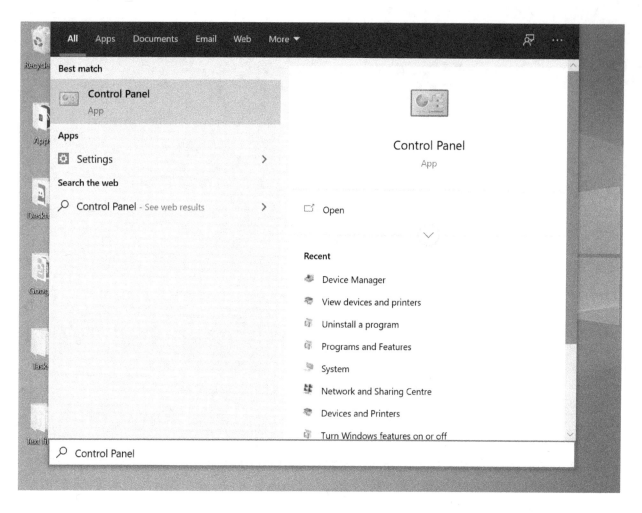

- When Control Panel opens, on the **Network and Internet** group, click **View network status and tasks**.

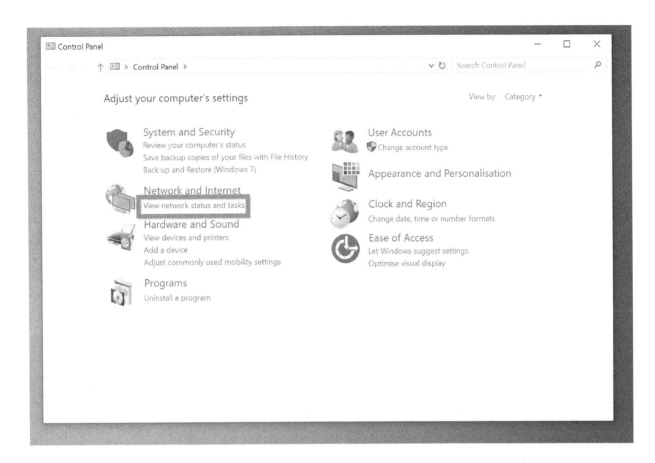

- Then, click **Change adapter settings**.

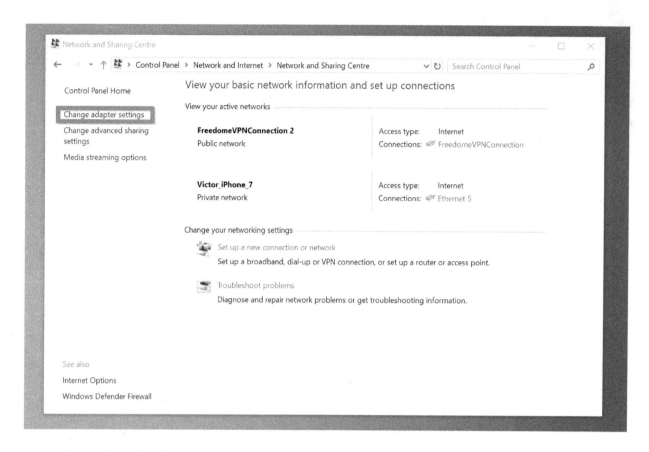

- **Right-click** the adapter you use to connect to the internet and click **Disable** – this will disable your Wi-Fi.

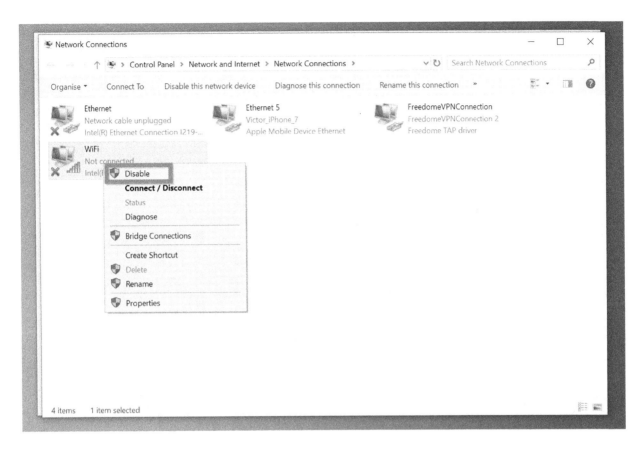

- Right-click the disabled Wi-Fi and click **Enable**.

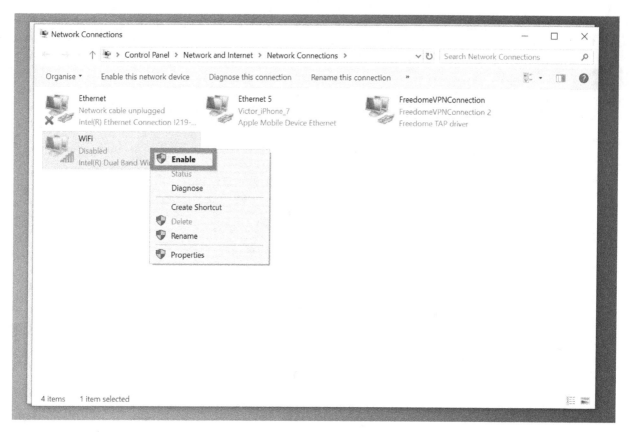

Disabling and re-enabling your Wi-Fi effectively forces it to reconnect to the router and refresh its IP settings.

Check to see if the "DNS Server Not Responding" error. If not, try the next fix.

Fifth Solution: To fix "DNS Server Not Responding" error, Restart your router

Another quick solution to the "DNS Server Not Responding" error message is to restart your internet router. This solution is very straight-forward. Simply turn off your Wi-Fi router and turn it back on. When it comes back on try connecting to the internet. If the error message still appears, try my next recommended solution.

Important Tip
For most routers (or modems), the power switch should be behind or underneath the router.

Sixth Solution: Update your Network Card driver

My next solution for the "DNS server is unavailable" error message is to update your network card driver. The steps below will guide you through the steps:

- **Right-click** Windows 10 Start Menu (Windows logo on the left of your taskbar). From the displayed menu options, click **Device Manager**.

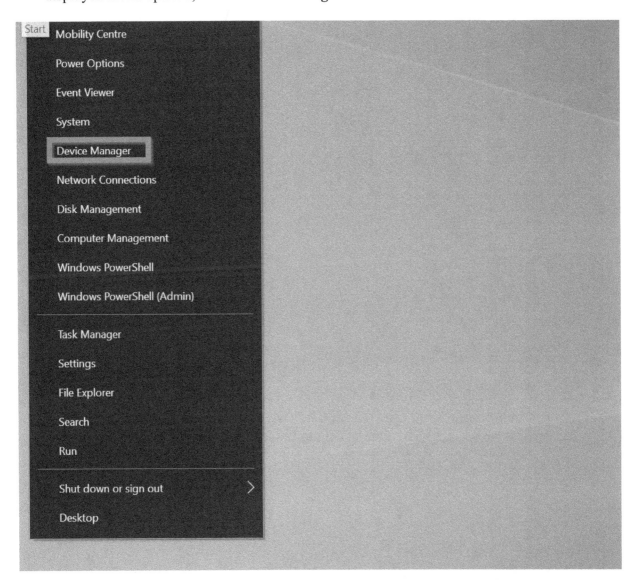

- When **Device Manager** opens, locate the **Network adapters** group and expand it.

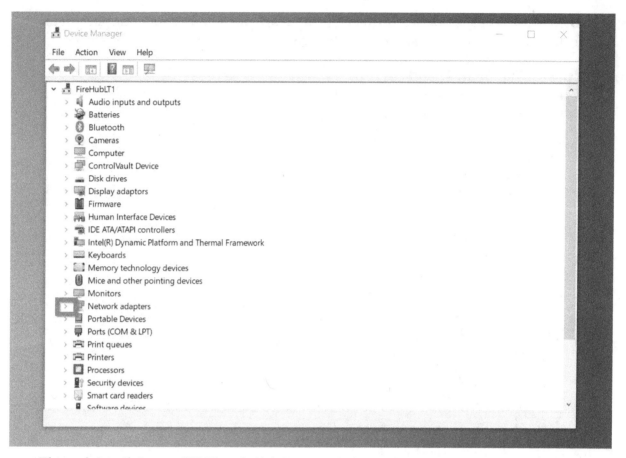

- Then, **right-click** your Wi-Fi and click **Update Driver.** If you use a cable to connect to your router, update the adapter with "Ethernet" in its name.

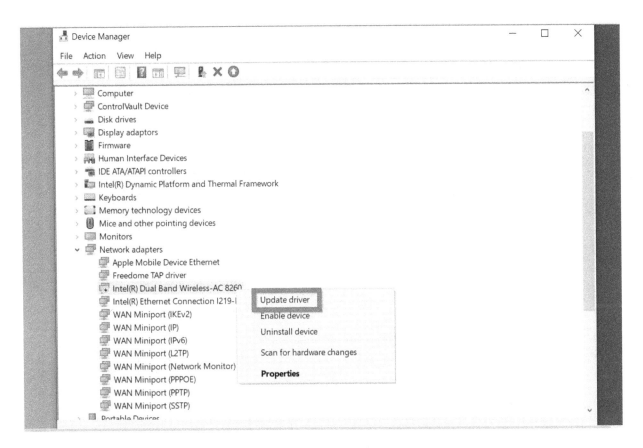

- Click the first option..."**search automatically for updated driver software**...". If that option does not update your network card drive, download the driver. Then use option 2 to update the driver manually.

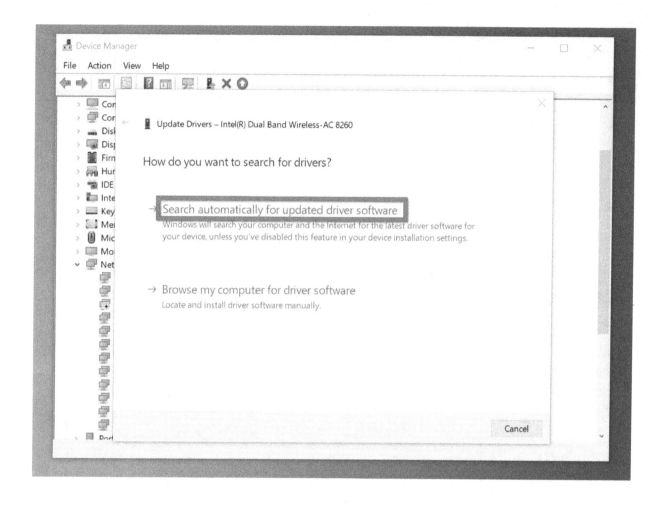

If the problem is still not resolved, try the next solution.

Seventh Solution: To resolve "DNS Server Not Responding" error, Temporarily Turn off firewalls

Sometimes firewalls may prevent you from connecting to the internet and potentially lead to the "DNS server is unavailable" error. The walk-around will be to turn off firewalls, test whether you can connect then turn the firewall back on.

Here is how you turn firewalls off in Windows 10:

- In Windows 10 search box on the taskbar, type **Command prompt.** Then, right-click **Command prompt** and select **Run as Administrator**.

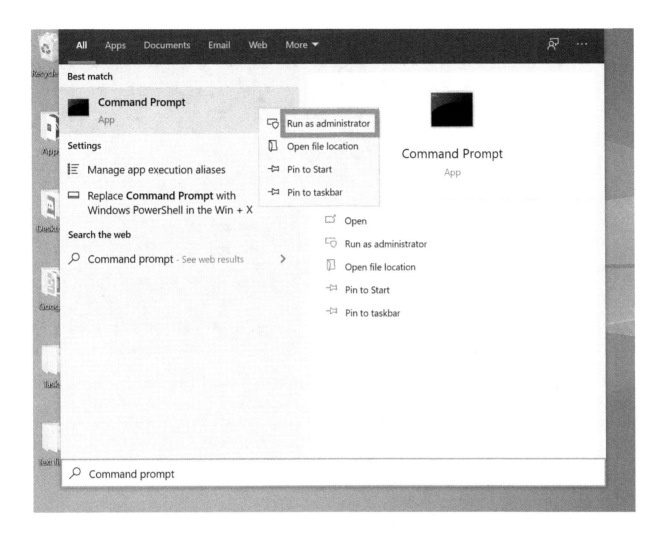

- If you receive the **User Account Control** prompt, click **Yes**.
- When command prompt opens, type the command below, then press **Enter**.

```
netsh advfirewall set allprofiles state off
```

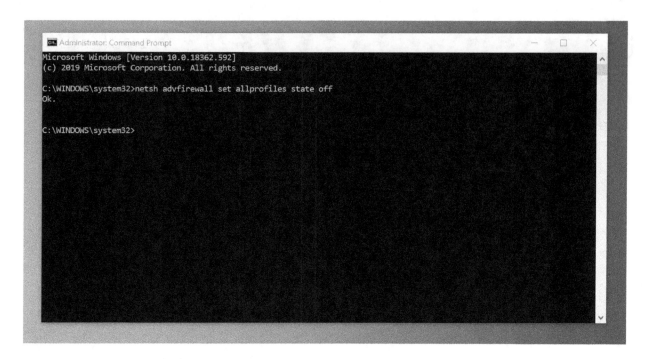

After running this command, try connecting to the internet. If you can, then the firewall was preventing you from connecting to the internet. If you made any recent changes, reverse those changes. Whatever happens, it is recommended to turn your firewall back on. To do this, type the command below into the command prompt window. Then press **Enter**.

```
netsh advfirewall set allprofiles state on
```

Below is the screenshot of the last command.

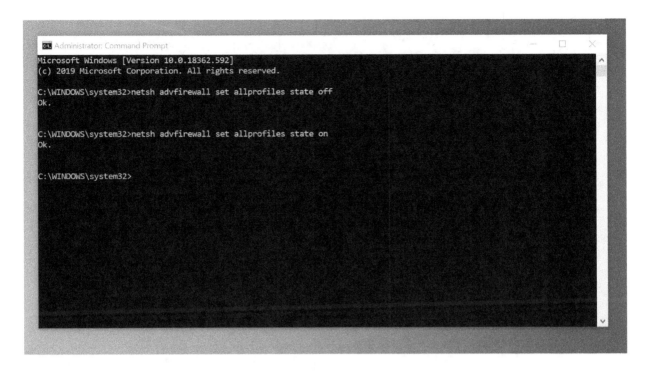

Eight Solution for "DNS Server Not Responding": Turn off Antivirus

Your antivirus could also cause the "DNS Server Not Responding" error message and stop you from connecting to the internet.

The steps to turn off your antivirus will depend on your antivirus software. Use the document for your antivirus software to determine how to turn it off and on.

Ninth Solution: To resolve "DNS Server Not Responding" error, check that flight mode is off

If flight mode is turned on, it will prevent you from getting to the internet. The next thing to check is that it is turned **OFF**. To do this on Windows 10, follow the steps below:

- On the right side of your taskbar, click your network icon then confirm that the flight mode is grey. If it is blue, click it once. If it turns grey, it is off and you should now be able to get to the internet.

Tenth Solution: Finally, to resolve "DNS Server Not Responding" error, Restart your computer

This is my final recommendation. If none of the earlier recommended solutions resolved the error message, restart your computer.

How to Fix "BootMgr is Missing" Error in Windows 10

This guide provides 3 options to fix "bootmgr is missing" error.

For all the options discussed in this guide, you will require a Windows 10 installation media. You will also need to boot to Windows 10 Recovery Environment.

Follow the steps below to boot Windows 10 to recovery environment:

- Insert Windows 10 installation media (USB, DVD, etc) into your computer.
- Boot to BIOS and modify boot sequence to boot from the above media.
- Boot your computer. You will receive a prompt to boot from the installation media. Press any key to continue boot.

- When your computer boots to this screen, click Next.

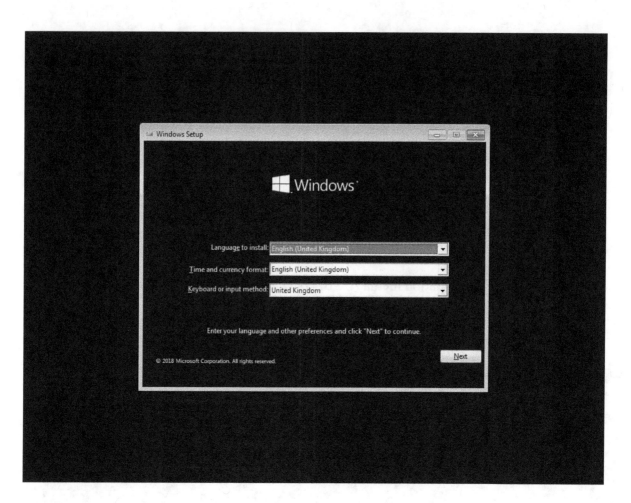

- At this screen, click *Repair your computer*.

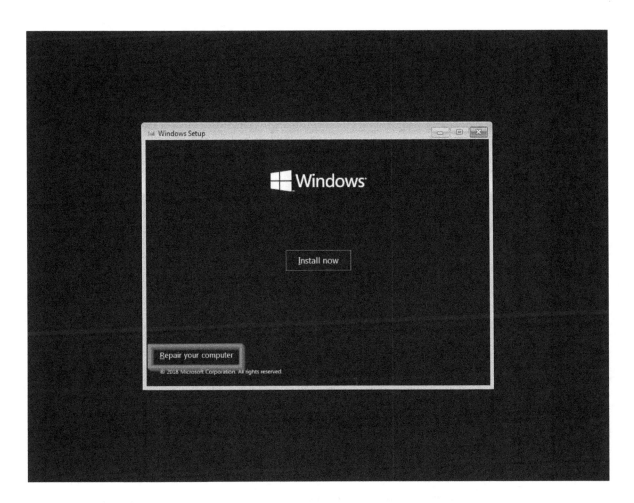

- Windows will boot to the recovery environment. See the image below:

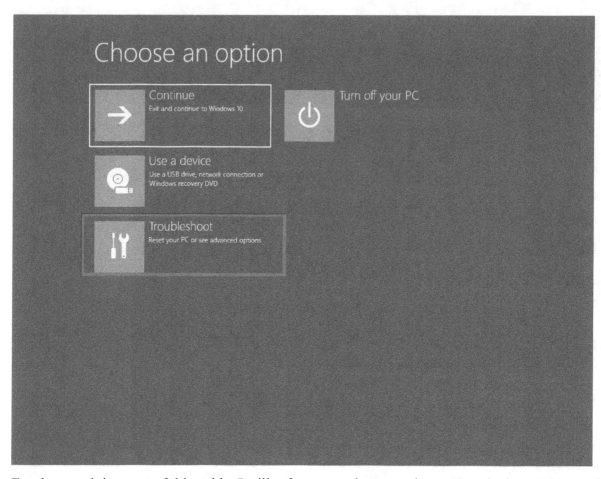

For the remaining part of this guide, I will refer you to the steps above. Here is the summary of the above steps: **1**, Boot into Windows 10 installation media. **2**, click Next. **3**, click Repair your computer.

Here are the methods you can apply to fix "BootMgr is Missing" in Windows 10:

Method 1: Perform Start-up and Repair

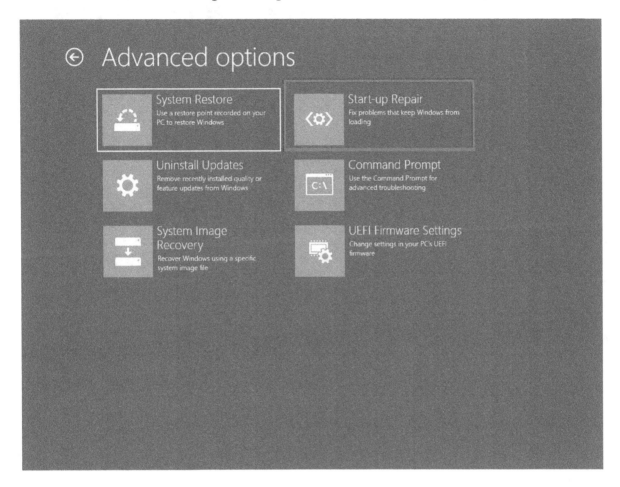

This is my first recommended option to fix "bootmgr is missing" in Windows 10 error. Here are the steps:

- Boot to Windows 10 Recovery Environment. Then click **Troubleshoot**. The **Advanced options** screen will load.

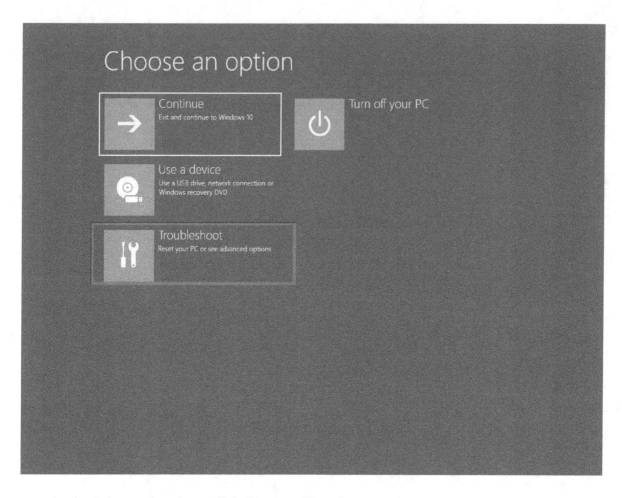

- At the Advanced options, click **Start-up Repair**.

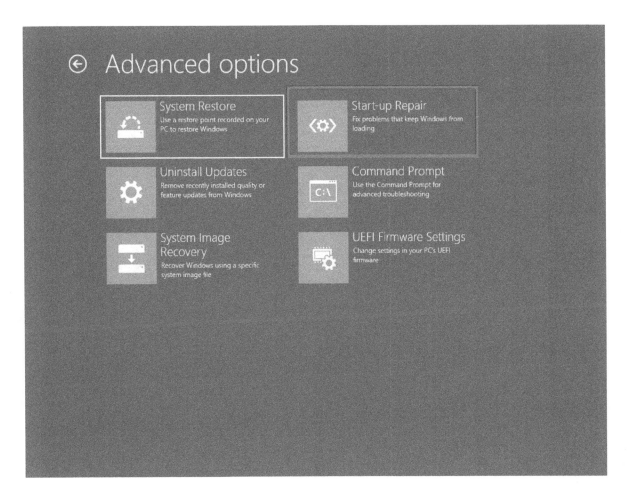

- Finally, select the target Operating system to repair. In this example, I will click on *Windows 10*. Then follow the steps to complete the repair.

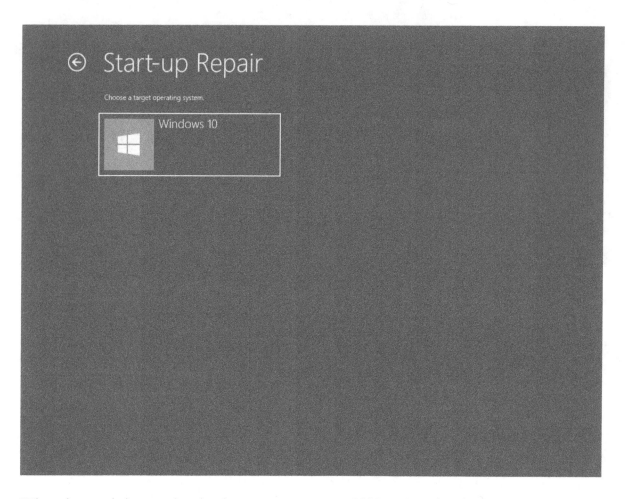

When the repair is completed, reboot your computer. If "BootMgr is missing Windows 10" error is not fixed, try the next fix below.

Method 2: Rebuild the Boot Configuration Data (BCD)

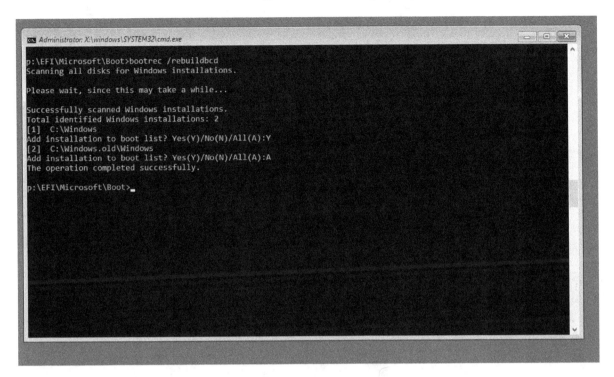

- Boot to Windows 10 Recovery Environment. Then click **Troubleshoot**. The **Advanced options** screen will load.

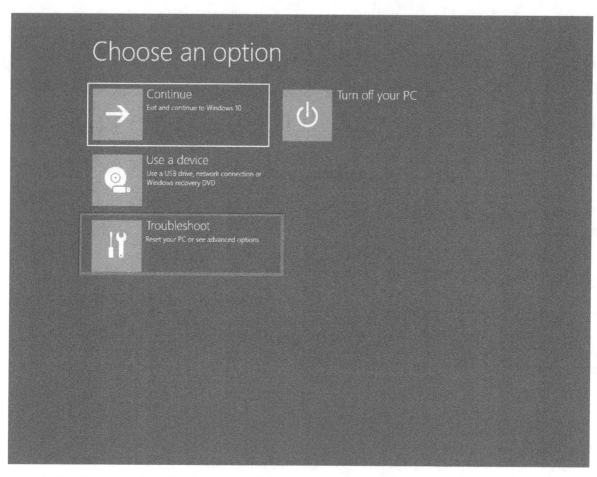

- At the **Advanced options** screen, click **Command Prompt**. Windows Command Prompt will open.

⊕ Advanced options

 System Restore
Use a restore point recorded on your
PC to restore Windows

 Start-up Repair
Fix problems that keep Windows from
loading

 Uninstall Updates
Remove recently installed quality or
feature updates from Windows

 Command Prompt
Use the Command Prompt for
advanced troubleshooting

 **System Image
Recovery**
Recover Windows using a specific
system image file

 UEFI Firmware Settings
Change settings in your PC's UEFI
firmware

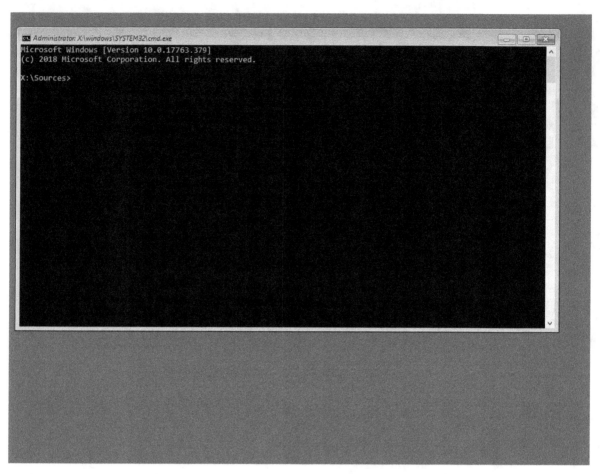

In the next steps, you will run some commands that will repair the Boot Configuration Data (BCD). This assumes that "BootMgr is missing Windows 10" is caused by corrupt or damaged Boot configuration.

This guide covers 2 options to rebuild BootMgr: **1** if your computer has BIOS with MBR systems. **2** if your computer uses the new UEFI Systems.

Steps to Rebuild BootMgr for MBR Systems

If your computer uses MBR, follow the steps below to fix "BootMgr is missing Windows 10" error.

- At the previous command prompt, enter the following commands one at a time. When you type a command, press Enter key on your keyboard. Then, enter the next one and press the Enter key.

```
bcdedit /export C:\BCD_Backup
attrib c:\\boot\\bcd -h -r -s
ren c:\boot\bcd bcd.old
```

56

```
bootrec /rebuildbcd
```

When the last command completes, you will receive this prompt:

Add installation to boot list? Yes/No/All:

Enter *A* after the ':' and press Enter.

Steps to Rebuild BootMgr for UEFI systems

If your computer runs the new UEFI, use the steps here to fix "bootmgr is missing" error in Windows 10:

This section has two parts: **part 1**, use diskpart to assign a drive letter to the EFI volume. **part 2**, rebuild BCD.

- Boot to Windows 10 Recovery Command Prompt. Then, at the command prompt, type the command below. Then press enter

```
DISKPART
```

Diskpart prompt will open.

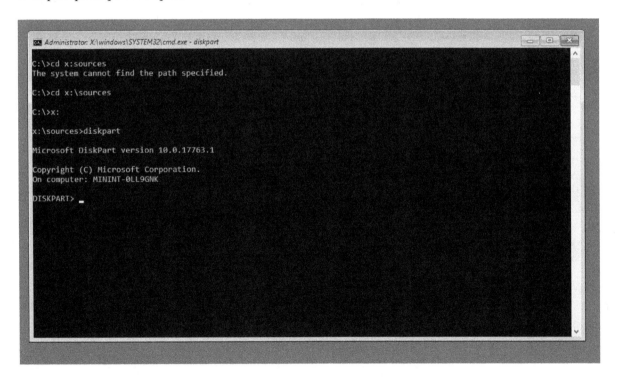

- At the DISKPART prompt, type this command and press enter.

```
list disk
```

All available disks on your computer will be displayed.

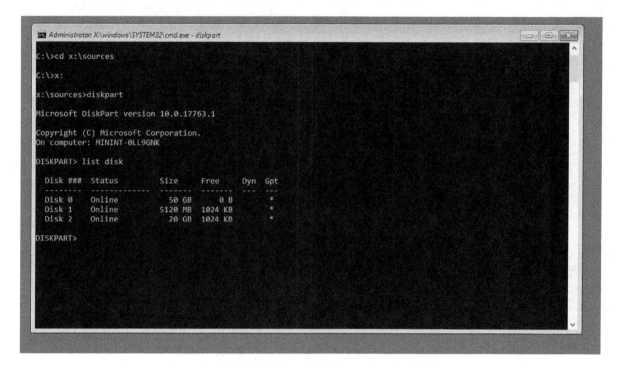

- Then type the command below to select the disk with your Windows installation.

```
Select disk 0
```

If your operating system is installed in a disk with a different number, change 0 to that number in the previous command. The command will return the result below:

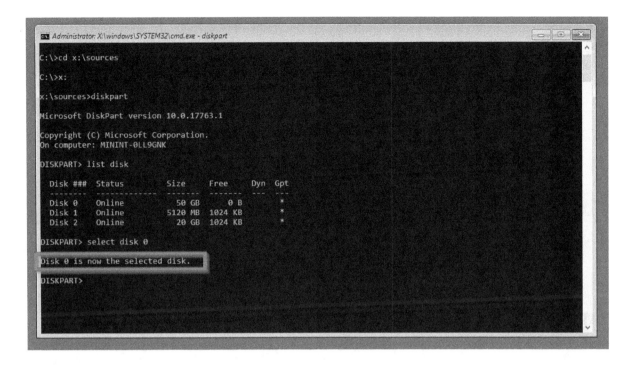

- To display volumes in the selected disk, type the command below and press enter.

```
list volume
```

Here is the result of the command...

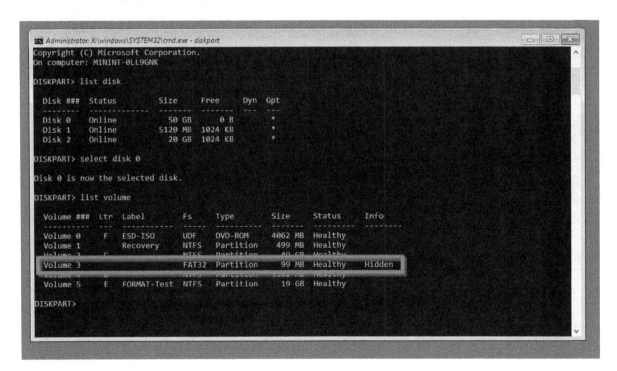

The next step is to select your EFI volume from the list. Here is how you identify the EFI volume:

1. It should be formatted with FAT32
2. Size is likely to be about 100mb (shown as 99mb in this example)

To select the EFI volume, run a command similar to this command:

```
select volume 3
```

Change 3 to your EFI volume number.

- Next, assign the volume a drive letter with this command

```
assign letter P:
```

Here are the results of the commands

- Finally, to exit DiskPart type *exit* then press Enter.

```
exit
```

You will be returned to the original command prompt.

Here is the second part to fix "bootmgr is missing" error in Windows 10 in EFI systems.

- Change directory to point to the EFI boot drive. Use the command below (if you assigned your EFI a different drive letter, change P to that drive letter):

```
cd /d p:\efi\microsoft\boot\
```

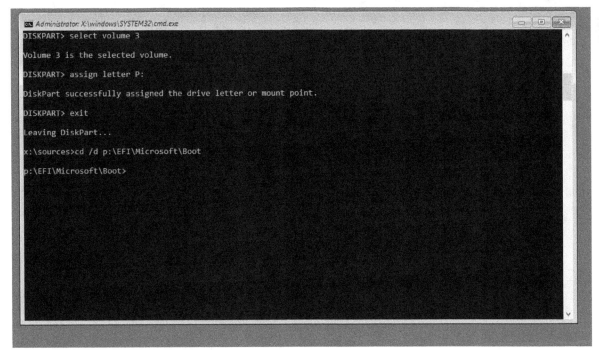

In the last command, P: is the drive letter you assigned the EFI volume.

Next, run the following commands in order:

```
bcdedit /export P:\efi\microsoft\BCD_Backup
ren bcd bcd.old
bootrec /rebuildbcd
```

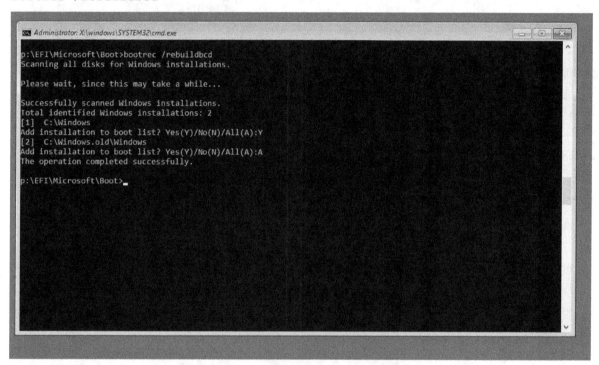

The last command will take a bit to recreate the BCD. When it completes the process, it will return this prompt:

Add installation to boot list? Yes/No/All:

Type *A* and press Enter.

In most instances, the fix in this section should resolve "bootmgr is missing" error in Windows 10. But if it doesn't, try the next fix.

Run System Restore (If Previously Enabled on Your Computer)

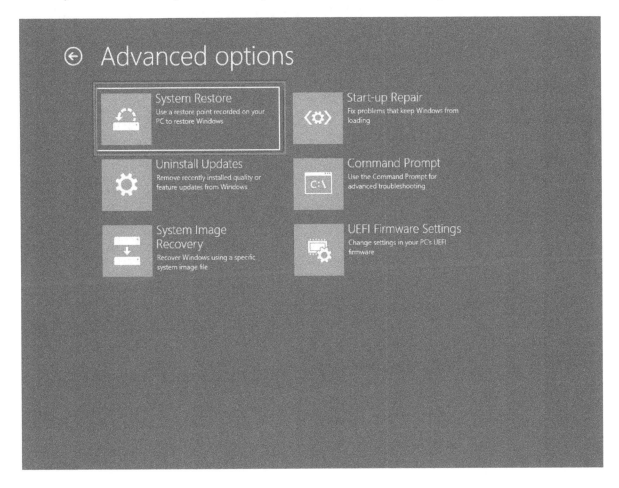

To use this repair option, you would have enabled **System Restore** before your computer had the "bootmgr is missing" error. If you did not enable System Restore before this problem, there is no need to try this fix.

Here are the steps to fix "bootmgr is missing" error with System Restore:

- Boot your computer to the recovery environment. Then click Troubleshoot.

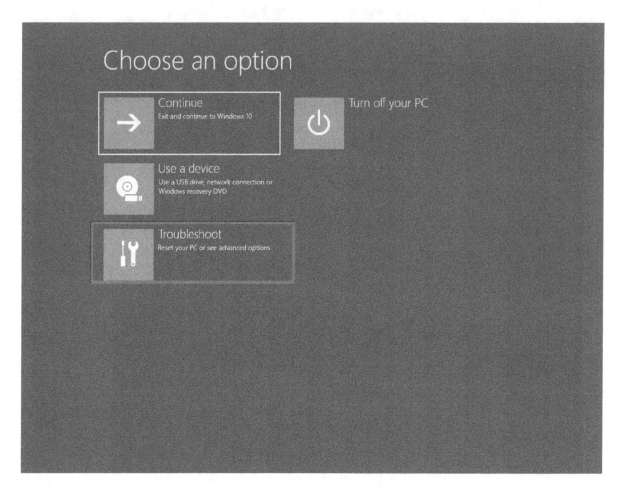

- At the *Advanced options* screen, select *System Restore.*

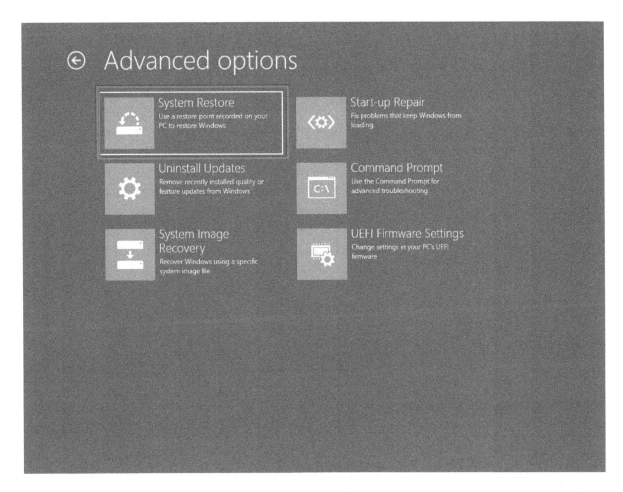

- Follow the wizard to select a previous restore point.

How to fix Your Printer if Status is "Offline"

Your printer may be offline due to a driver problem or some other more serious problem. This guide covers 5 options to get a printer online if it is offline.

If your printer is offline try these fixes. If the first method does not work, try the next and then the next until the problem is fixed for you.

Method 1: Check that the Printer is On and Connected to your Computer

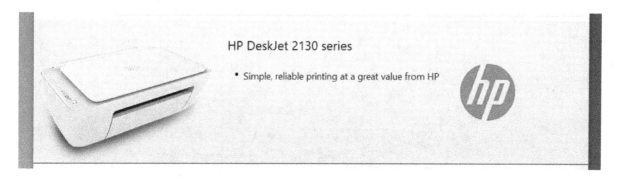

Before you do anything, the first step to resolve printer offline issue is to perform some physical inspections:

1. Check that your printer is connected to power and is turned on.
2. If you connect to the printer using a USB cable, check that the cable is properly connected. Resit the cable at the printer and on your computer.
3. However, if you connect to the printer using Wifi check that you are connected as well.

Once you complete physical inspection and are happy it is properly connected, check the printer status. If Printer offline issue is not resolved, proceed to the next fix below.

Method 2: Manually Force the Printer Online

To manually force offline printer online:

- On the search bar, type *printers & scanners*. Then select it from the search result.

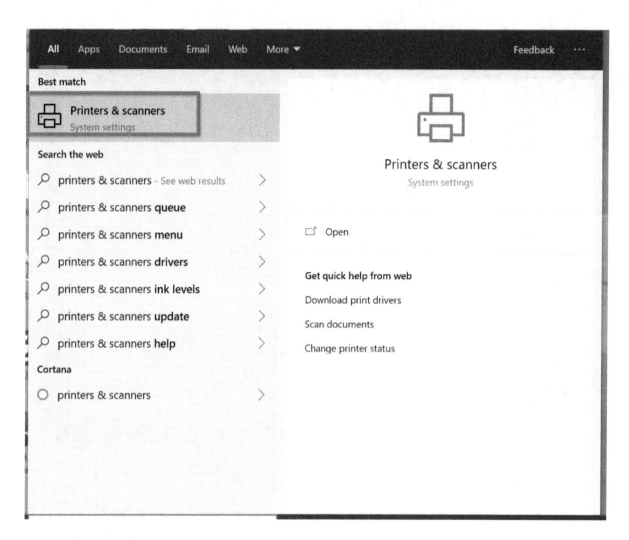

- When *Printers & Scanners* settings open, click the printer that is offline, then click *Open queue*.

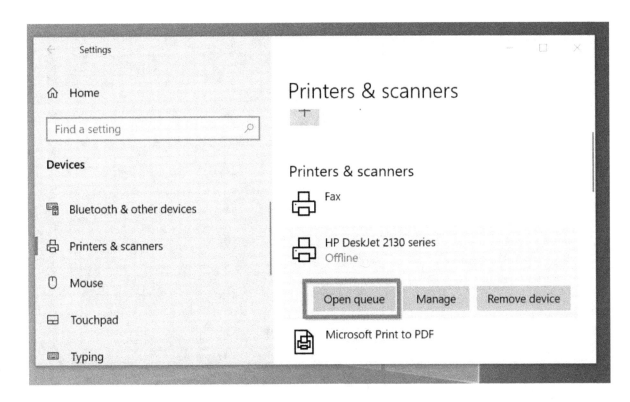

- Next, click *Printer* then click *Use Printer Offline.*

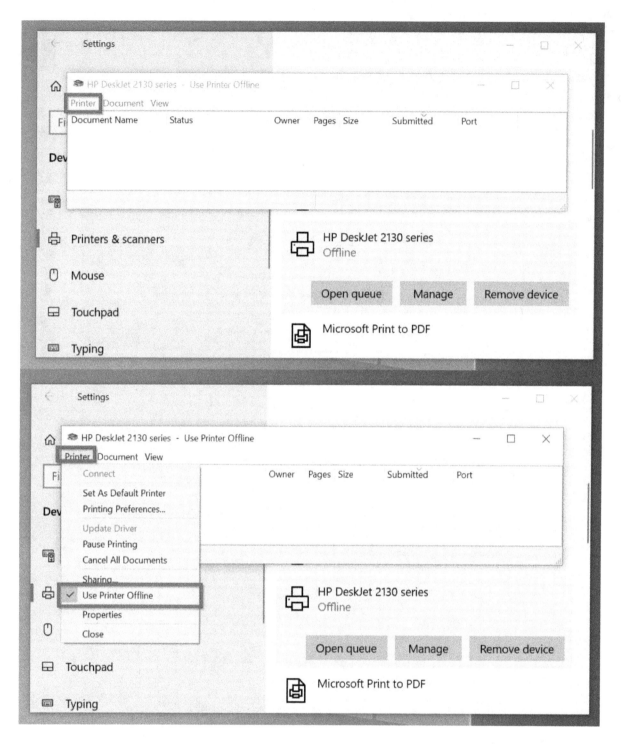

If there is nothing else wrong with your printer, the status will change from *Offline* to *Online*.

However, if there is an underlying problem, the last method will not fix the problem. Try my next recommended fix below:

Method 3: Update Printer Driver

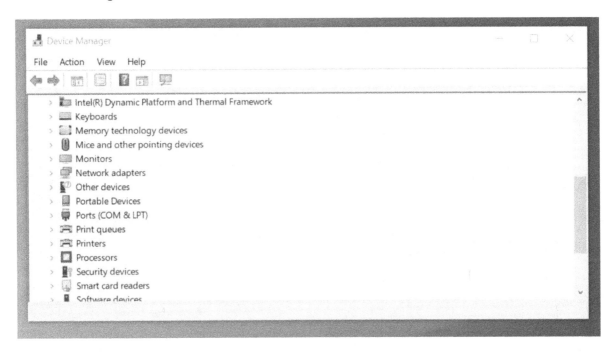

To perform the steps for this fix:

- Press **Windows + R** (Windows logo on your keyboard simultaneously with the R key). This will open the RUN command.
- At the RUN command, type *devmgmt.msc*. Then press OK to open Device Manager.

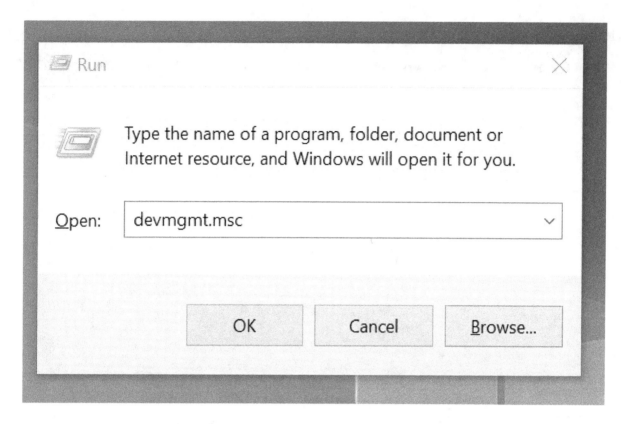

- To get to the printer drivers, expand the arrow pointing towards Printers (see the image below). You may need to scroll down a bit to get to *Printers*. You will then see a list of all printers currently installed on your computer.

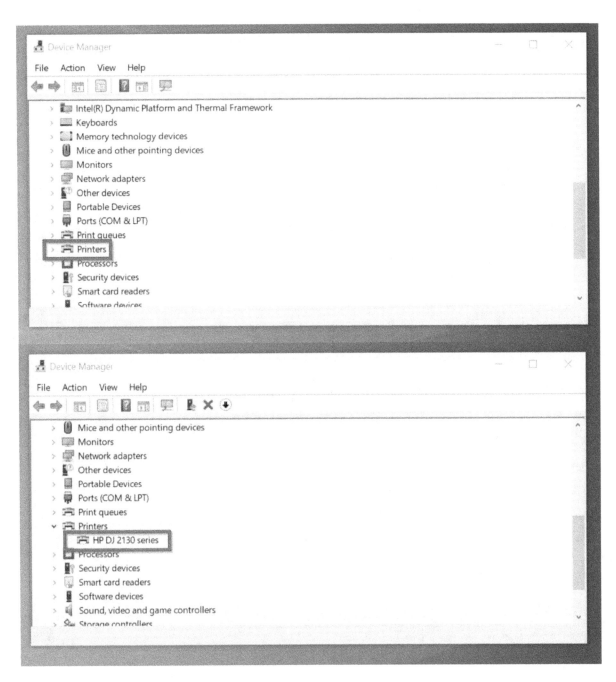

- Right-click the printer that has the problem. Then select *Update Driver*.

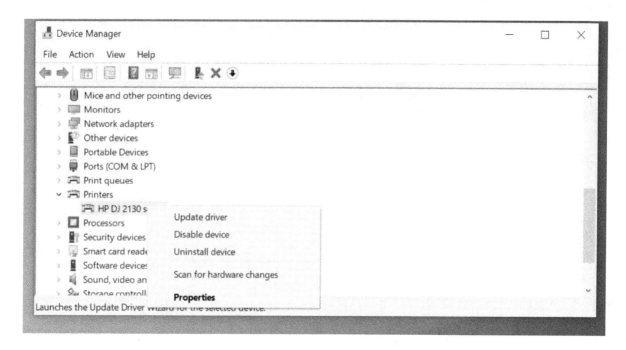

- At the *Update Drivers - <printer name>*, click the first option - *Search automatically for updated drivers*.

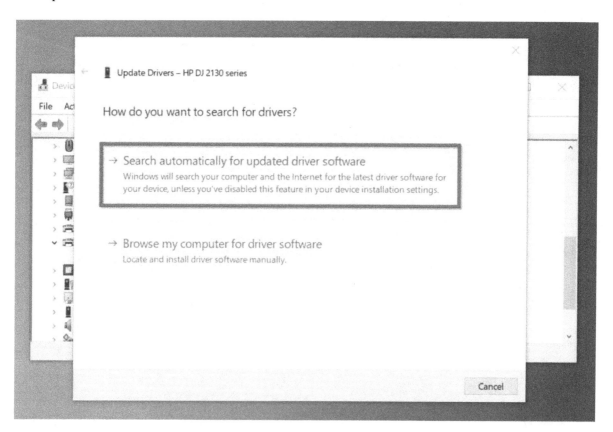

Windows will attempt to find an updated driver for your printer online. If there is a driver newer driver than what you have and Windows is able to find it, the driver may be updated.

When the update completes successfully (Or if it completes successfully!), check your printer. If it comes back online congratulations! But if it is still offline, try the next fix.

Method 4: Uninstall and Reinstall Printer Driver

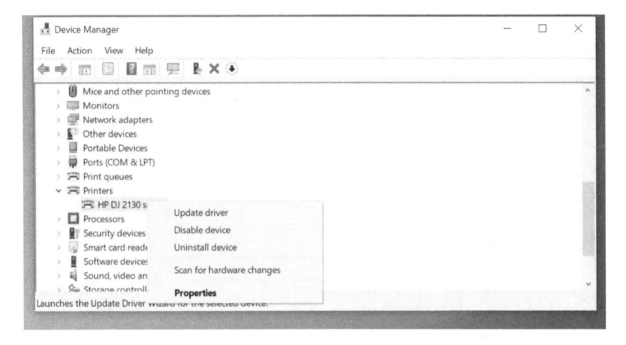

This method is like the last one. But instead of updating the driver, you uninstall it. Then reinstall it. Here are the steps:

- Right-click Windows start menu (Windows logo at the bottom left of your taskbar). Then, click **Device Manager**.

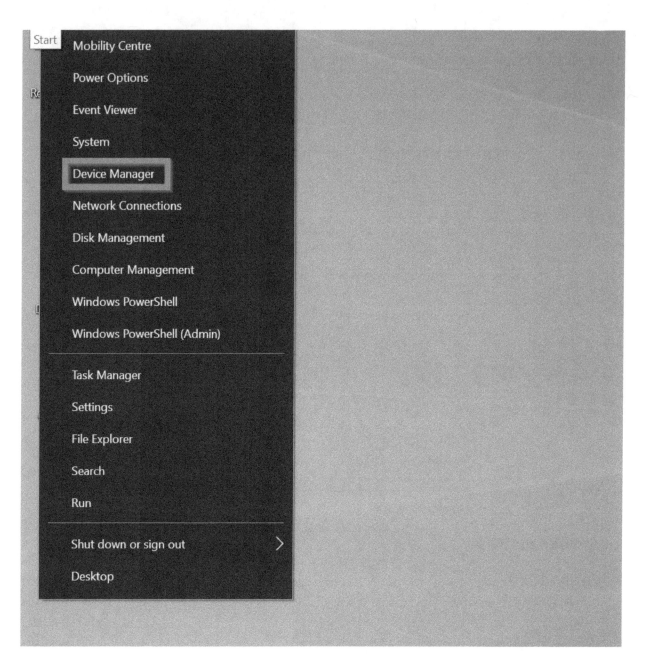

- When **Device Manager** opens, scroll down to **Printers**, then expand it. To expand **Printers**, click the arrow beside it.

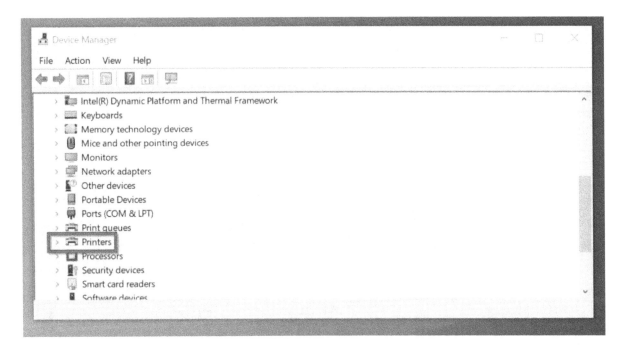

- Right-click your printer select *Uninstall device.*

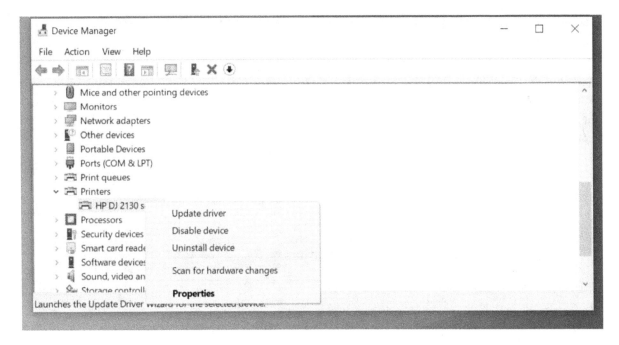

- At the Uninstall device prompt, check the box beside *Delete the driver software for this device.* Then click *Uninstall.*

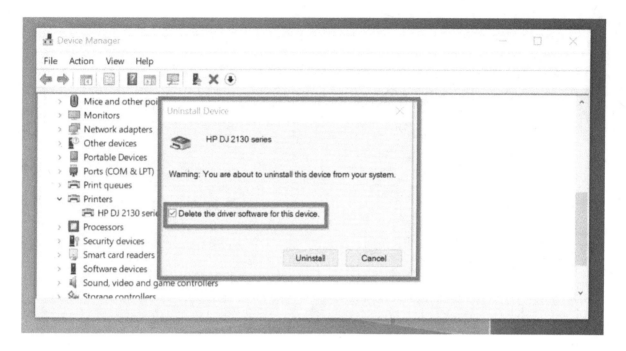

- When the uninstall completes successfully, disconnect the printer from your computer. Then restart your computer.
- When your computer starts, download the latest printer driver from the printer manufacturer's website. Then reinstall the driver.

If the printer re-installation prompts to restart the computer, restart it. Then check your printer status. It should now be *Online*. If in the rare instance that you still have printer status showing offline, try the last method below.

Method 5: If Everything Else fails...Check these…

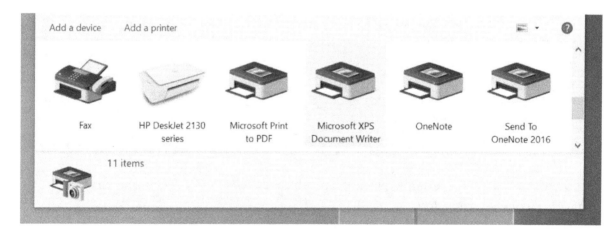

1. Change the cable you use to connect the printer to your computer. If the cable is bad, changing it may fix this problem.

2. Swap your connection method. If you connect using USB and your printer has a Wifi option, use it and try if it works. Alternatively, if you have been connecting via Wifi, try using a USB cable.
3. Finally (and this is very possible), your printer may be bad and need to be fixed or replaced! If you have the option to take it to the manufacturer or reseller, take that option.

How to Fix "Windows Could not Automatically Detect This Network's Proxy Settings"

You suddenly lose the ability to connect to the internet. Then you run network troubleshooter and it returns "Windows could not automatically detect this network's proxy settings"!

You have not made any changes to your computer. And you are wondering "what is going on?". I know this is frustrating but "Windows could not automatically detect this network's proxy settings" error could be caused by the following:

- The proxy may have been set incorrectly
- Your network card has the wrong settings
- A Malware may have infected your computer

Here are my 6 recommended fixes for "Windows could not automatically detect this network's proxy settings":

Method 1: Check Automatic Proxy Setup

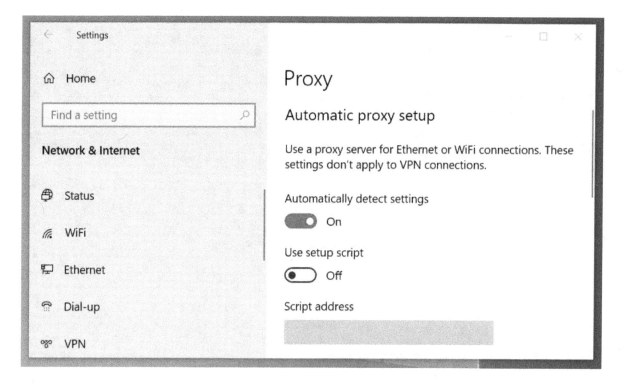

Windows 10 includes proxy setup within Windows settings. This is the first place to look. Here are the steps to check whether your proxy settings have changed:

- Right-click Window 10 start menu and click *Settings*.

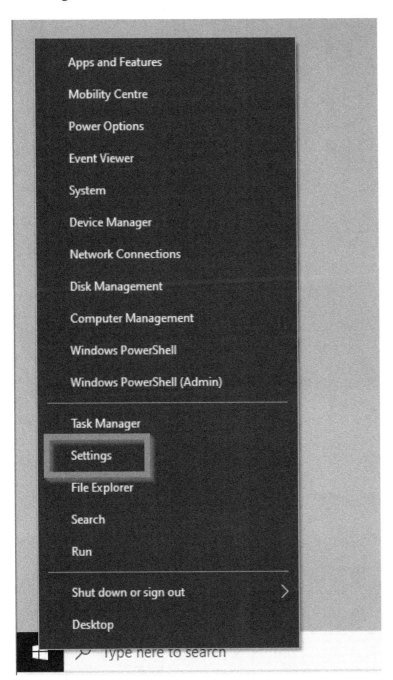

- When Settings opens, click *Network & Internet*.

- Then click *Proxy*.

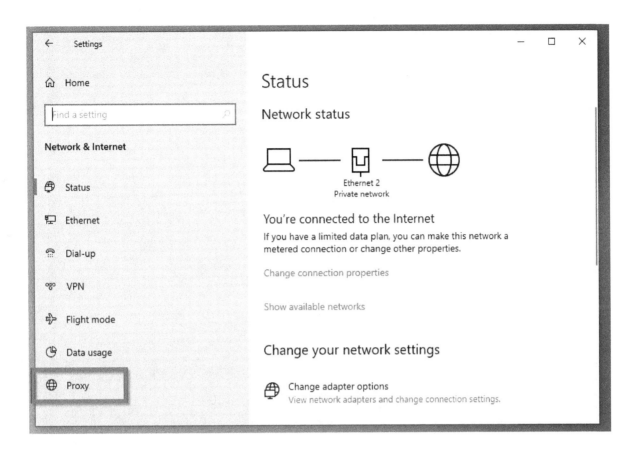

- Refer to the image below. For most settings: *Automatically detect settings* should be on. On the Manual proxy setup section, *Use a proxy server* should be off.
- If you are a home user, ensure that yours is set up as shown in the image. For office users, contact your network administrator.

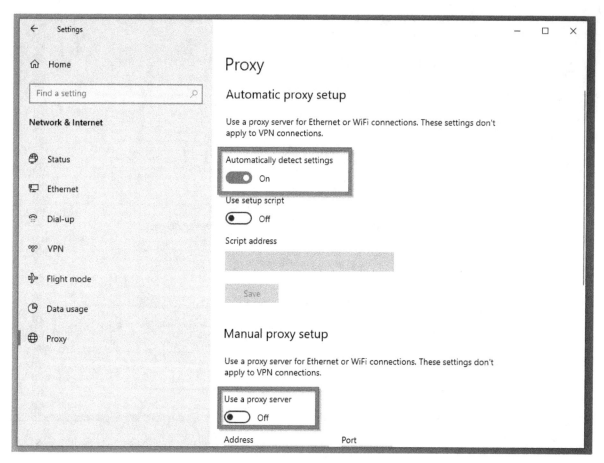

If you made changes to the proxy setup above, check whether you can connect to the internet. But, your settings are exactly as shown above, try the next fix in this guide.

Method 2: Perform Network Card Reset

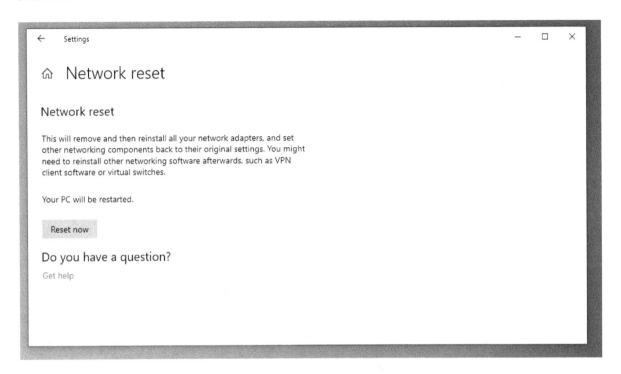

The next easy fix for "Windows could not automatically detect this network's proxy settings" is to perform a network reset.

A reset will remove all network drivers and restore them to the original state. Unless your computer is infected by malware or otherwise badly damaged, this should fix the problem and get you back on the internet! Here are the steps:

- Follow the steps in Method 1 until you get to *Network status*.

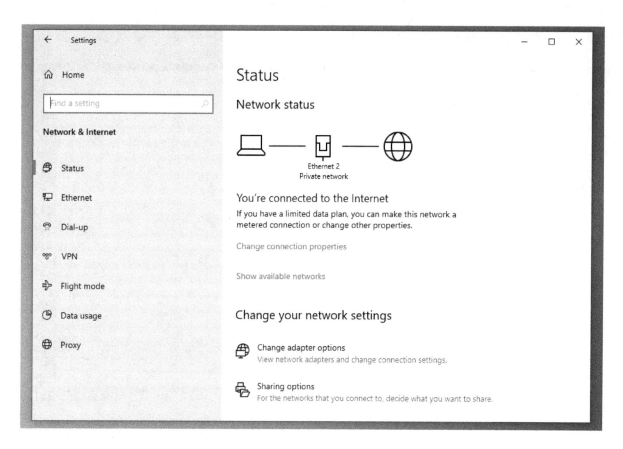

- Then scroll down until you get to *Network reset* and click it.

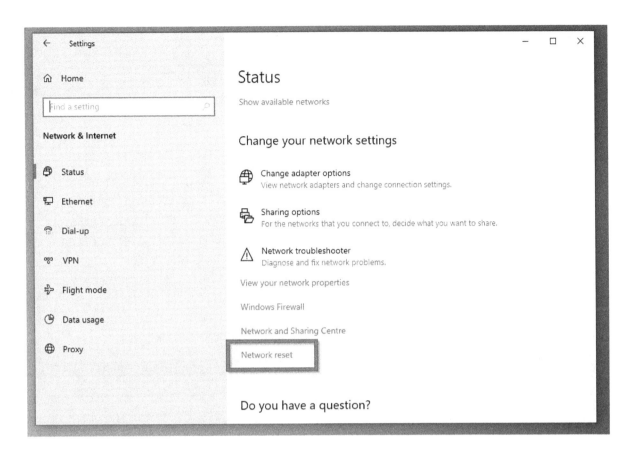

- When **Network reset** opens, click *Reset now*. Then, on the Network reset confirmation, click Yes.

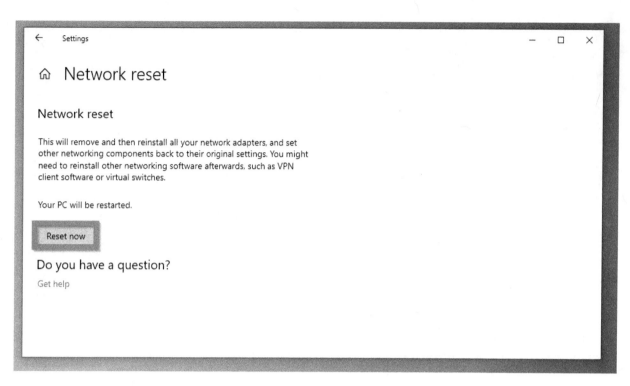

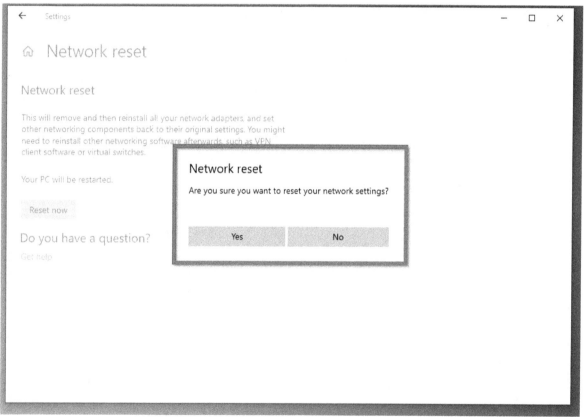

After some time your PC will restart. You will receive a shutdown notification prior to the restart.

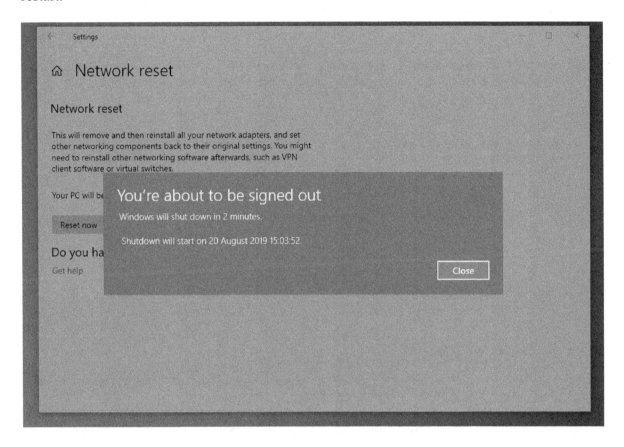

When the network reset is completed, try connecting to the internet. If the problem is still not resolved, try the next fix.

Method 3: Run Malware removal tool

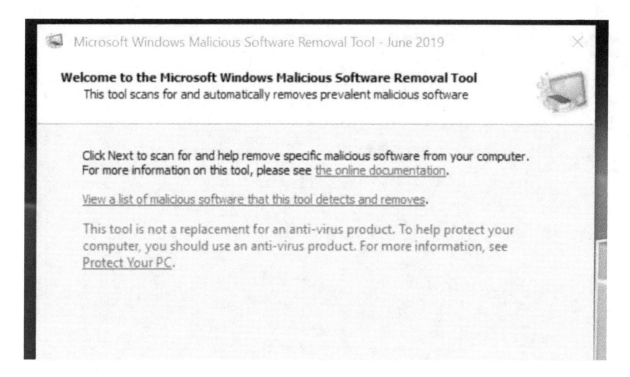

If the last two fixes have not resolved "Windows could not automatically detect this network's proxy settings" error, then there may be more trouble!

My next fix is to Download and Run *Microsoft's Malicious Software Removal Tool (MSRT)*. Follow the last link for details.

- Search *Microsoft's Malicious Software Removal Tool (MSRT)* in Google. Click the MSRT link.

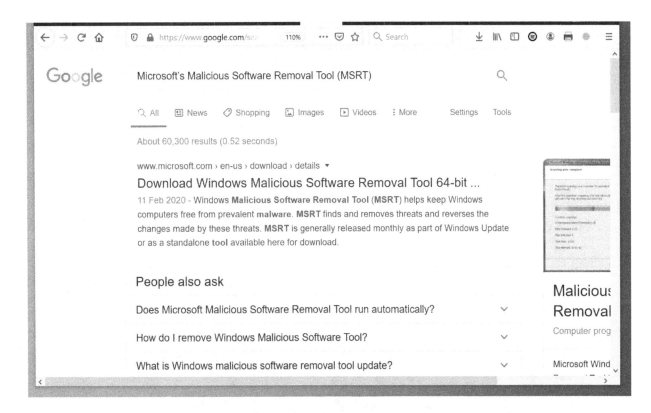

- Scroll down the page and click **Download**. Save the file in a folder on your computer.

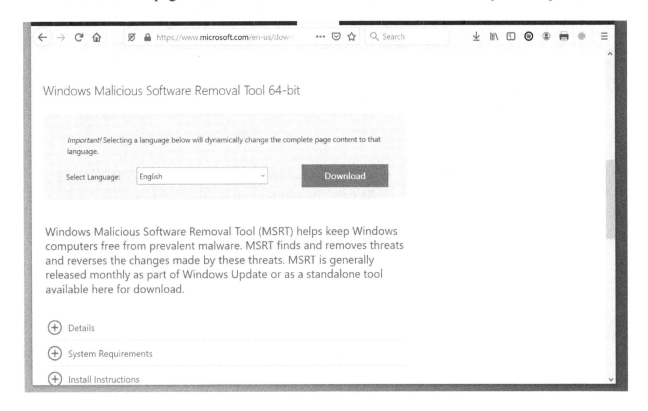

- Finally, install the tool. When it is installed on your computer, open the tool and follow the wizard to check and clean your computer if necessary.

Once you run the malware removal tool, reboot and check whether the problem is resolved. If it is still not fixed, then you need to repair, reset or restore Windows 10!

The last 3 recommended fixes are intended to repair or restore your operating system.

Here they are.

Method 4: Repair Windows 10 with DISM /Online and SFC /scannow

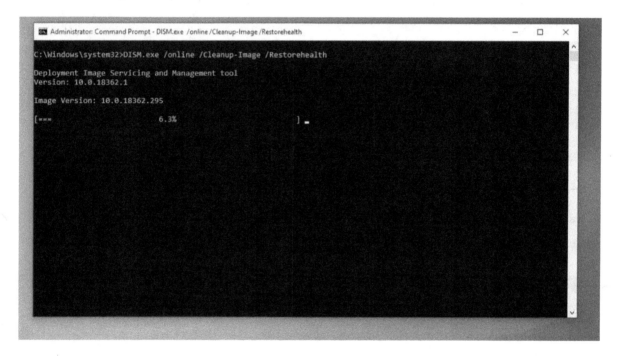

This method resolves most Windows 10 problems. I suspect that whatever triggered "Windows could not automatically detect this network's proxy settings" error, the commands below will likely fix it!

- Search *Command Prompt*. Then right-click it and select *Run as administrator*.

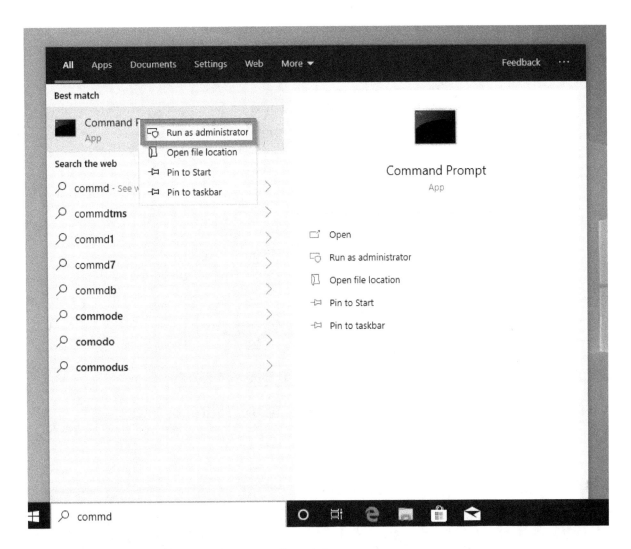

- Respond **Yes** to the **User Account Control** prompt.

- When Command Prompt opens, type the command below. Then press enter.

```
DISM.exe /Online /Cleanup-Image /Restorehealth
```

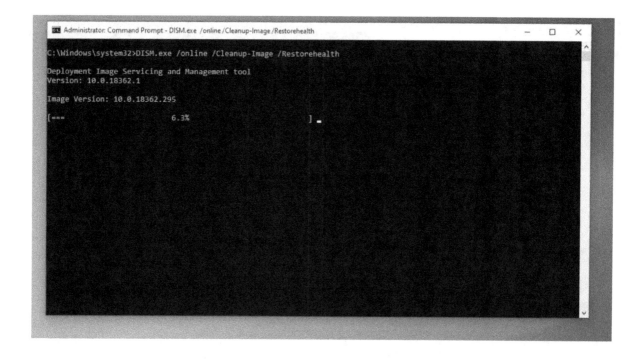

- Wait for the DISM command to complete. Then on the same command prompt, type this command and press enter.

```
SFC /scannow
```

When the SFC command completes, restart your computer. If this does not fix "Windows could not automatically detect this network's proxy settings" error, then try the last 2 fixes in this guide.

Method 5: Use System Restore

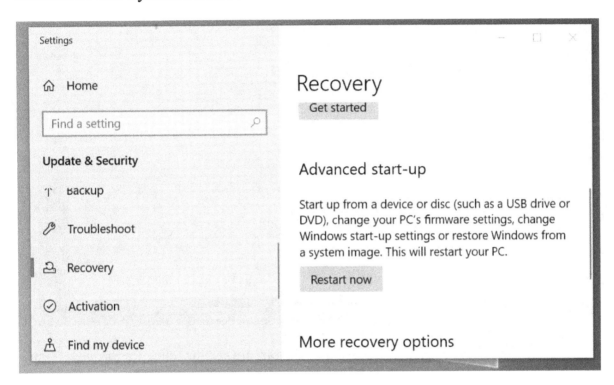

To use this option, you must have enabled system restore before your computer had this problem.

Most users that received "Windows could not automatically detect this network's proxy settings" resolved it by performing a system restore. Here are the steps to restore Windows 10 to a previous restore point:

- Search *Recovery*. Then click *Recovery options*.

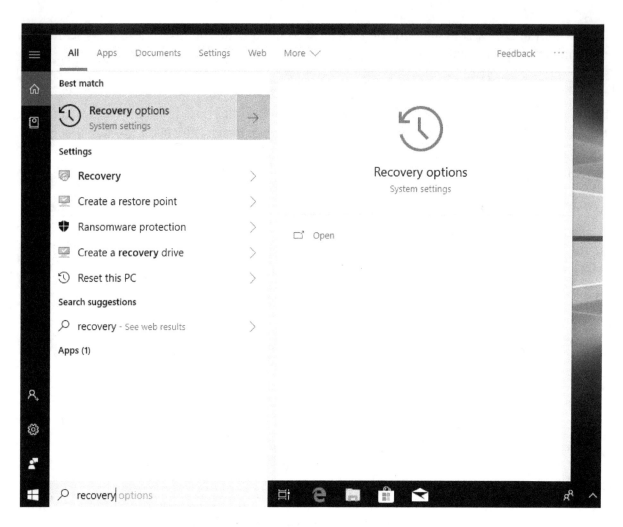

- When **Recovery settings** open, at the **Advanced start-up** section, click *Restart now*. Your computer will restart, and Windows 10 will boot to **Automatic recovery**.

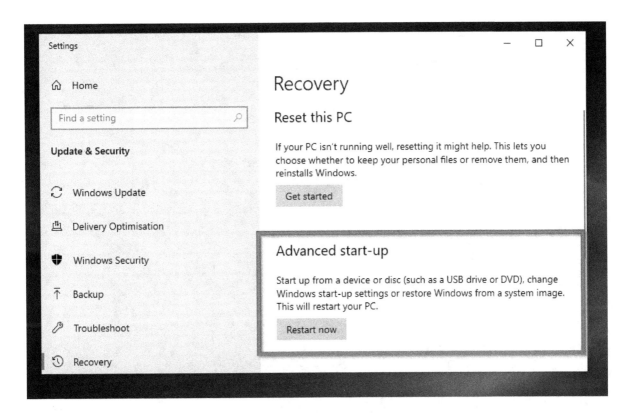

- When Windows 10 boots to recovery environment, click **Troubleshoot**.

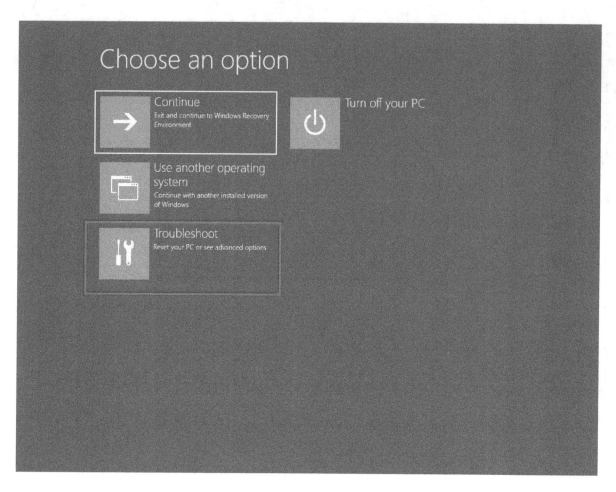

- Then on the Troubleshoot screen, click **Advanced options**.

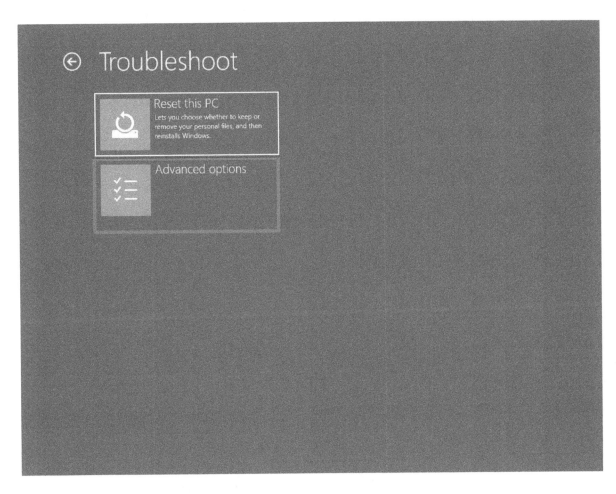

- When **Advanced options** screen opens, click **System Restore**. Windows may take some time to display the next screen.

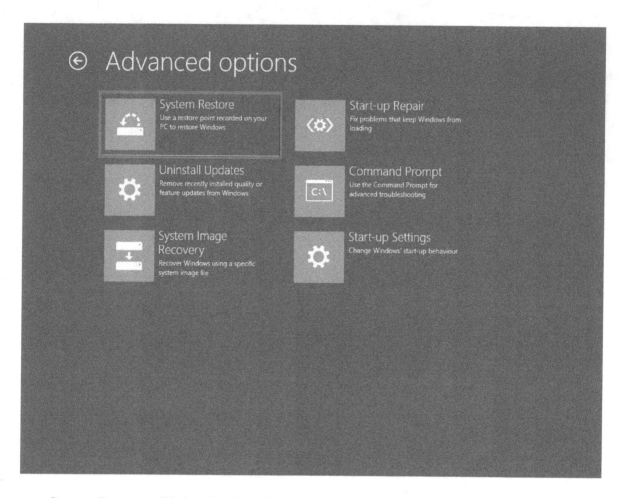

- System Restore will then display all users on the computer. Select the user with administrative privilege to perform the restore.
- Then enter the password for the account you selected and click **Continue**.

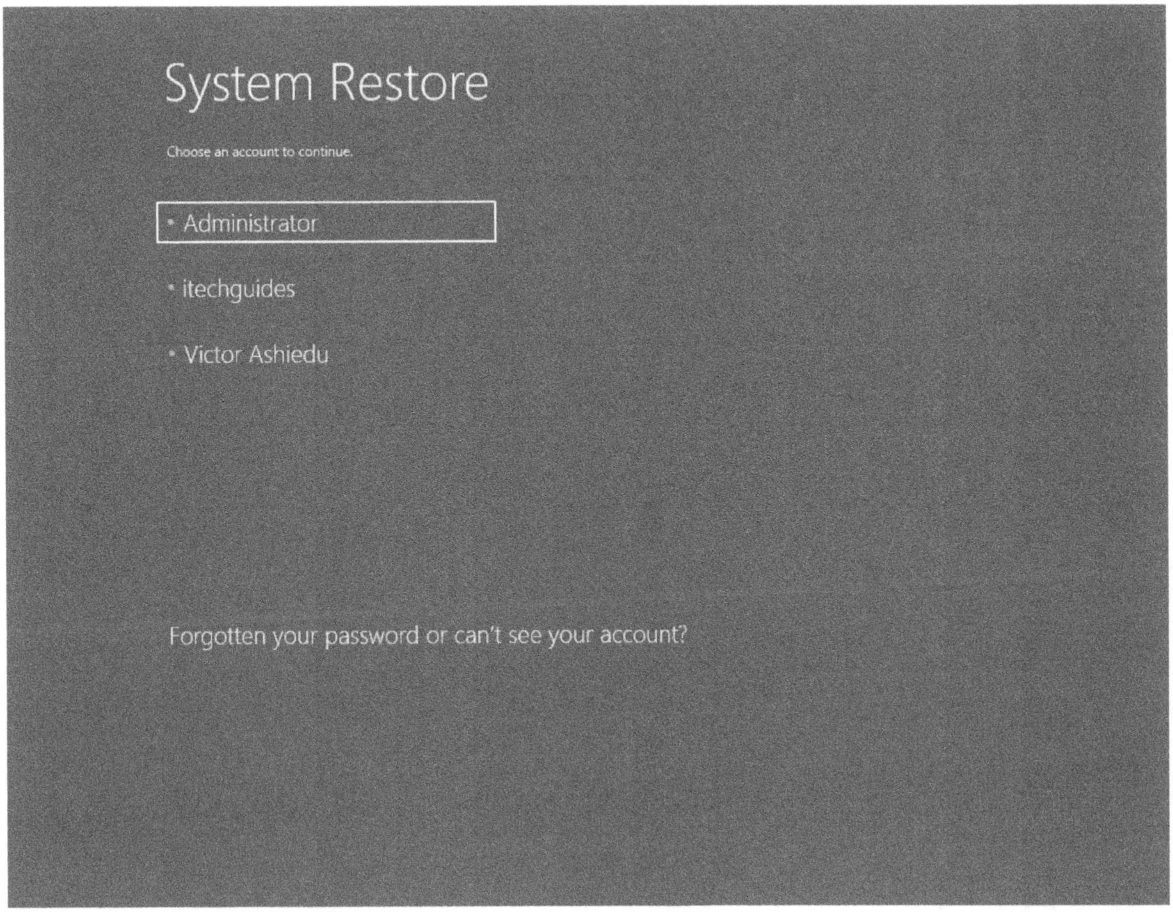

System Restore

Choose an account to continue.

- Administrator

- itechguides

- Victor Ashiedu

Forgotten your password or can't see your account?

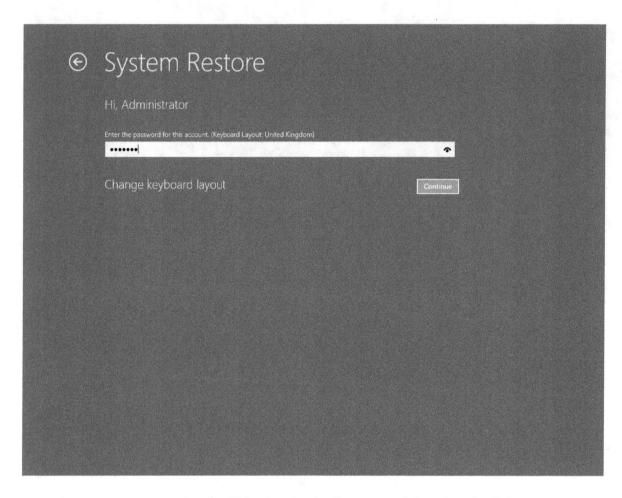

- The system restore wizard will begin. On the first page of the wizard, click **Next**.

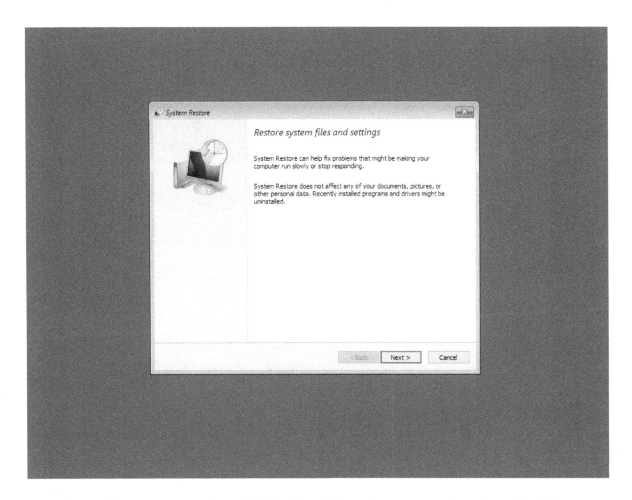

- Then, select a restore point and click Next. If you have not previously enabled System Restore, no restore point will be enabled.

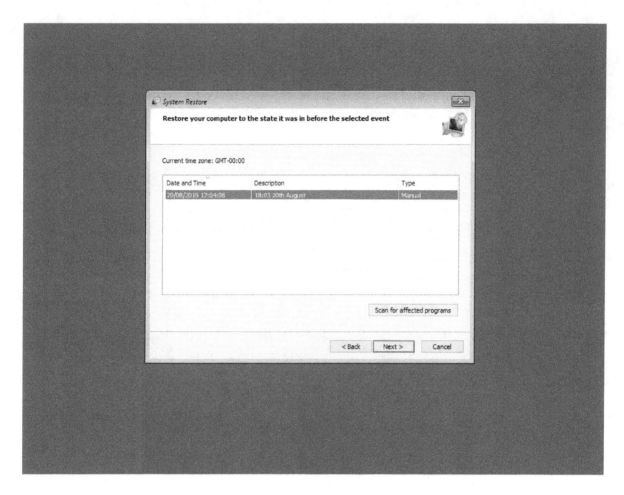

- To initiate the restore, click Finish. Then to confirm the restore, click *Yes*.

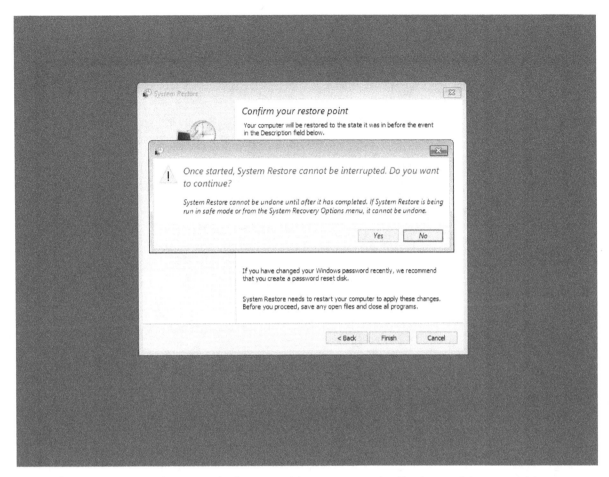

When the restore completes, "Windows could not automatically detect this network's proxy settings" should be resolved - assuming whatever caused the error happened after the restore point was created!

If the error is not fixed, then you may have to reset your PC. See the steps on the next page.

Method 6: Reset Windows 10

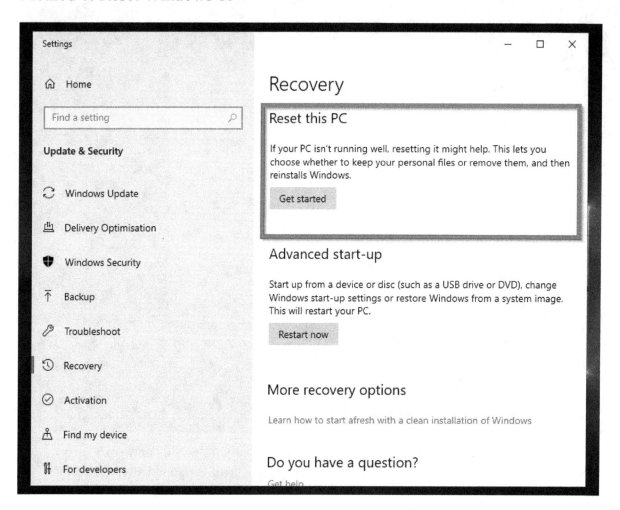

Warning!
When you reset your PC using the steps in this section, you will have to reinstall all your applications. Your data will not be lost. Please select your options carefully.

Steps to reset your PC.

- Log in to your Windows 10 PC and search for *Recovery*. Then click *Recovery options*.

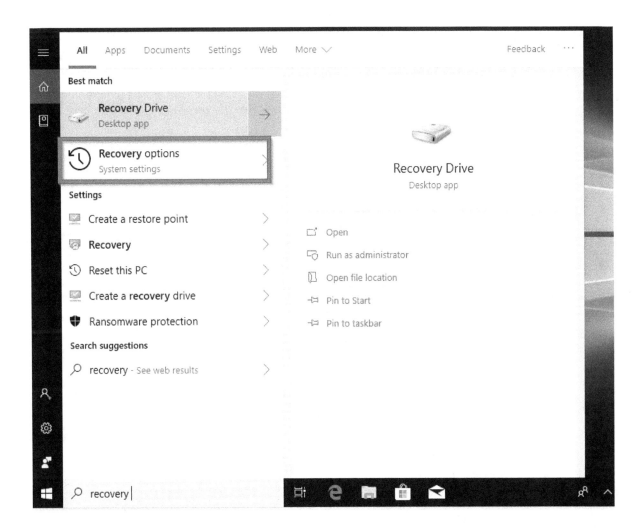

- At **Recovery options** settings, on the *Reset this PC* section, click *Get started*.

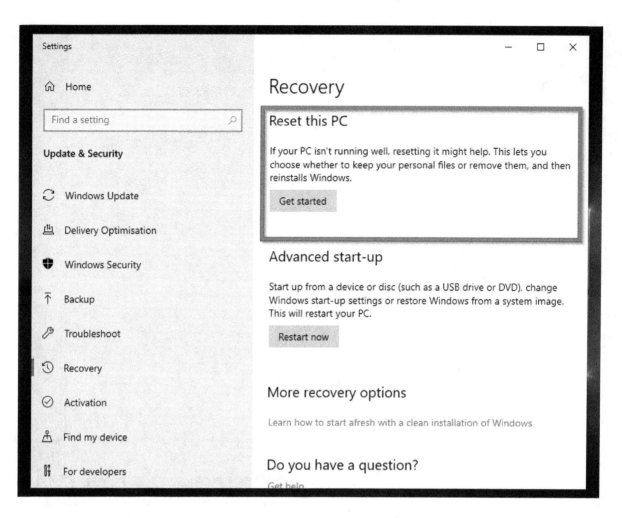

- On the **Choose an option** page, select **Keep my files**. If you select the second option, ALL your personal files will be deleted!

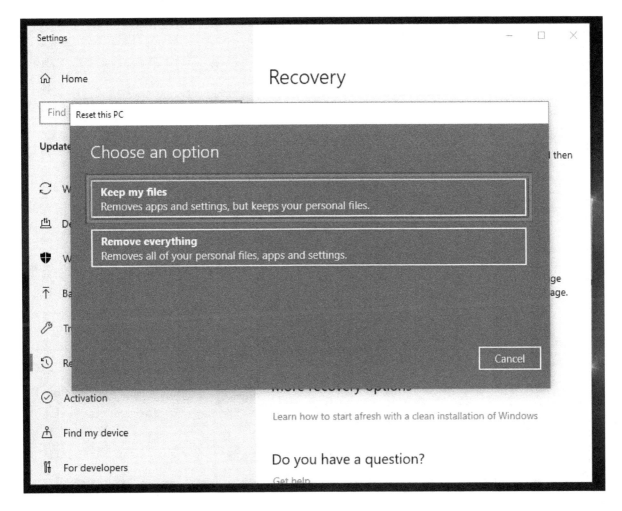

- The reset process will commence. Wait...

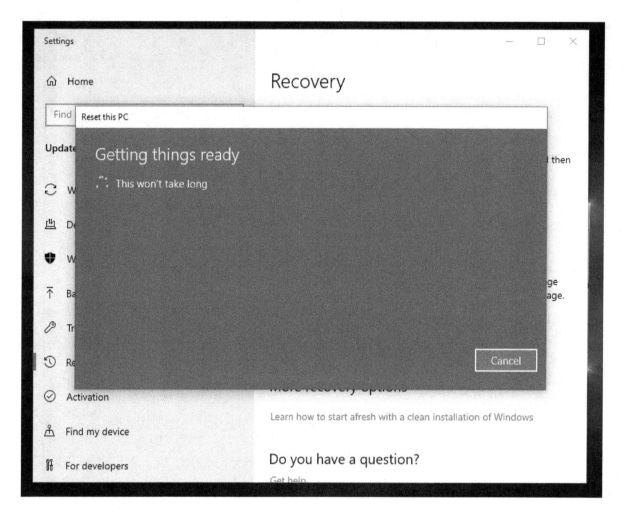

- When the next screen is displayed by the Reset wizard, click Next.

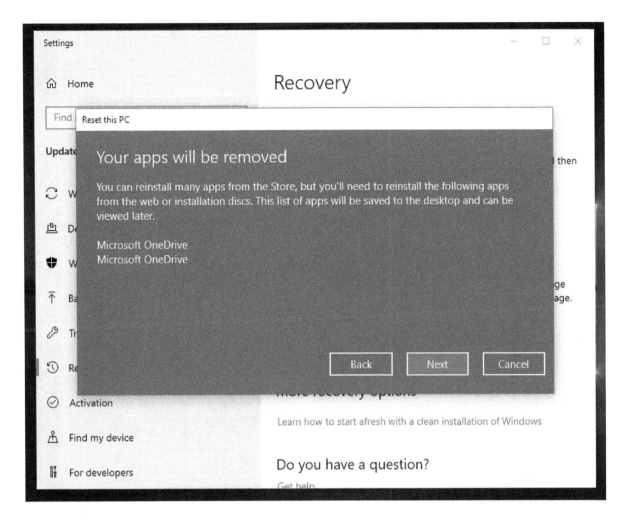

- Then, to start the Reset click *Reset*.

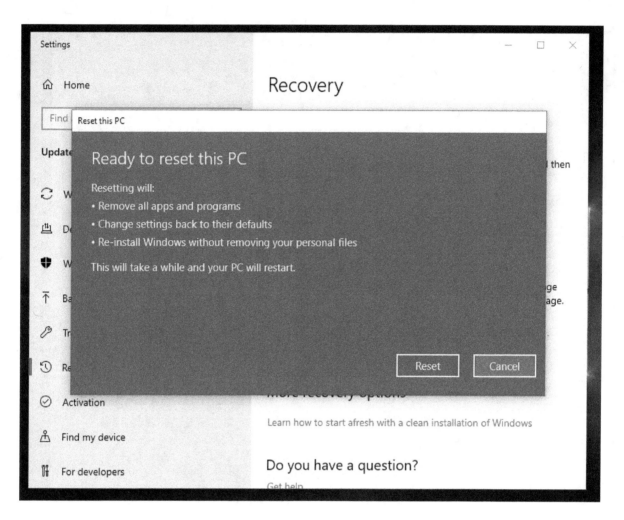

- Now, wait for the Reset to complete.

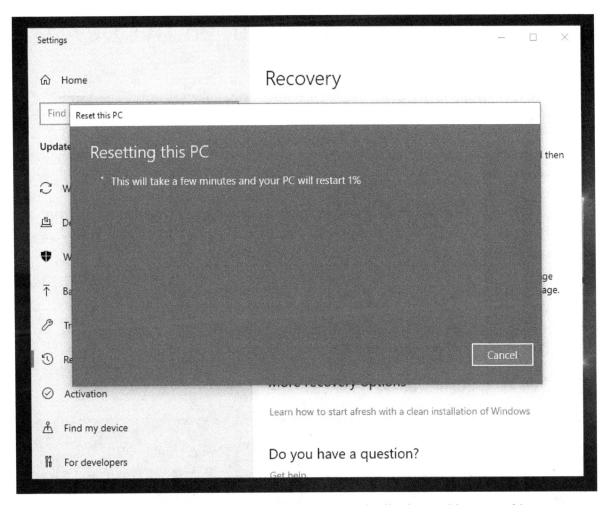

When the reset completes, "Windows could not automatically detect this network's proxy settings" should be fixed for good.

One of the 6 fixes discussed in this guide should fix "Windows could not automatically detect this network's proxy settings".

How to Fix "Windows Has Stopped This Device - Code 43" Error

Sometimes you may receive "Windows has stopped this device code 43" error. This error is likely to come up when you plug in a USB device into your computer.

9 out of 10 times, this error is caused by improperly ejected devices. My first two recommended fixes will address this.

Some other time, code 43 windows error may be because your device has an outdated driver. Code 43 windows error may also come up if your Operating System is not running the latest Windows update.

This guide presents 5 fixes for "Windows has stopped this device code 43".

The recommended fixes are based on the know causes of this error. Most of the fixes have also resolved this error for so many other Windows users.

Method 1: Properly Eject All USB Devices

To properly eject an attached USB device:

- Plug the USB device into **another** computer and wait for the device to be completely detected.
- Then, at the bottom right of your Windows 10 taskbar, click the ***Safely Remove Hardware and Eject Media*** icon.

- Finally, click *Eject Flash Disk...*or whatever your USB device displays.

- Once the USB device is properly ejected in another computer, plug it back into the original computer. It should work without errors unless there is something else wrong with the device.

If your device is still showing error code 43, try the next fix.

Method 2: Unplug all Devices from Your PC and Restart it

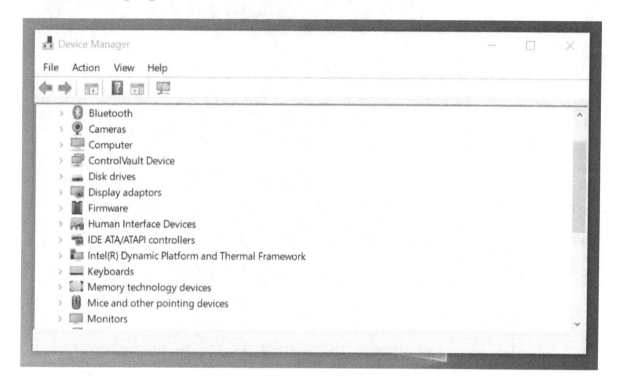

The steps described below have proven to fix this error for so many Windows users:

- Unplug all devices from your computer. Nothing should be connected to the computer including mouse.
- Shutdown the computer.
- If it is a laptop, disconnect the battery
- Leave the computer off for about 5 minutes
- Insert the battery back (if it is a laptop)
- Restart the computer
- Plug all devices back, one at a time including the USB device that gave error code 43

If the error is still not resolved, try the next fix.

Method 3: Check for and Install Windows Update

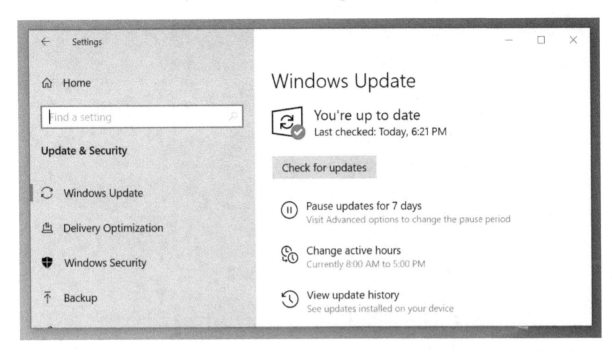

Sometimes installing the latest Windows update may resolve "Windows has stopped this device code 43". Here are the steps to check for and install all available Windows update…

- Right-click Windows 10 start menu (Windows logo at the bottom left of the taskbar). Then click **Settings**.

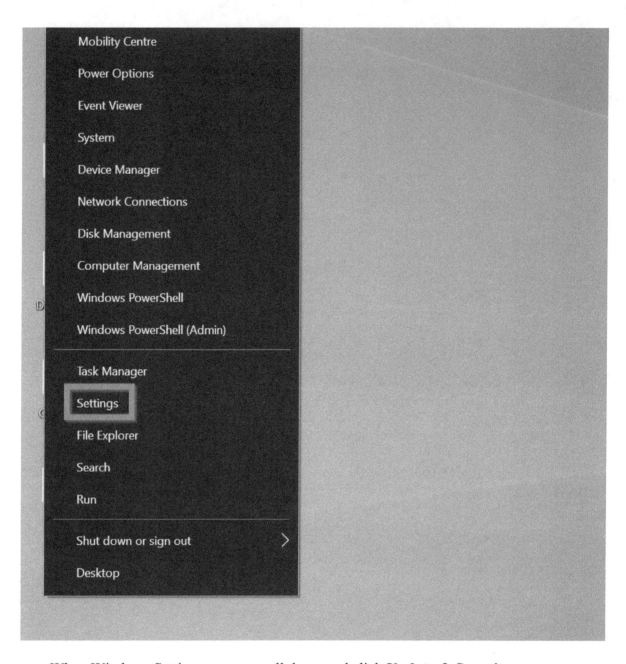

- When Windows Settings opens, scroll down and click **Update & Security**.

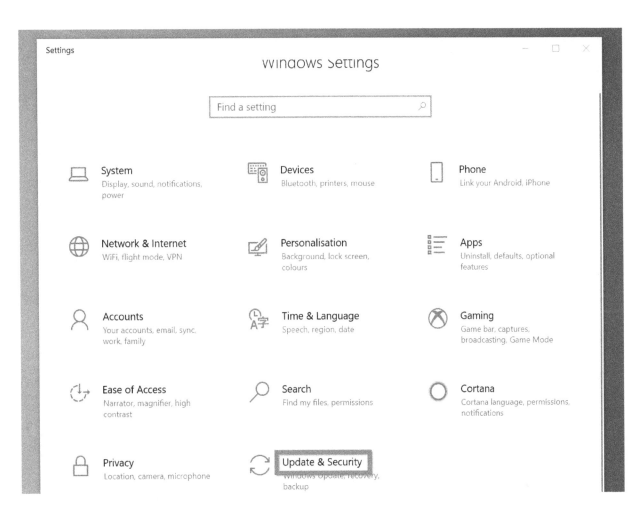

- If there are pending Windows updates, the Windows update screen will either display **Restart** or **Download**. Click the available option. Your computer will restart.

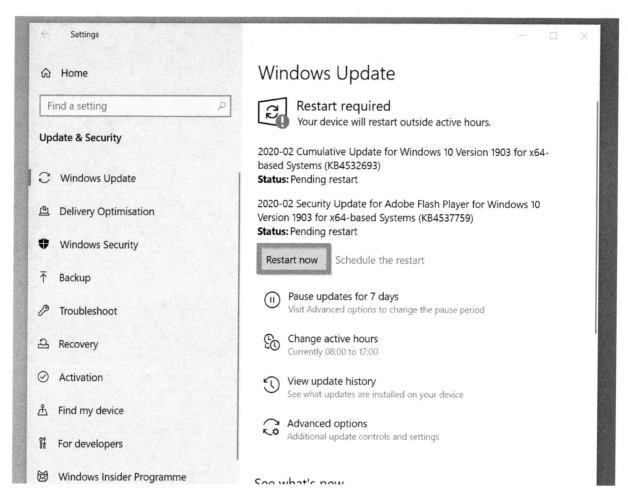

If installing Windows update does not fix "windows has stopped this device code 43", try the next fix.

Method 4: Reinstall Universal Serial Bus (USB) Controllers

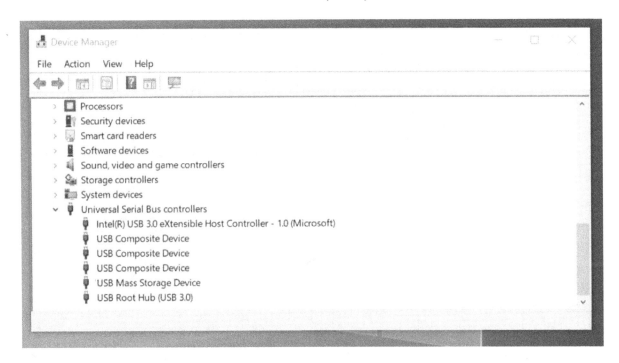

Warning!

If your mouse is connected to your computer via a USB port, performing the steps below will temporally stop your mouse from working. If you are using a laptop, use the mouse pad. For a desktop try to uninstall the USB device driver your mouse is attached to last.

To reinstall USB controllers drivers:

- Press **Windows + R** (Windows logo and R key pressed simultaneously). The *run* command will open.
- At the Run command, type *devmgmt.msc* and press OK to open Device Manager.

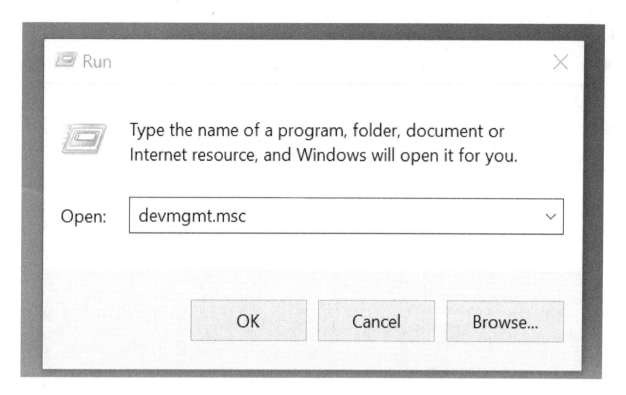

- When Device Manager opens, scroll down until you locate *Universal Serial Bus controllers*. Expand it to display all installed USB drivers.

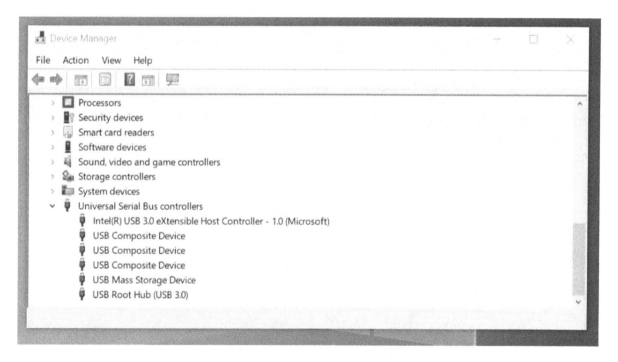

- For each Driver in the list, right-click, then select *Uninstall Device*. To confirm that you wish to remove the device driver, click Uninstall (see the second image below).

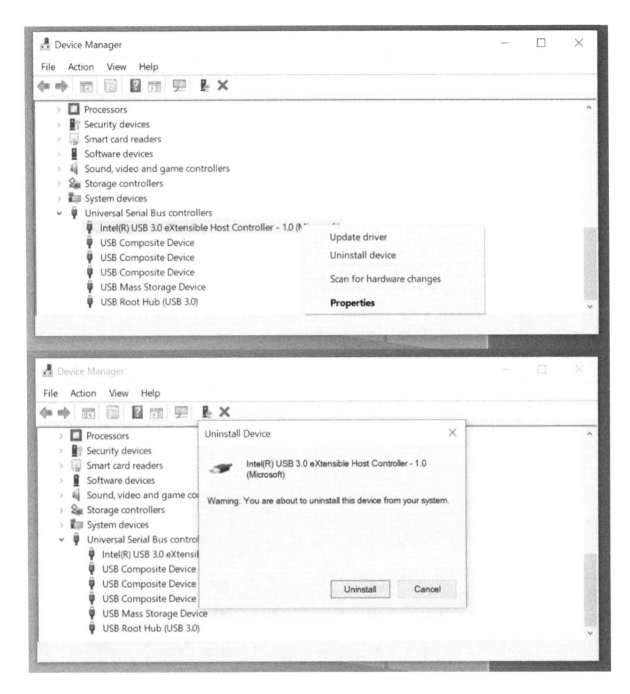

- Repeat this process until you have removed all the devices under *Universal Serial Bus controllers*
- Restart your computer. USB drivers will reinstall automatically.

If reinstalling your USB drivers does not fix "windows has stopped this device code 43", proceed to the next recommended fix.

Method 5: Disable "USB Selective Suspend" Setting

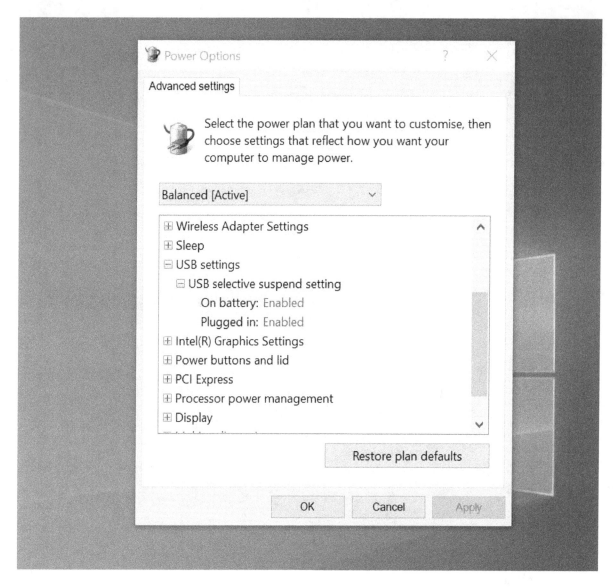

This last recommended fix applies to laptops. Here is my last effort to fix "windows has stopped this device code 43" for you:

- Type *power plan* in the Search box, and then select *Choose a power plan*.

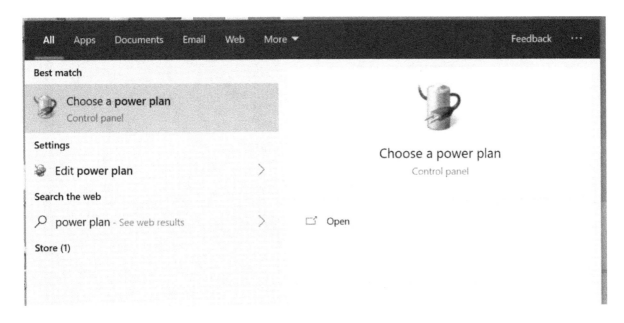

- Beside your current power setting, click *Change plan settings*.

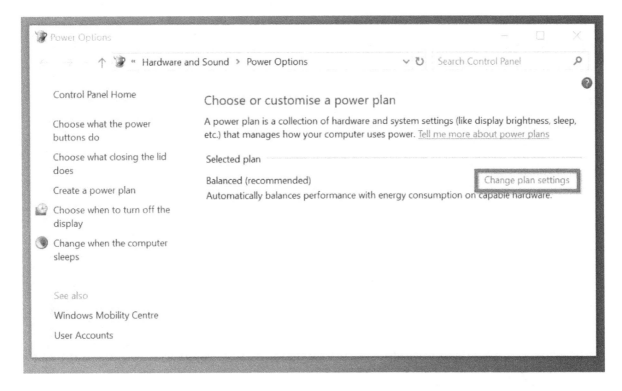

- Then on the *Change settings for plan <plan-name>* settings, click *Change advanced power settings*.

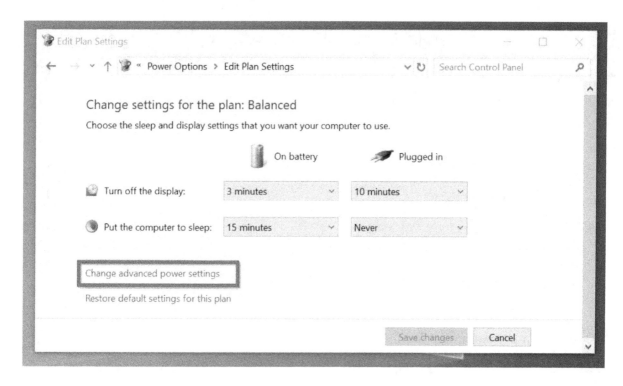

- When Advanced Power option settings open, expand *USB settings*. Then expand *USB selective suspend setting*.

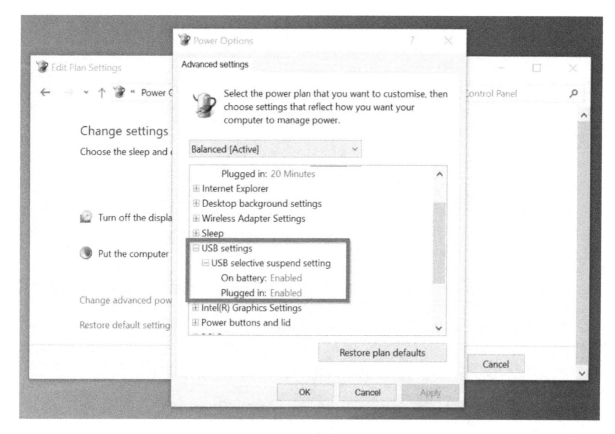

- Finally, if **On battery** is Enabled, click **Enabled** and select **Disabled**. To save your changes, click Apply.

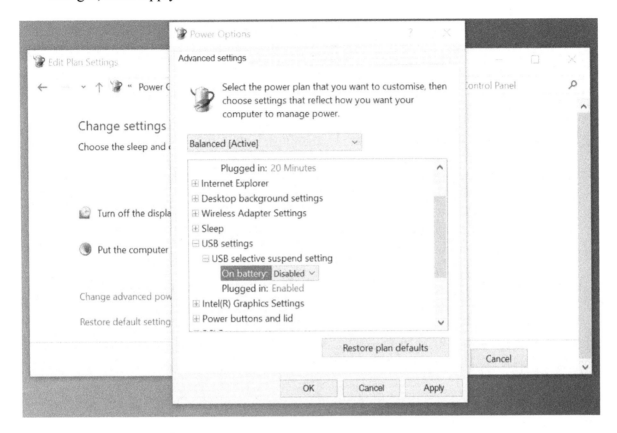

Hopefully, this last fix resolves "Windows has stopped this device code 43" for you!

How to fix "0xc000021a: Status System Process Terminated" Error

"0xc000021a (STATUS_SYSTEM_PROCESS_TERMINATED)" error may be triggered by any of the following:

1. After installing a new device on your Windows computer.
2. You may also receive this error after a Windows update or a new software installation.
3. This error may also occur if some critical Operating System files are missing.

Based on these, this guide offers the following fixes for "STATUS_SYSTEM_PROCESS_TERMINATED" error, based on the following:

One, if 0xc000021a (STATUS_SYSTEM_PROCESS_TERMINATED) error is caused by a driver, windows update or new software installation.

Two, if 0xc000021a (STATUS_SYSTEM_PROCESS_TERMINATED) is caused by missing or corrupt Windows files.

Method 1: Fix for 0xc000021a (STATUS_SYSTEM_PROCESS_TERMINATED) Error

Important Note
Because your computer will not boot if it has error 0xc000021a, you need a Windows 10 disk to boot your computer to Safe mode. Once in safe mode, you can remove any driver or software causing the problem.

If you receive 0xc000021a (STATUS_SYSTEM_PROCESS_TERMINATED) after installing Windows update, a new driver or new software, here is the fix:

- Insert Windows 10 DVD into your computer. Then boot to BIOS and change the boot sequence to boot from CD. You may also use a Windows 10 USB.
- Reboot your computer. When you receive the message below, click any key to boot from the Windows CD or USB drive.

```
Press any key to boot from CD or DVD....
```

- Your computer will boot as if you are reinstalling Windows 10.
- On the first screen, click Next.

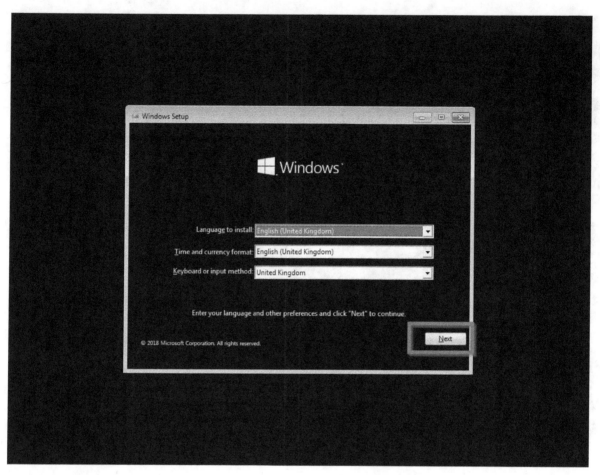

- Then click **Repair your computer**.

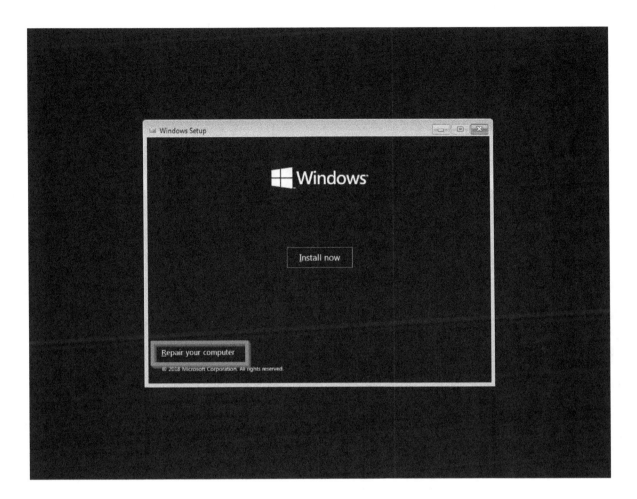

- On the boot options screen, click **Troubleshoot**.

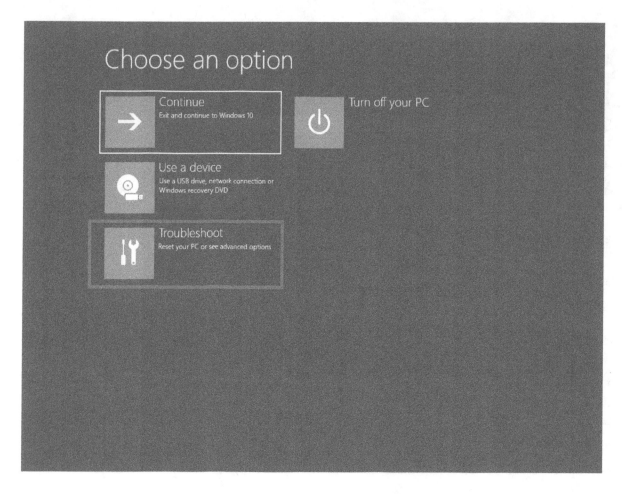

- What you click on the next screen depends on the cause of this error.
- If you recently installed Windows updates, click **Uninstall Updates**. Then follow the screen to uninstall any update that may have caused error 0xc000021a (STATUS_SYSTEM_PROCESS_TERMINATED).
- Alternatively, if error 0xc000021a (STATUS_SYSTEM_PROCESS_TERMINATED) was caused by a recent driver or software update, click **Command Prompt**. Then, follow the steps beneath the image below.

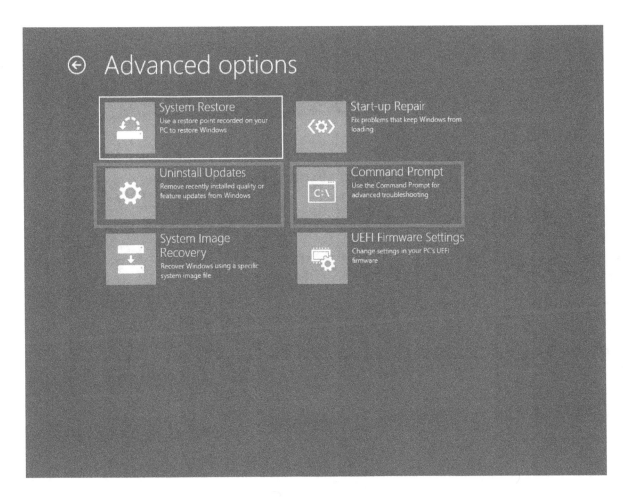

- When Command Prompt opens, type the command below. Then press Enter key on your keyboard.

```
bcdedit /set {default} safeboot minimal
```

If you typed the command correctly, it should return the message "The operating completed successfully".

- When the command completes successfully, close command prompt. Then click **Continue** to reboot your computer.

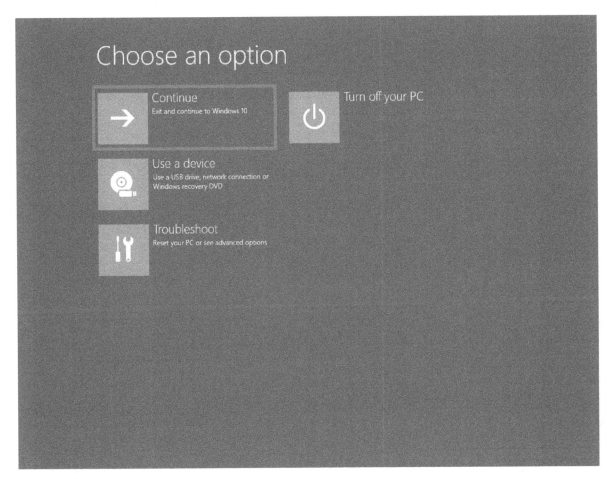

Important Tip

When you reboot your computer this time, DO NOT boot with Windows 10 DVD. Allow the computer to boot up to safe mode.

- Log in to your computer as normal. Notice that your computer booted in safe mode (second image below).

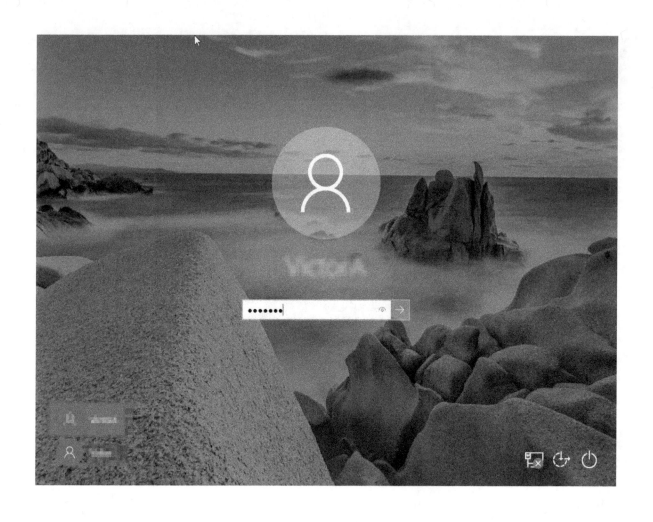

From this point, you can uninstall a device driver you believe may have caused error 0xc000021a (STATUS_SYSTEM_PROCESS_TERMINATED). You may also uninstall any recently installed software.

To uninstall a device driver:

- Right-click the Windows logo on the left of your taskbar. Then click **Device Manager**.

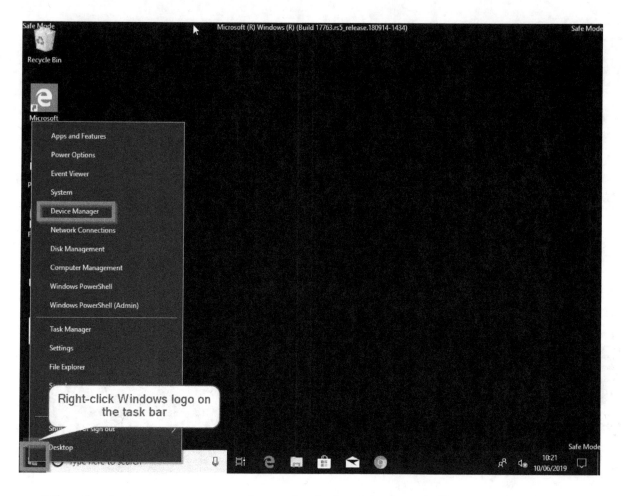

- When the device manager opens, locate the device driver you believe may have caused error 0xc000021a (STATUS_SYSTEM_PROCESS_TERMINATED). Right-click the device driver. Then click **Uninstall device**.

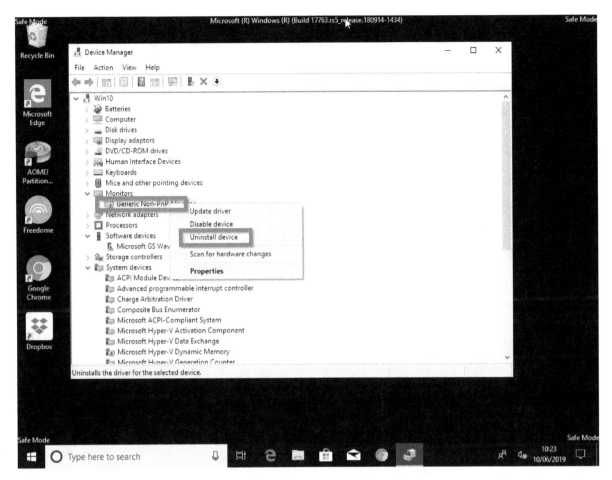

Important Tip

As a guide, try uninstalling any device driver(s) you installed before you experienced error 0xc000021a.

If you recently installed software, follow the steps below to uninstall the software:

- Type *Apps* into Windows 10 search bar. Then select **Apps & features**.

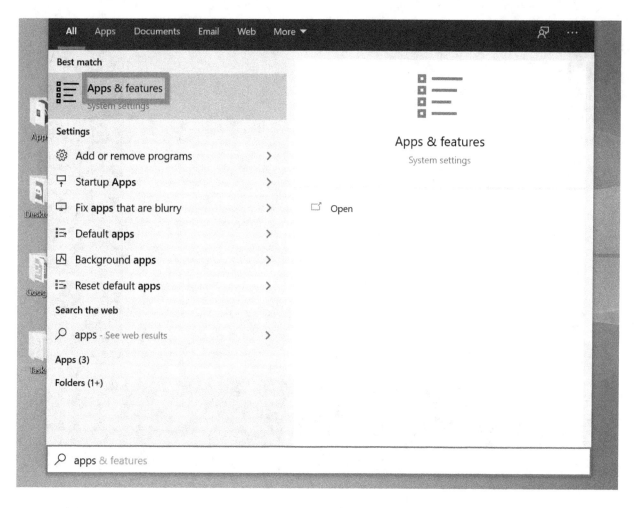

- When **Apps & features** open, scroll down to the app you recently installed before the error message and click on it.
- When you click the app, the Uninstall option will become available. Click Uninstall.

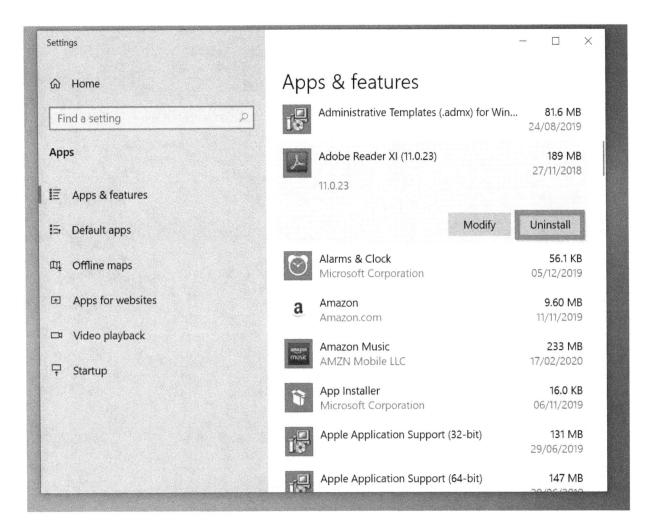

- To confirm that you want to uninstall the App, click **Uninstall** again.

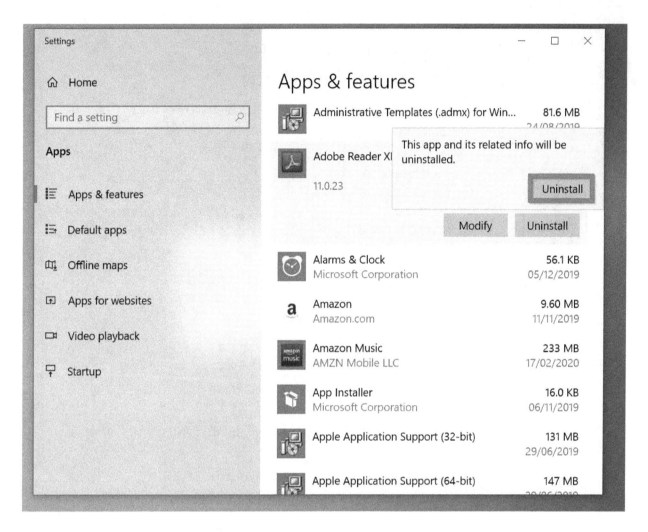

- Restart your computer.

Very Important Note
Except you need to apply the solution outlined in Method 2 below, you MUST remove your computer from safe mode. Otherwise, it will continue to boot to safe mode.

- To stop your PC booting to safe mode, open command prompt as administrator, type the command below and press enter.

```
bcdedit /deletevalue {default} safeboot
```

Method 2: Fix for 0xc000021a: STATUS_SYSTEM_PROCESS_TERMINATED Error

Error 0xc000021a may not be resolved by uninstalling recently installed updates. If uninstalling updates do not fix your problem, it is possible that some important windows files may be missing or corrupt.

If this is your situation, the following steps may help resolve your 0xc000021a (STATUS_SYSTEM_PROCESS_TERMINATED Error):

While still booted to safe mode and logged on to Windows:

- Right-click the Windows logo on your taskbar. Then click **Run**.

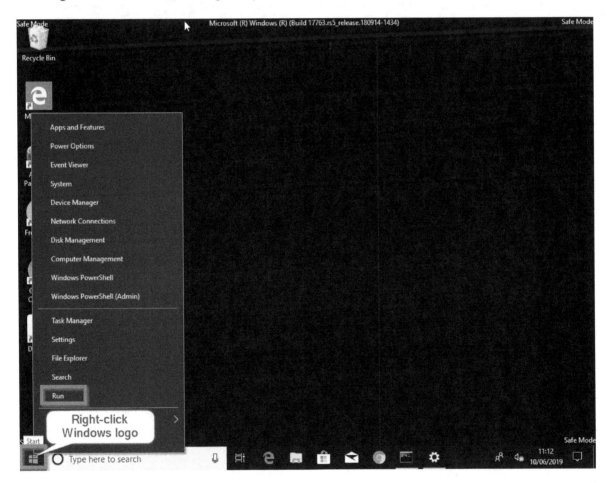

- When **Run** opens, type **cmd** then click Ok. This will open **Command Prompt**.

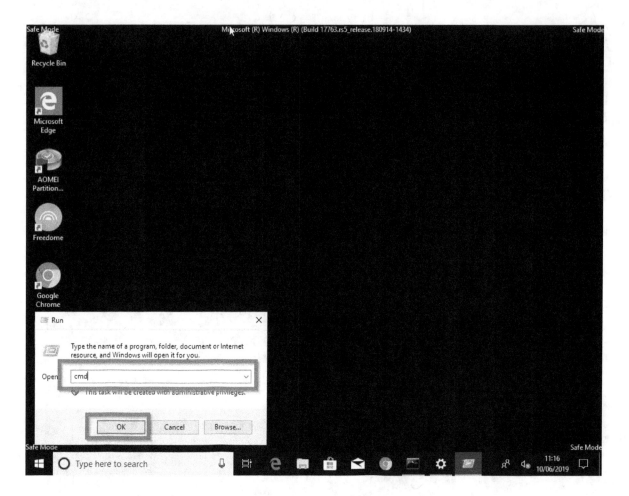

- When command prompt opens, type the command below and press Enter.

```
SFC /scannow
```

Remove Windows from Safe Mode

When you finish these tasks, to make sure your computer boots normally, open Command Prompt as administrator. Then, type the command below and press Enter key.

```
bcdedit /deletevalue {default} safeboot
```

145

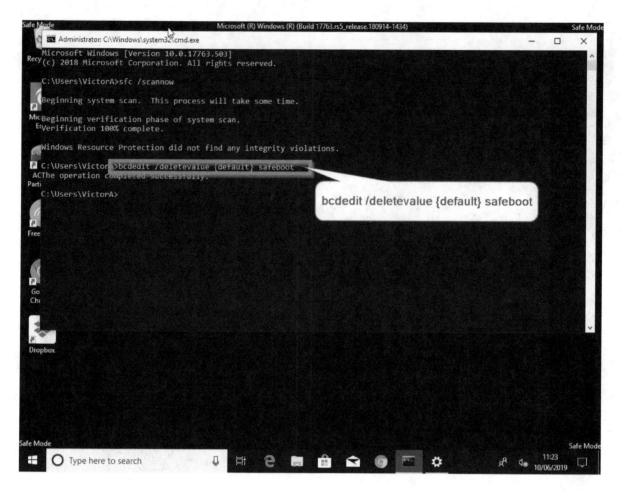

- Reboot your computer.

How to Fix "C:\WINDOWS\system32 \config\systemprofile\Desktop Is Unavailable" Error"

You may receive the error message "WINDOWS system32 config systemprofile Desktop is unavailable" after upgrading to Windows 10.

The reason for the error is that the default desktop profile was not found in its usual location. This meant that your desktop could not be loaded.

This guide offers 3 methods to fix "WINDOWS system32 config systemprofile Desktop is unavailable" error:

1. Copy the default Desktop folder to C:\WINDOWS\system32\config\systemprofile
2. Create a new user, login with the new user name and copy your files
3. Perform a fresh install of Windows 10

Method 1: Copy the default Desktop Folder

Use the steps below to copy default Desktop to C:\WINDOWS\system32\config\systemprofile:

- Press **Windows** + **E** (Windows logo simultaneously with **E** key) on your keyboard. This will open *File Explorer*.

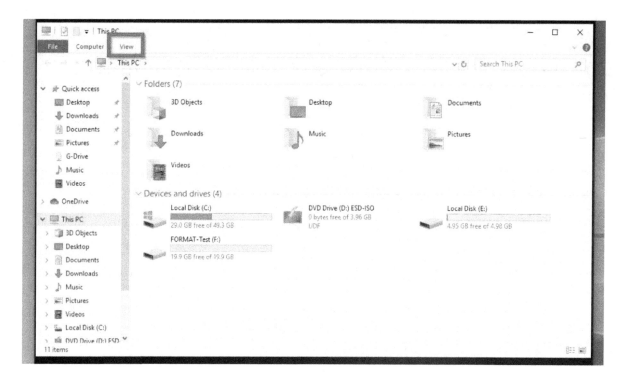

- On the top left of File Explorer, click the *View* tab.

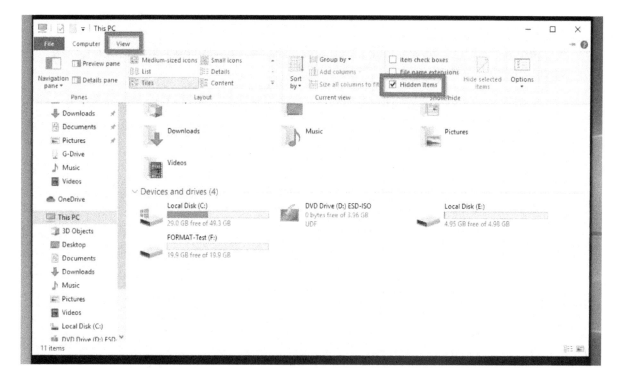

- On the View tab, check the box beside *Hidden items*. This will show hidden files and folders.
- Then navigate to *C:\Users\Default* and copy the *Desktop* folder.

148

- Next, click *This PC*. Then open the path C:\Windows\System32\config\systemprofile and paste the Desktop folder you copied earlier.

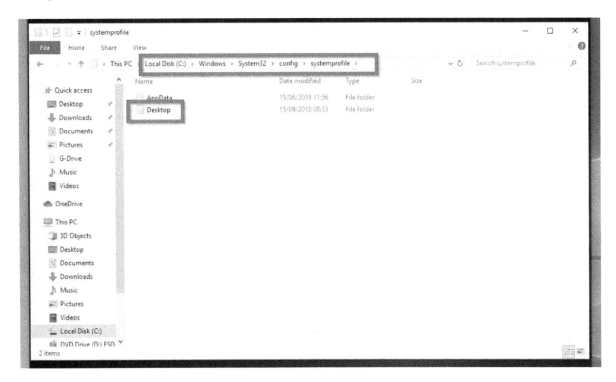

149

- Restart your computer. Then login with the user name where you received the error message. If you log in successfully, congratulations! Otherwise, try method 2 below.

Method 2: Create a New User and Copy Your Files

This method is more of a workaround: You will create a new local user. Then login with the new username and copy your files from the "corrupt" profile to the new profile. Here are the steps.

- Search *cmd* into Windows 10 search bar. Then right-click **Command Prompt** and click **run as Administrator**.
- You will receive a User Account Control prompt. Click Yes.

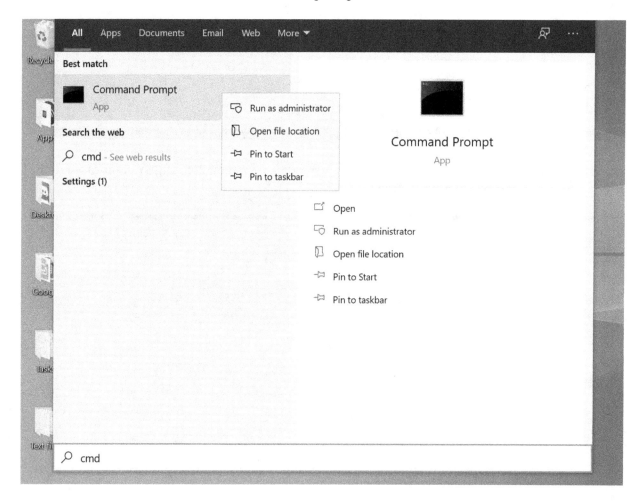

- When Command Prompt opens, type the command below and press Enter.

```
control userpasswords2
```

- The previous command will open the User Account tool.

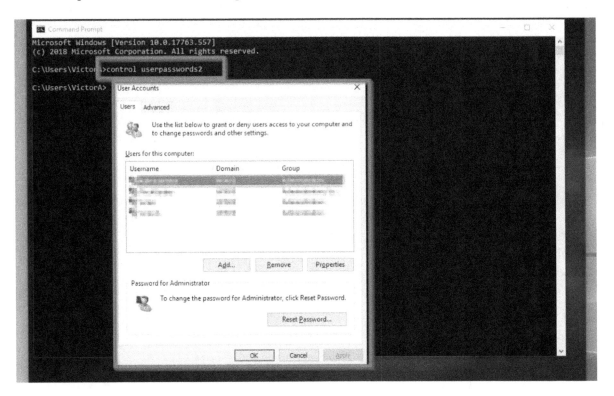

From this point, you can either add an existing domain user or create a new local user.

To add an existing domain user:

- Click **Add**.

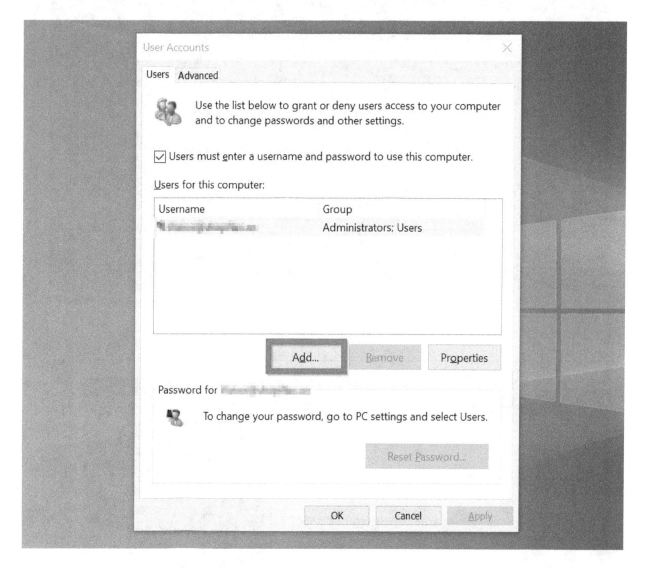

- When the *Add a domain account* wizard opens, click *Browse*. The *Select User* menu will be displayed.

- On the *Enter the object name to select* box, type the name of the domain account you want to add. Then click *Check Names*. Verify your domain credentials. Then click OK.

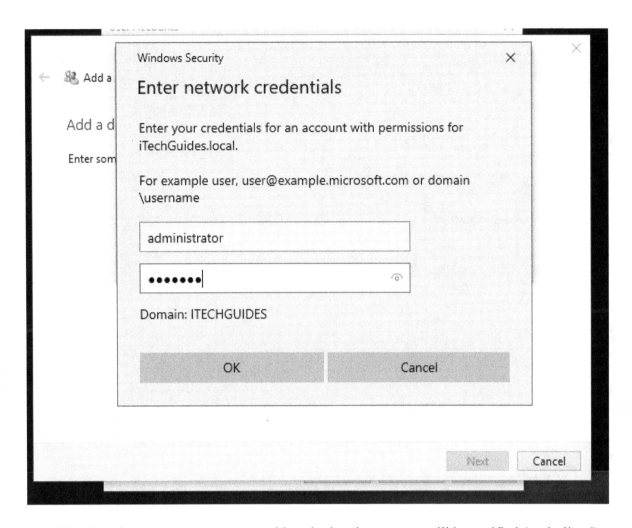

- The domain account you want to add to the local computer will be verified (underlined).
- To proceed, click OK.

- From this point, click Next. Then add the user as an administrator.

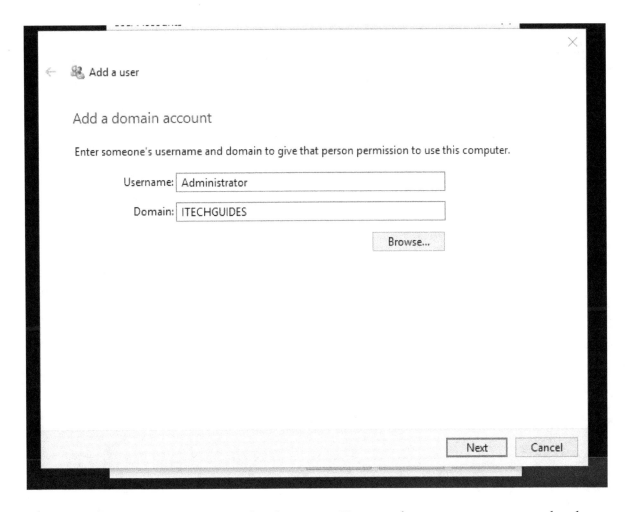

Alternatively, you can create a new local account. Here are the steps to create a new local user account in Windows 10:

- On *User Accounts*, click the *Advanced* tab.

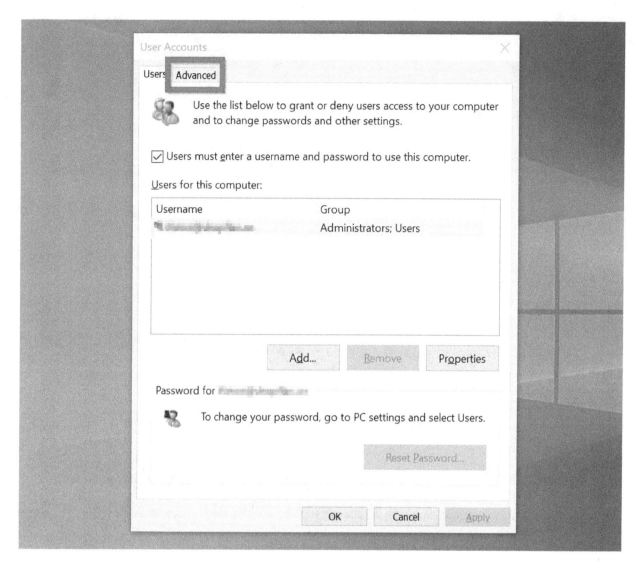

- Then, on the *Advanced user management* section, click *Advanced. Local Users and Groups* MMC will open.

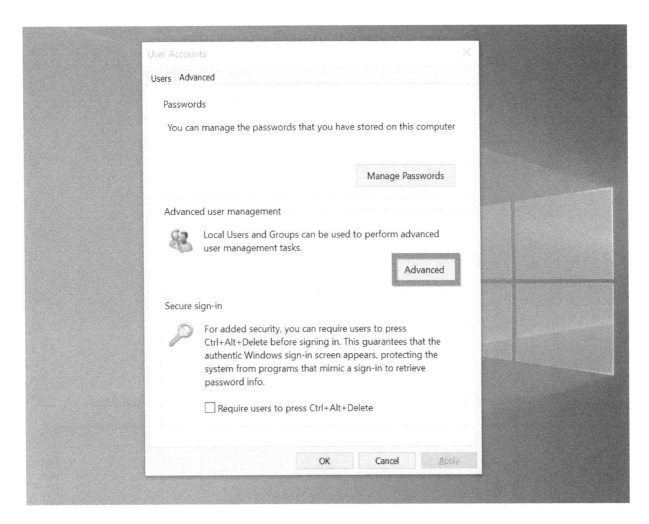

- To create a new local user account, right-click *Users* and click **New User**...

- Finally, type a username for the new user. Enter a password for the new account, uncheck **User must change password at next logon**. Then, to create the new user, click **Create**.

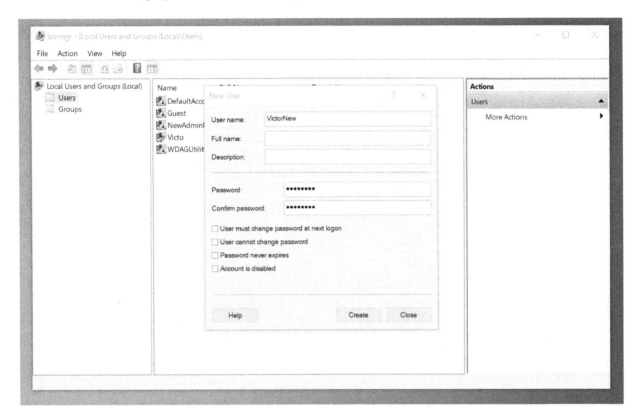

- Close the new user window.

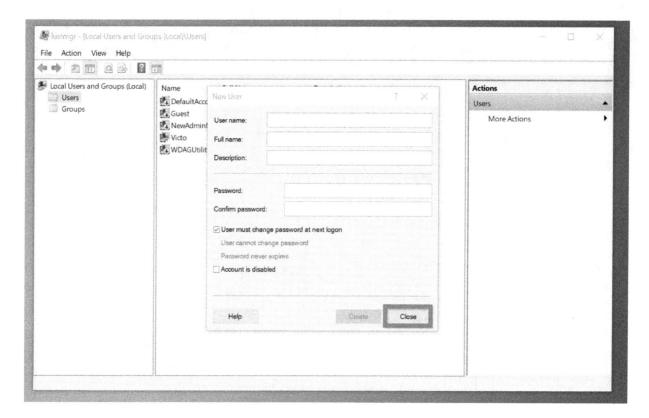

- Double-click the new user to open its properties.

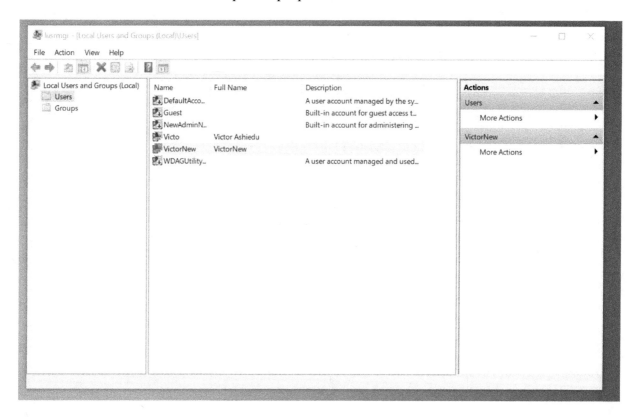

- Then, click the **Member of** tab.

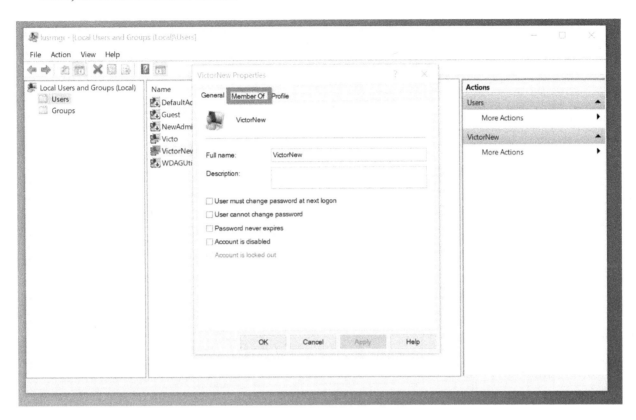

- When the tab opens, click Add

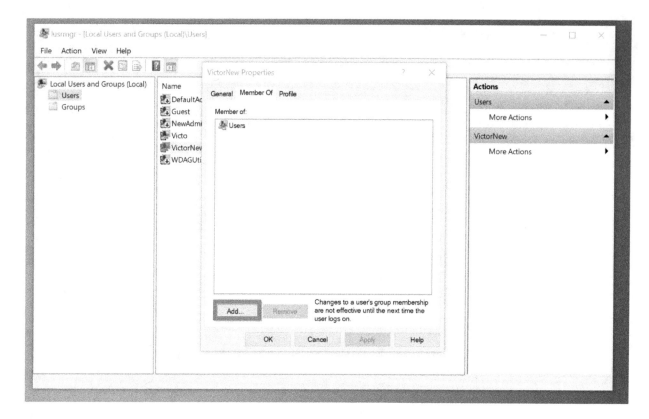

- Then, type *administrators* and click **Check Names**.

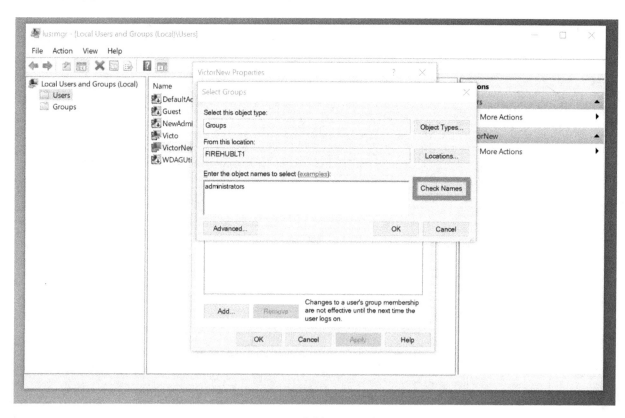

164

- The name will resolve as shown – *ComputerName*\Administrators. Click OK.

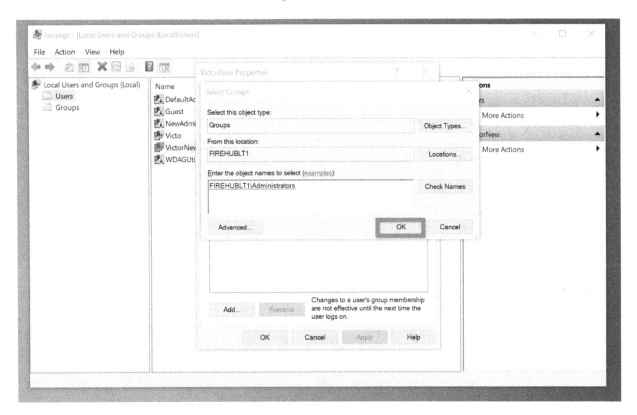

- The new user you created is now added to the local administrators group. To save your changes, click OK.

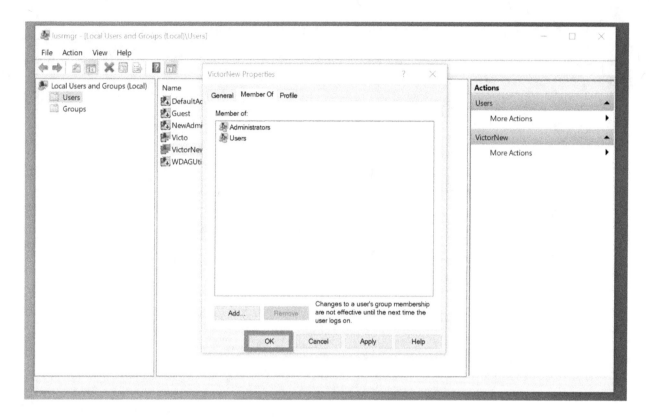

- Log out of the computer. Then log back as the new user you created. When you log in to the new account, you will be required to select some privacy settings. When your desktop is displayed, proceed to the next step.
- Right-click Windows 10 menu and click *File Explorer*.

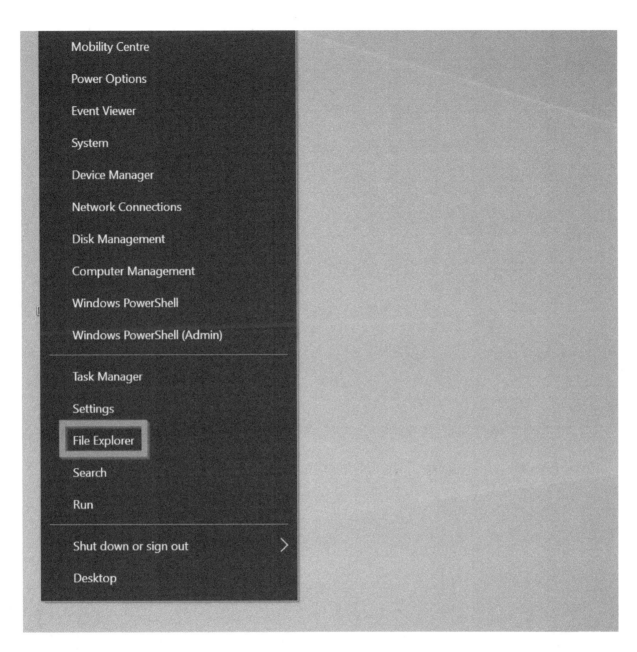

- When File Explorer opens, click the *View* tab.

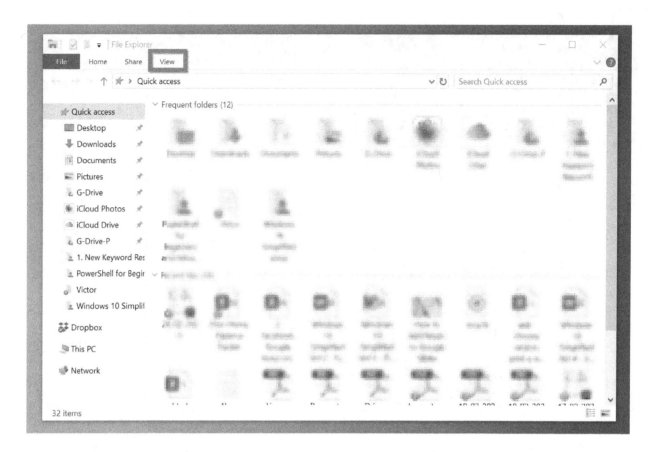

- At the *View* tab, click the box beside **Hidden Items**.

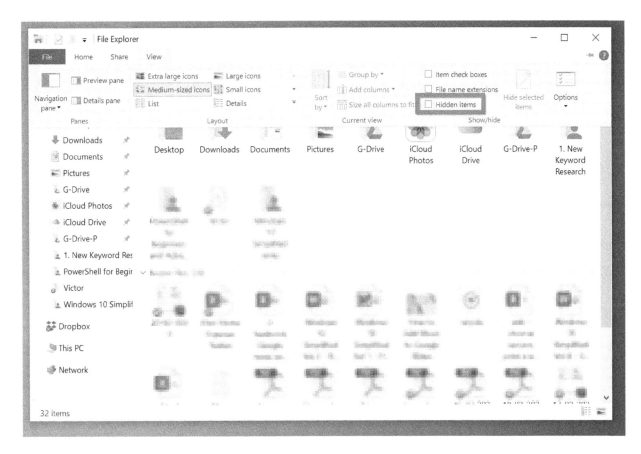

- Then, at the bottom left of File Explorer, click **This PC**.

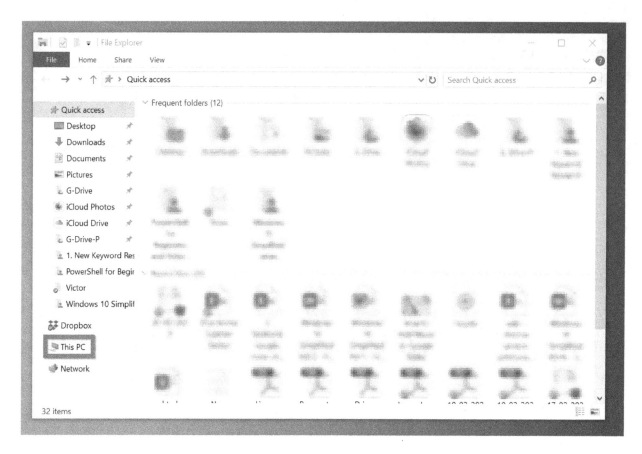

- Finally, click **Local Disk (C:).**

170

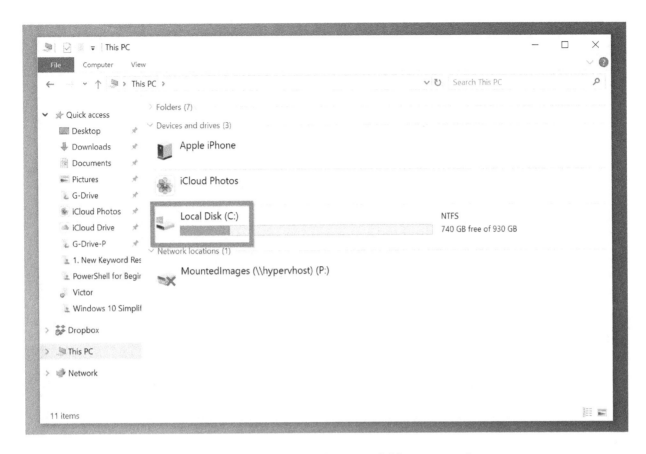

- When Drive C opens, locate and double-click Users folder to open it.

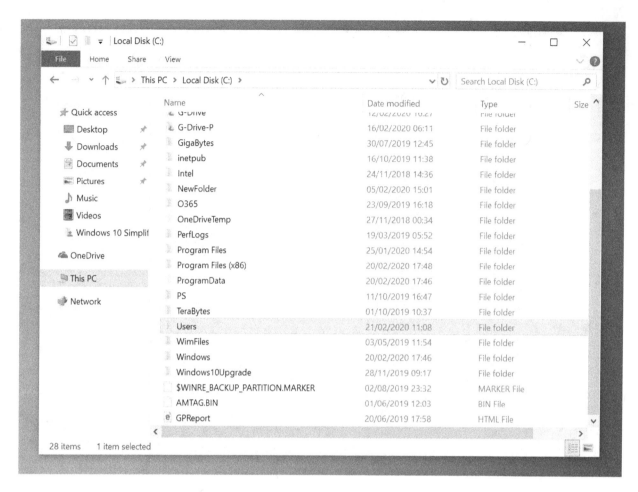

- All users that have logged on to the PC will be listed. For this illustration, *Victo* is my old corrupt profile; *VictorNew* is the new account I just created. Click your old account folder.

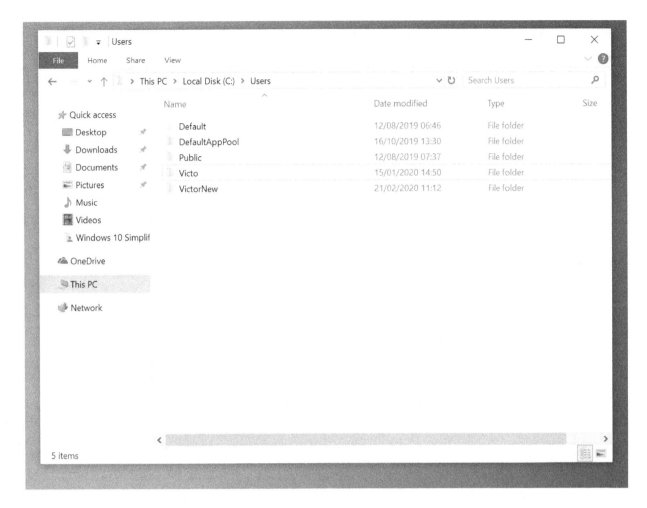

- On the permission pop up, click **Continue**. The wait for the folder to open.

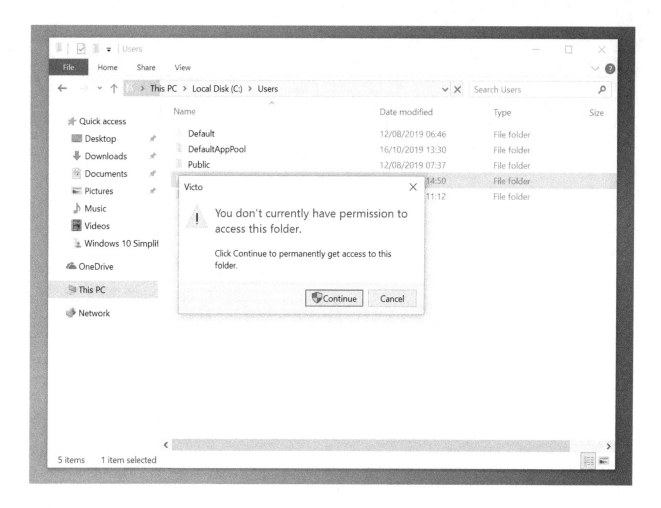

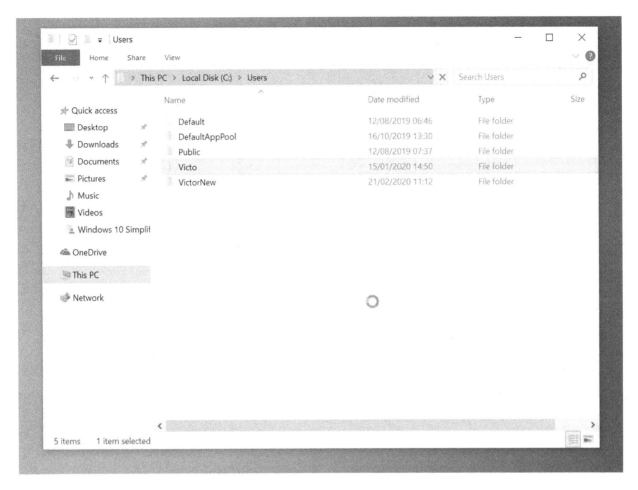

- When the folder opens, click **Ctrl** and **A** keys on your keyboard to select all items in the folder. Then, click **Ctrl** and **C** to copy all the items. Finally, use the back button to return to the **Users** folder.

V

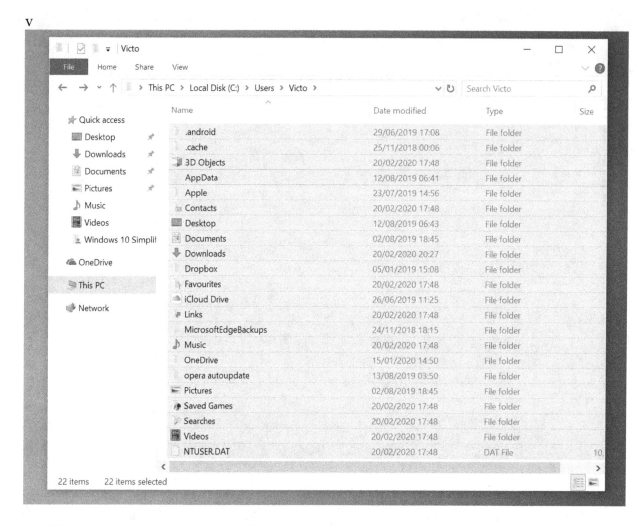

- When you return to the Users folder, double-click to open the folder for the new account you are currently logged in to.

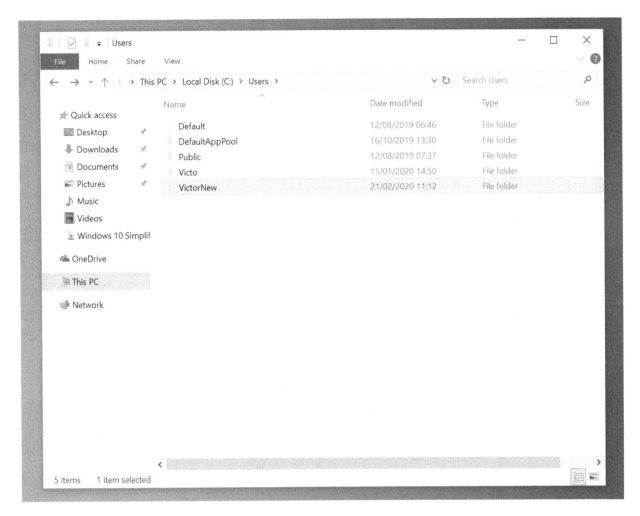

- Paste (**Ctrl** and **V** keys) all the contents you copied from the old profile. If you receive a prompt to replace existing files or folders, click Yes.

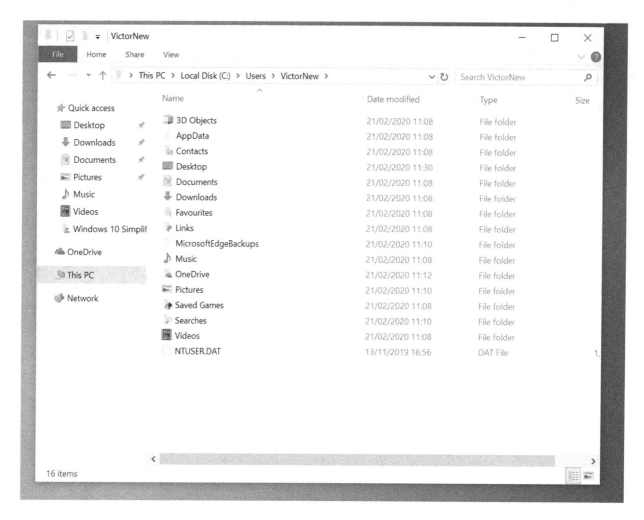

- Finally, log out and log back in. "WINDOWS system32 config systemprofile Desktop is unavailable" error should be resolved.

How to Fix "Windows Update Error 0x8024401c" in Windows 10

Follow these steps in this guide in order. After each step, try running Windows Update. When Windows Update 0x8024401c error is fixed, you do not need to proceed with the rest of the steps.

It is important to follow the steps in this guide in order. I have ordered the suggested fixes from the simplest to the most complex. In listing these fixes, I considered most scenarios that could cause Windows Update 0x8024401c error.

So, even though all the steps may not apply to your situation, it is important to follow the steps sequentially. Most of the steps are very simple and straightforward.

Method 1: Confirm that Your Copy of Windows 10 is Activated

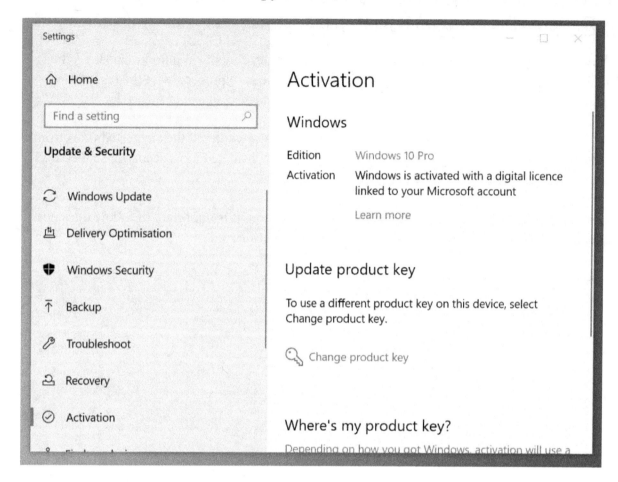

If your copy of Windows 10 is not activated, you may NOT be able to download and install updates. Microsoft is seriously cracking down on non-activated Windows, and for good reasons too.

To check your Windows activation status:

- Search *Activate*. Then click *Activation settings*.

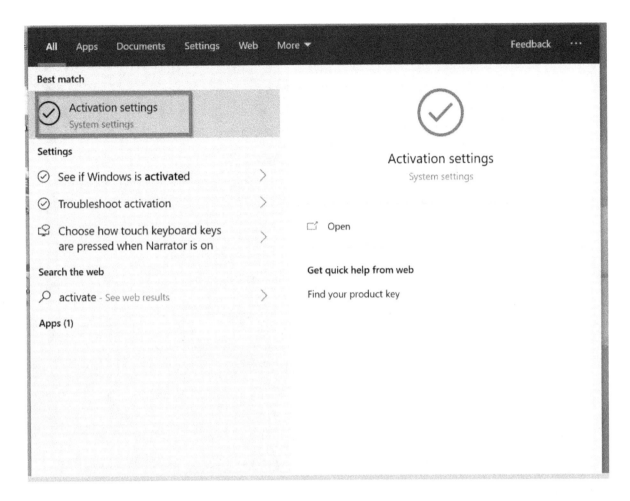

- If Windows is NOT activated, click change product key. Then complete the activation process.

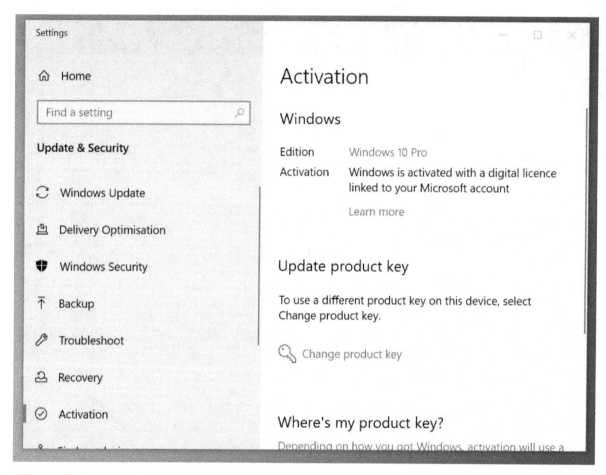

When Windows 10 is activated, try downloading Windows update. If error 0x8024401c is not fixed, not proceed to the next suggested fix.

Method 2: Check Your Internet Connection

You may receive Windows Update 0x8024401c error if you are not connected to the internet. One way to check that you are on the internet is to visit a website using your favorite browser.

Once you have confirmed that you are connected to the internet but still cannot update your computer, proceed to step 3 below.

Method 3: Restart Your Computer

Most Windows problems may be resolved by a simple reboot. Do this and try again.

Method 4: Disable IPv6

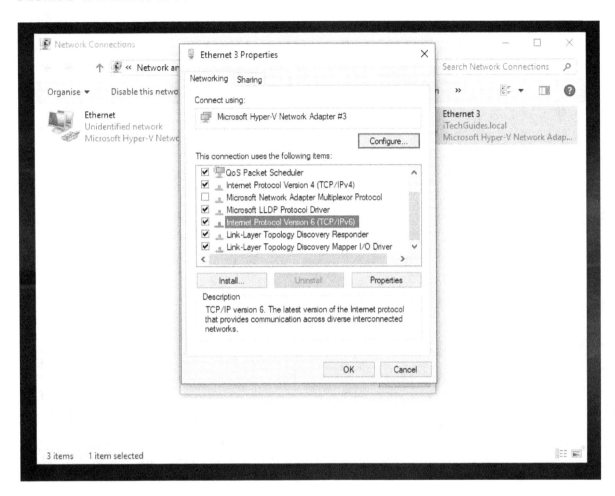

Disabling IP version 6 may fix Windows update error. Here are the steps to disable *Internet Protocol Version 6 (TCP/IPv6)*:

- Type *Control Panel* in the Windows 10 search box. Then select **Control Panel** from the result.

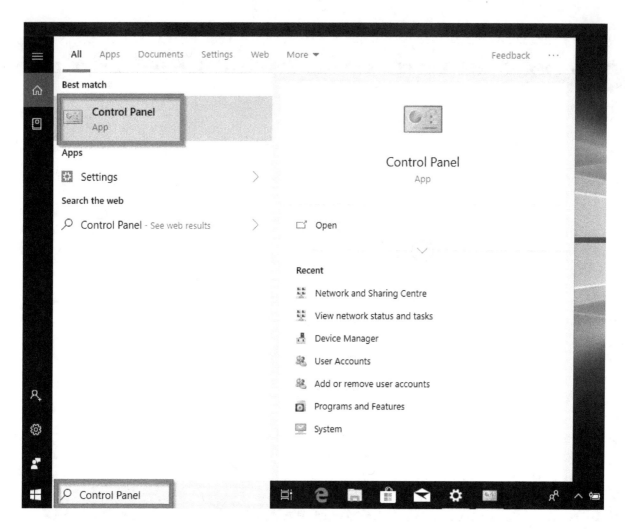

- When Control Panel opens, click *Network and Internet*. Then click the *Network and Sharing Centre*.

186

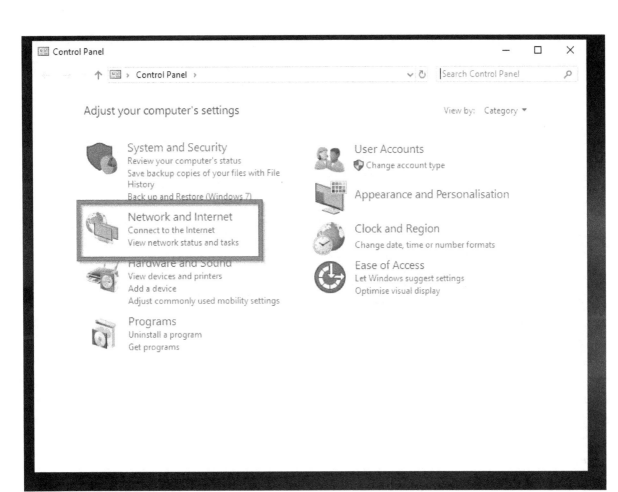

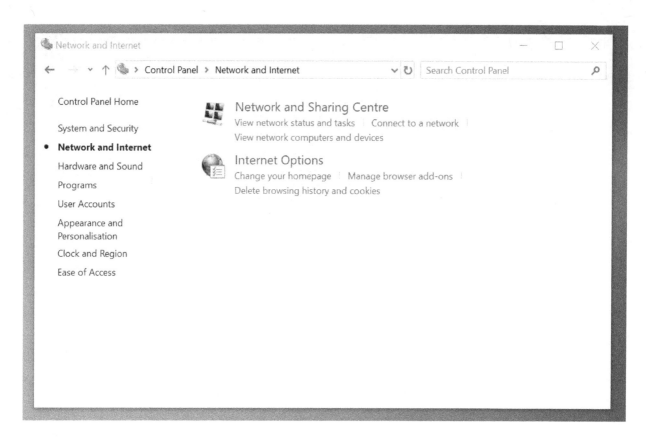

- Next, click *Change adapter settings*.

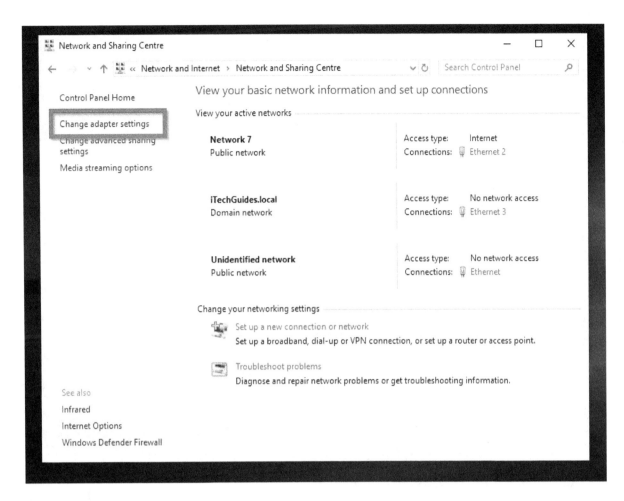

- Double-click the network adapter you use to connect to the internet. The Adapter status will be displayed.

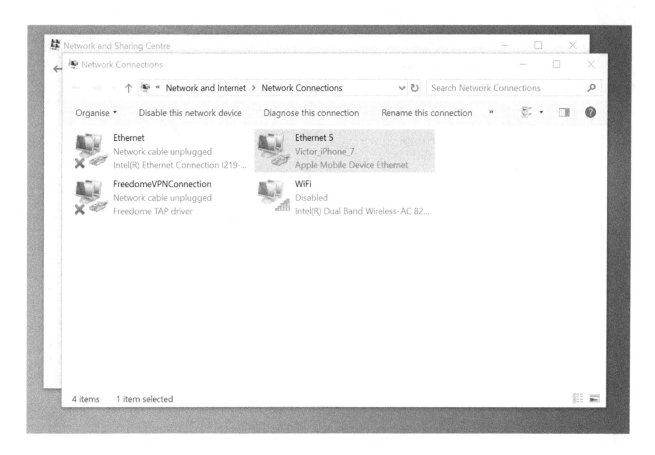

- Then click *Properties*. When the Properties of the network adapter opens, uncheck the box beside *Internet Protocol Version 6 (TCP/IPv6)*. Then click OK.

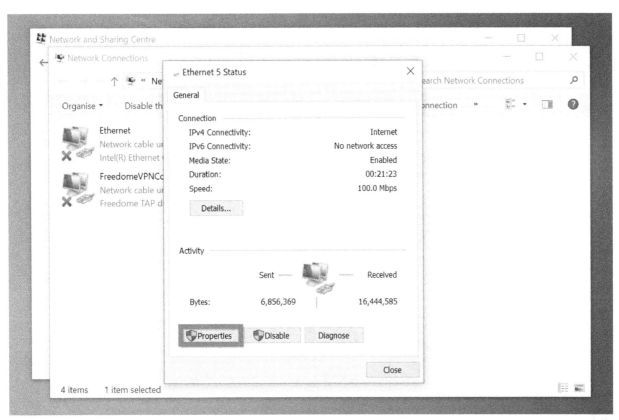

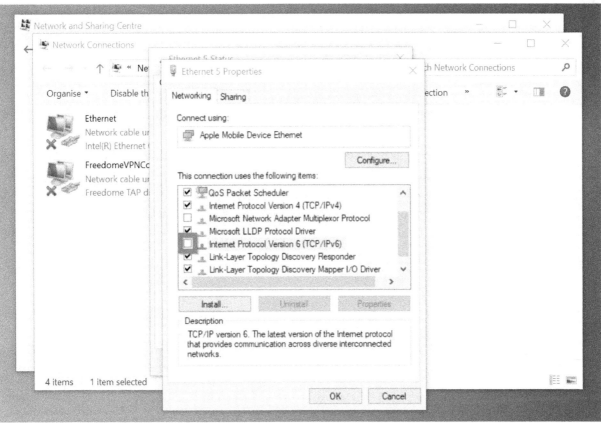

Restart your computer and retry the update. If you still receive the update error, try the next fix.

Method 5: Disable Metered Connection

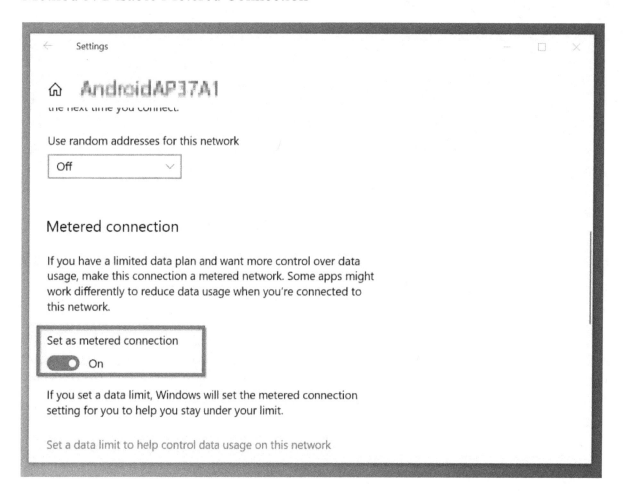

If your network adapter is set as a metered connection, you may not be able to download Windows updates. To rule this out, use the steps below to disable metered connection:

- Type *Network* in the Windows search. Then, select **Network status** from the search result.

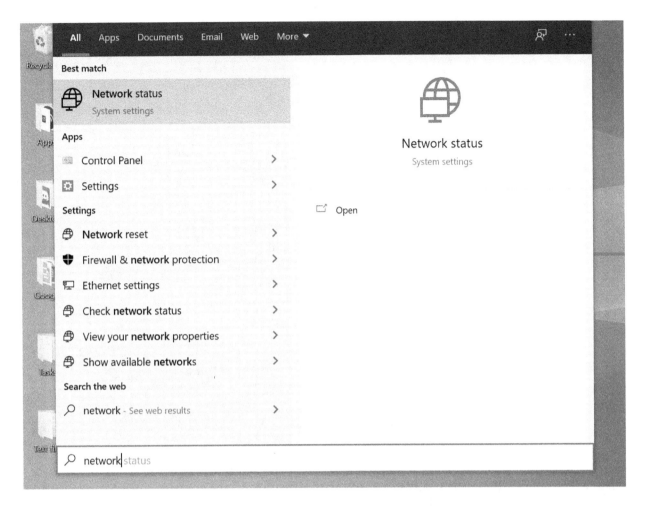

- When **Network status** opens, click **Change connection properties**.

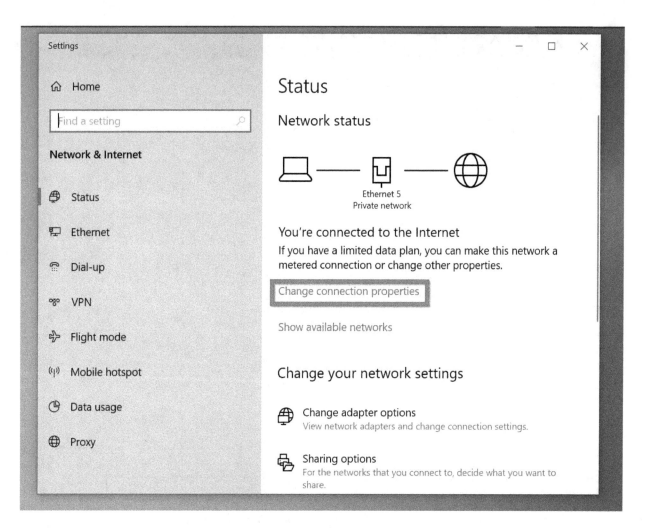

- Scroll down to **Metered connection**. If **Set as metered connection** switch is ON, click it to turn it OFF.

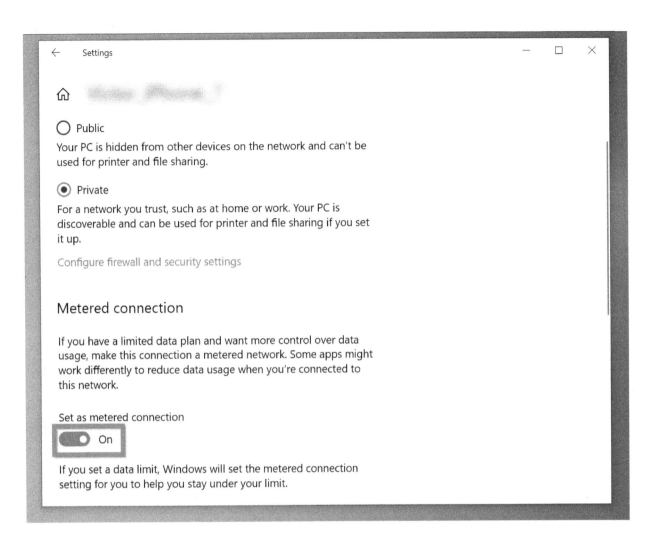

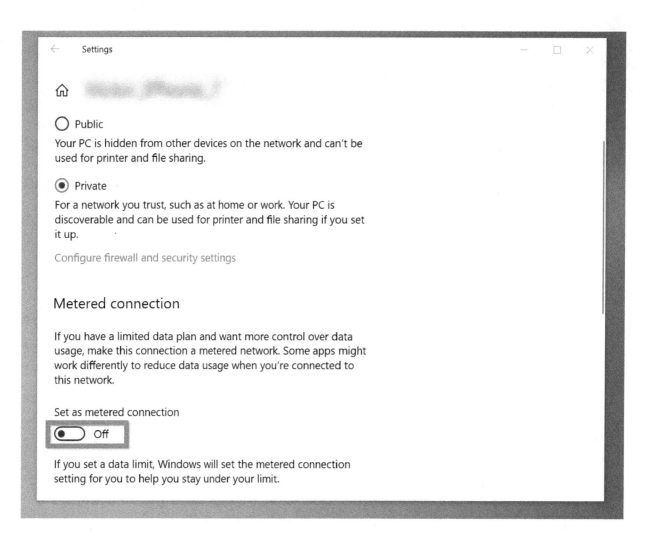

Check whether the Windows update error is resolved. If not, proceed to the next step.

Method 5: Change to a different Network

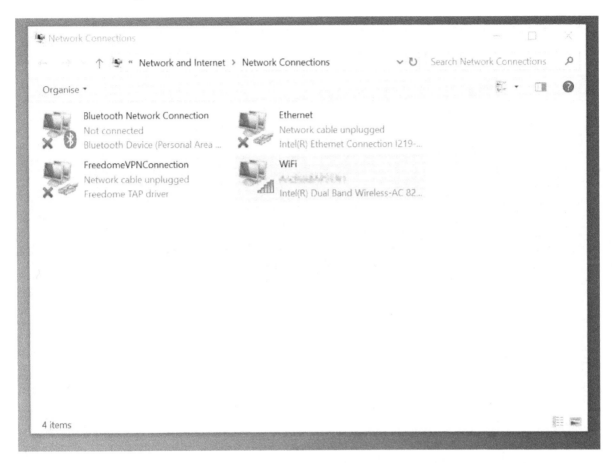

If you can access the internet from another connection type, change to another connection. For instance, if you are using Wireless, change to a wired connection.

Run Windows Update Troubleshooter

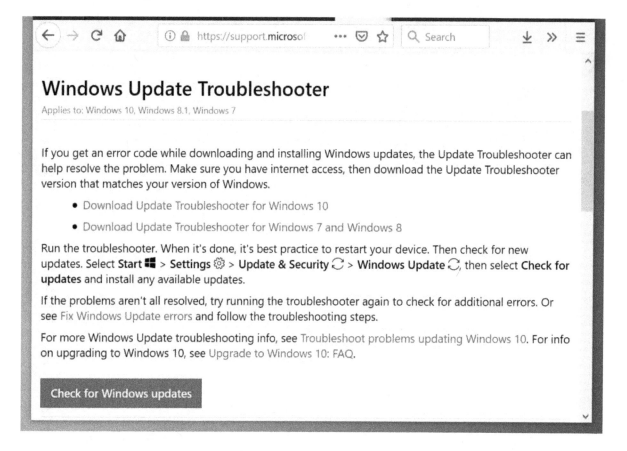

Windows Update Troubleshooter is designed to fix most Windows update problems.

To use this tool to fix error 0x8024401c:

- Search **Windows Update Troubleshooter** in Google. Then, click **Windows Update Troubleshooter – Microsoft Support** result – most likely the first result in the list.

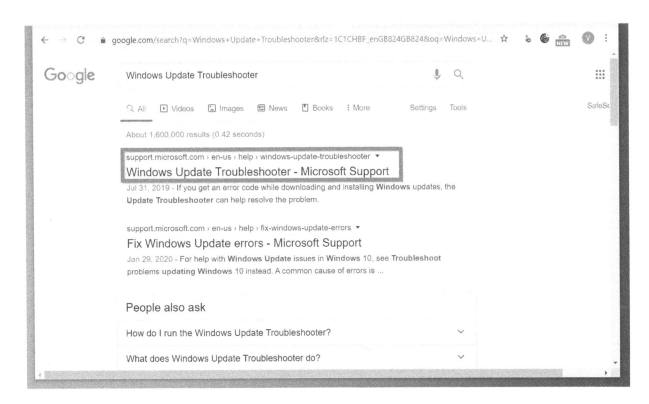

- When the **Windows Update Troubleshooter** page opens, click the link **Download Update Troubleshooter for Windows 10** or **Download Update Troubleshooter for Windows 7 and Windows 8.**

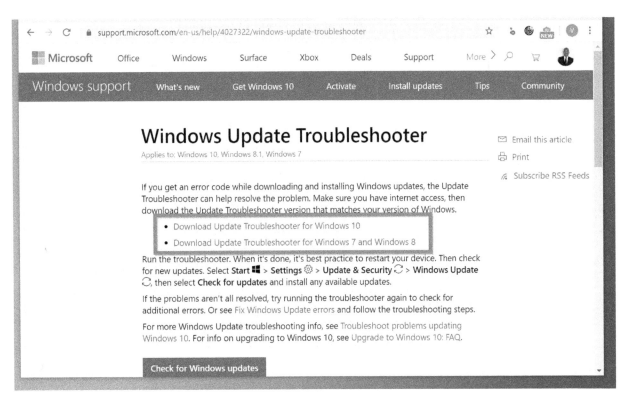

- Save the tool to a folder on your computer.

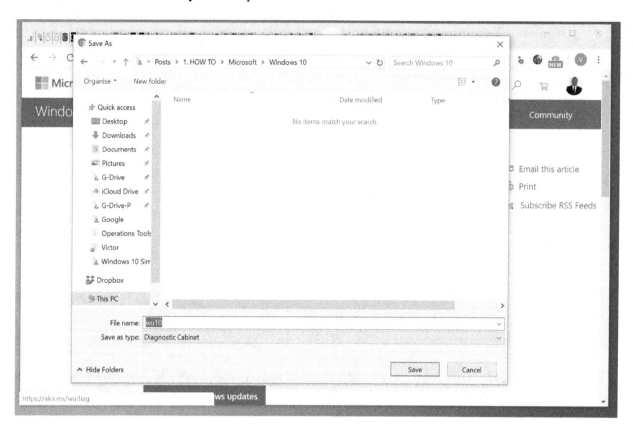

- Open the folder you saved the Troubleshooter and double-click it.

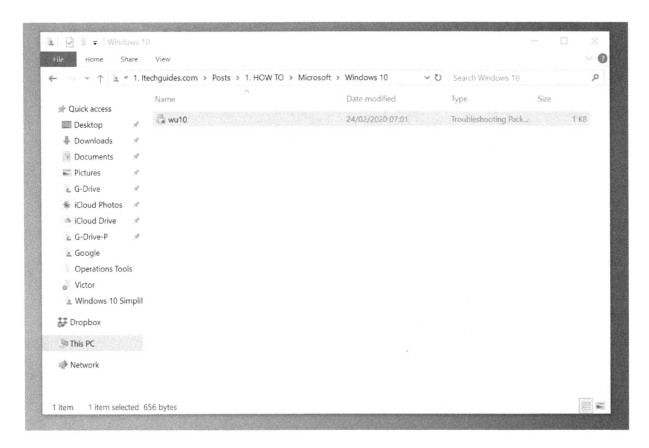

- On the first screen of the wizard, click Next.

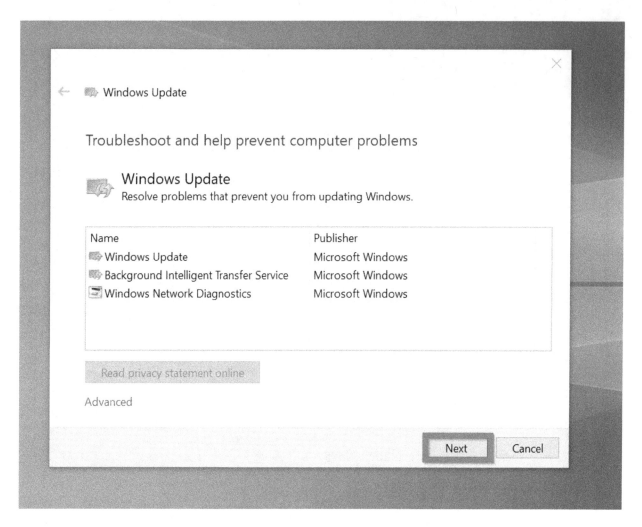

- If you receive a screen like the one below, click **Try troubleshooting as an administrator**.

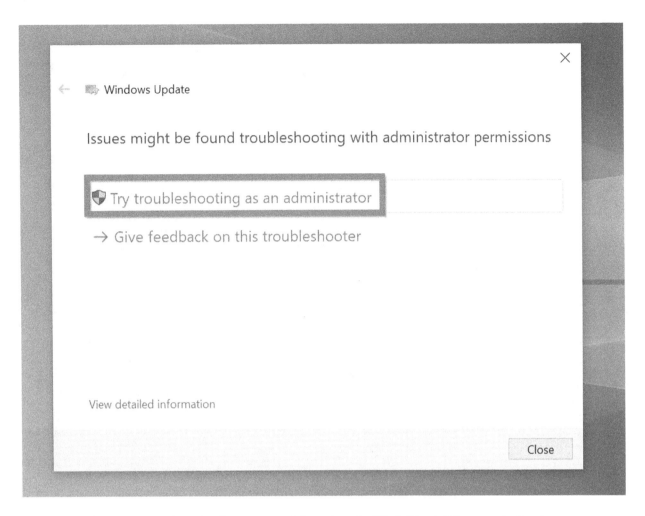

- You will be returned to the first page of the wizard. Click **Next**. Then, wait for the Troubleshooter to find potential problems that may be stopping Windows update from working properly.

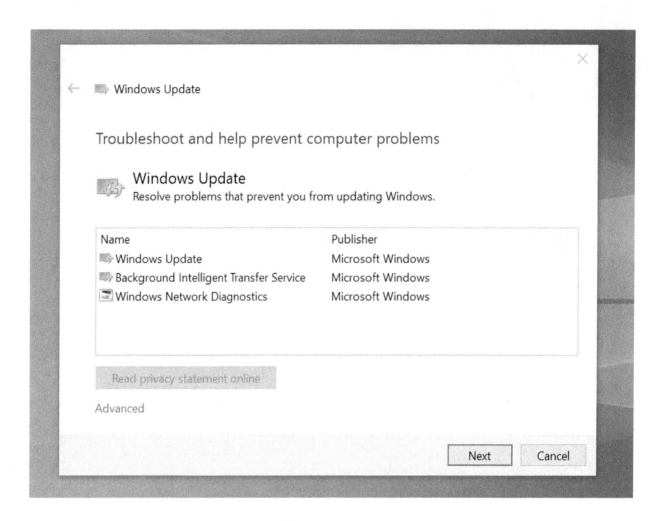

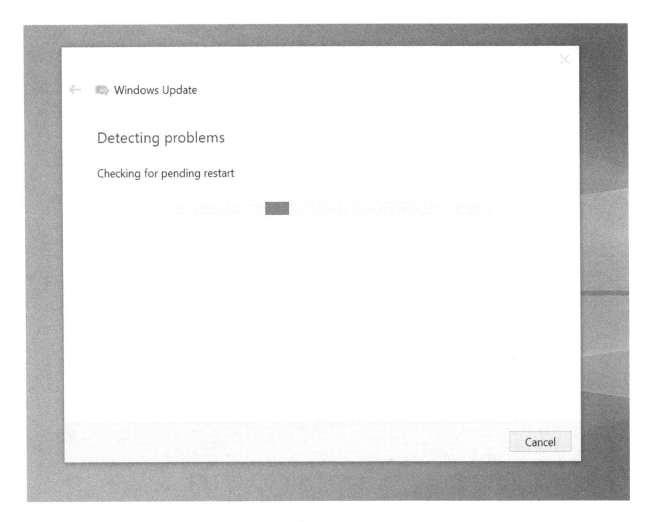

- The Troubleshooter will either display errors found and give you options to fix them. Or, it may return **Troubleshooting couldn't identify the problem**.

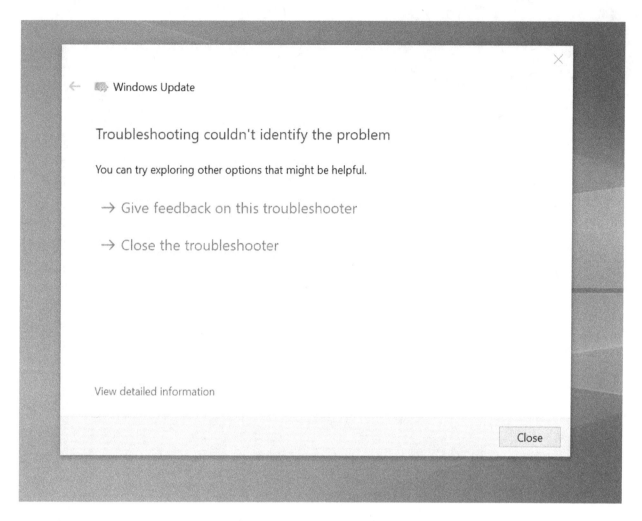

If you're still having trouble downloading and installing Windows update...try the next fix.

Method 6: Run DISM, then SFC /Scannow

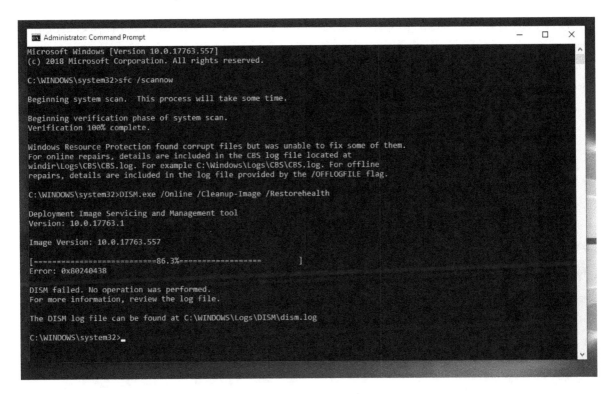

- Search Command Prompt. Then right-click it and select *Run as administrator*.
- When Command Prompt opens, type the command below. Then press enter.

```
DISM.exe /Online /Cleanup-Image /Restorehealth Explained
```

- When the above command completes, enter this command into command prompt and press Enter.

```
SFC /Scannow
```

Wait for the command to complete. Then retry downloading Windows update.

Method 7: If Everything Else Fails…Perform a Manual Update

- Open this link in a browser Microsoft.com/en-US/software-download/windows10 - type the link into a browser and click enter key.
- When the link opens, to download Windows 10 update assistant, click **Update now** link.

Info

As at the time of writing this guide, the latest Windows 10 update is the November 2019 update. When you are performing this task, the update may be different.

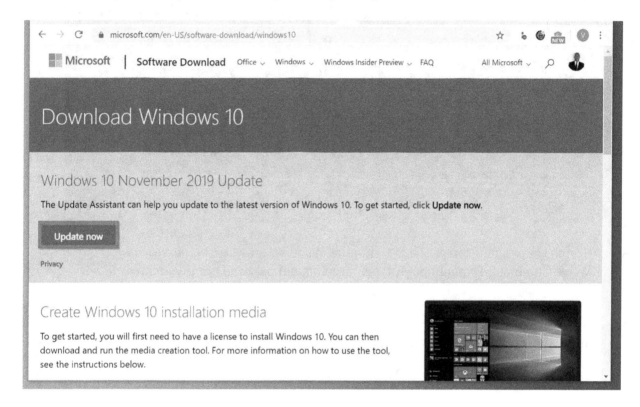

- Save the Windows update assistant application file into a folder on your computer.

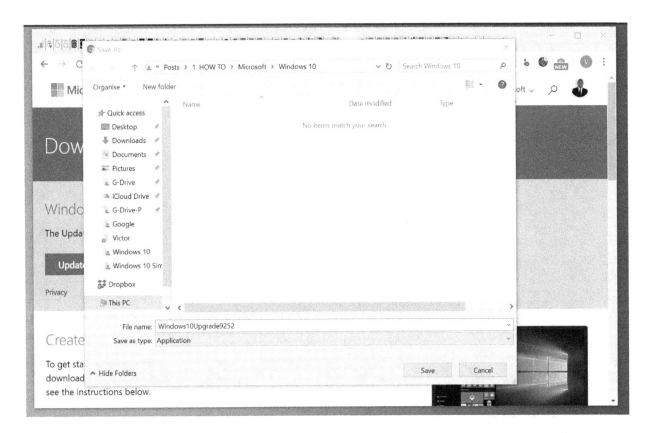

- Open the folder you saved the Update assistant and double-click to open it. If you receive a User Account Control confirmation pop up to allow the application to run, click **Yes**.

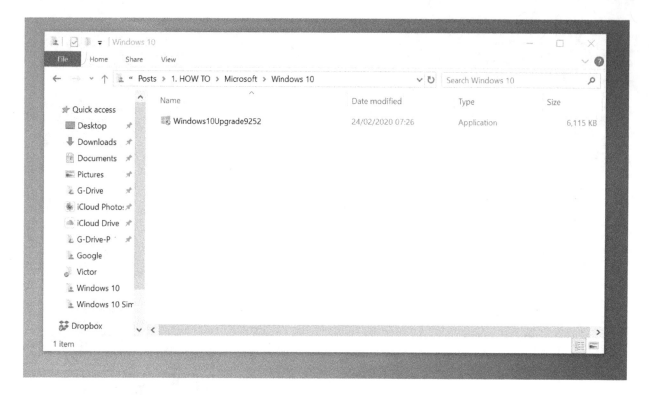

- When the first screen of the wizard opens, click **Update now**. The Update Assistant will perform a compatibility check on your PC. If your PC passed the check, click **Next**.

Update to the latest version of Windows 10

One of the best features of Windows 10 is that it keeps getting better with every update. This PC is not currently running the latest and most secure version of Windows 10. This PC is running version 1903. The latest version is 1909.

We can help you get the latest security enhancements and feature improvements. Click 'Update Now' to get started.

Do not update now

Update Now

Microsoft   Learn more

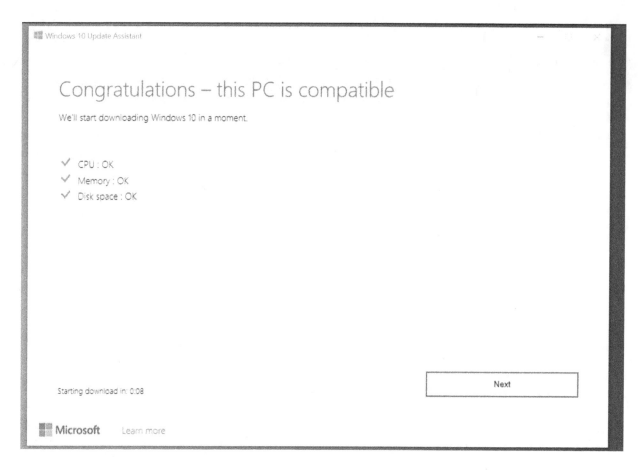

- Wait for Update assistant to download Windows 10 update. You can minimize the update assistant and continue using your computer.

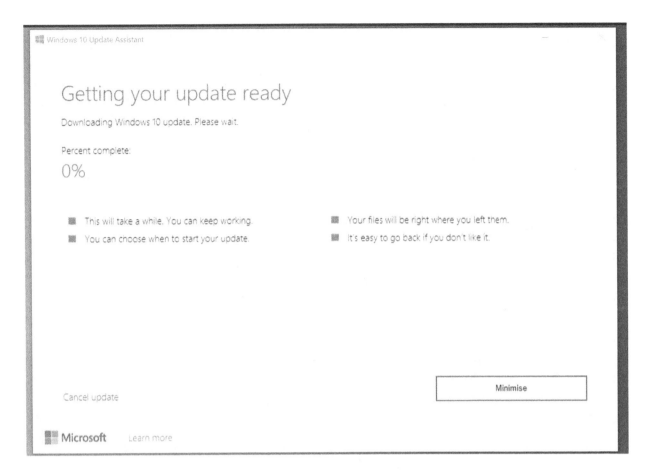

- To check the status of the download, open Windows 10 Update Assistant from the shortcut on your desktop.

When the update assistant downloads Windows 10 update, follow the wizard to install it. Your computer will restart several times during the update.

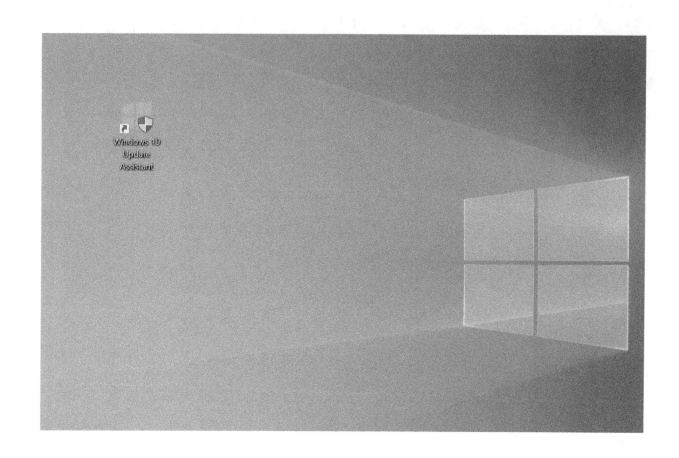

How to Fix "The Requested Operation Requires Elevation" Error

"The Requested Operation Requires Elevation" error may be caused by a number of reasons. Here are some of the reasons you may receive "The Requested Operation Requires Elevation" message, it may be that:

1. You are trying to run a command from cmd but the command needs to be run as an administrator.
2. Your folder permissions are not properly set. This may happen if you recently migrated or upgraded your operating system. Because it is now a new Operating system, the user with permission to run programs on the computer may have changed.
3. This error may also happen if you are trying to run a program from an external hard drive.

If you receive this error, follow the steps in this guide to fix it.

Method 1 Fix for "The Requested Operation Requires Elevation": Run as Administrator

If you received this error when you try to run a command via command prompt, follow the steps below to fix the error:

- Close the command prompt window.
- Then, Search *command prompt*, right-click it and select **Run as administrator**. You will receive a User Account Control prompt asking you to permit the program to run, click **Yes**.

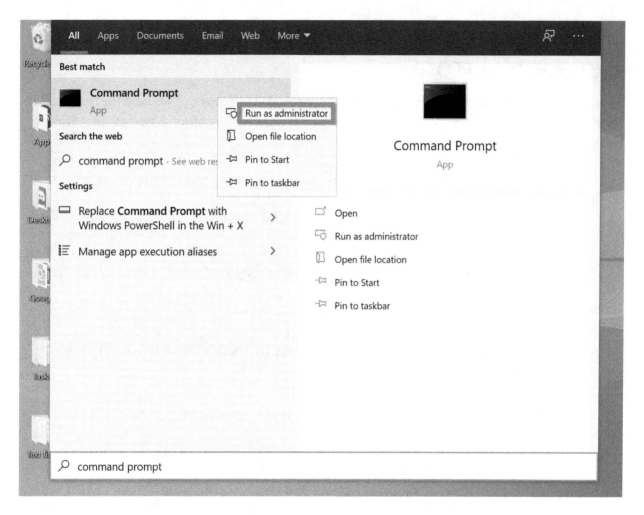

- Command Prompt will open with administrator privilege. Enter the command you ran earlier that gave the error message, it should work fine now.

```
Administrator: Command Prompt                                        —    □    ×

Microsoft Windows [Version 10.0.18362.657]
(c) 2019 Microsoft Corporation. All rights reserved.

C:\WINDOWS\system32>
```

Method 2 Fix for "The Requested Operation Requires Elevation": Replace Owner on subcontainers and objects

You MUST perform this operation while logged on to the computer as an administrator. The steps described in this section allows you to change the owner of files and folders on your computer

If you are recently upgraded your computer. Or migrated your computer to a new hard drive, follow the steps below to fix "The Requested Operation Requires Elevation":

- Right-click Windows logo and select *File Explorer*.

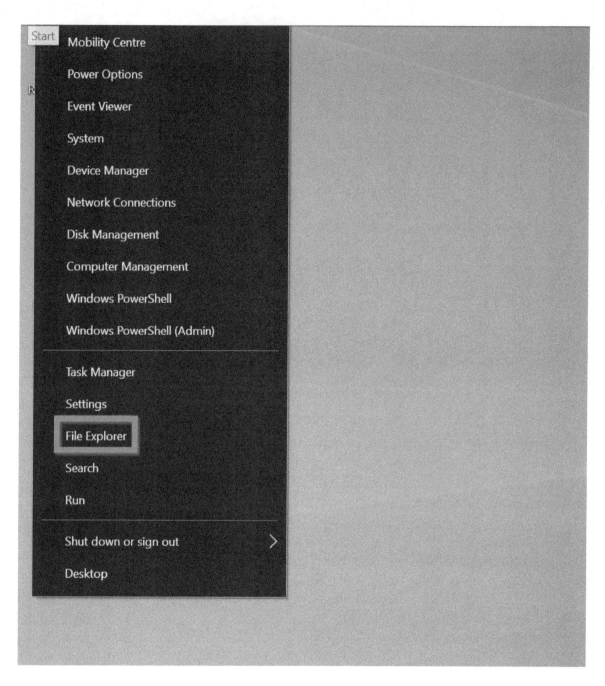

- When **File Explorer** opens, scroll down and click **This PC**.

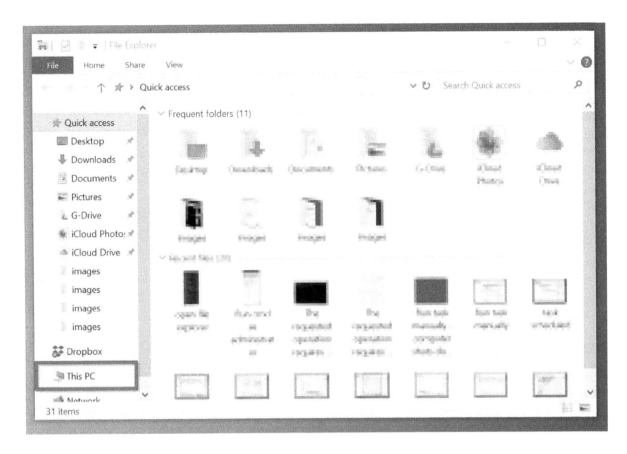

- When *This PC* opens, scroll down until you can see your Drive C: Then right-click Drive C and select **Properties**.

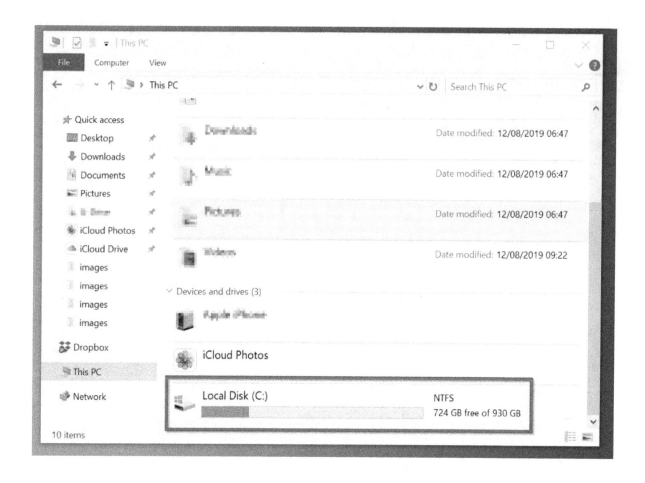

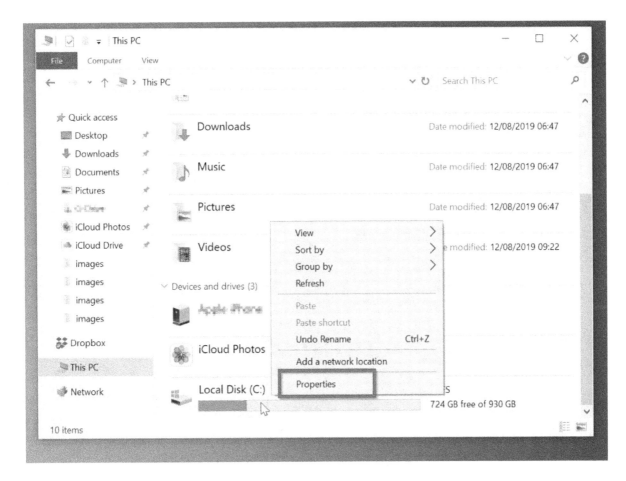

- On the drive C properties, click the **Security** tab. Then click **Advanced**.

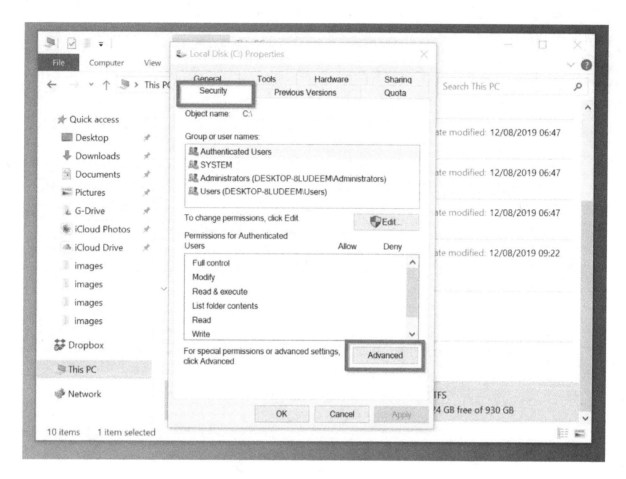

- When **Advanced Security Settings for Local Disk (C)** opens, click **Change.** The *Select User or Group* option will open.

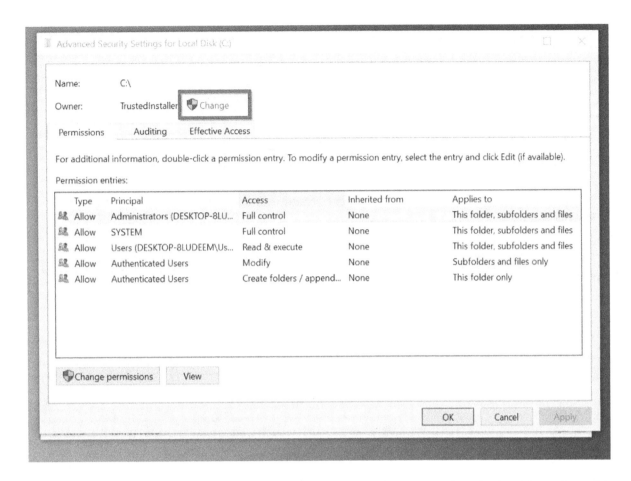

- Type your username. Then click **Check Names**. If the name exists, it should resolve without errors. Then click OK. The option to take ownership will open.

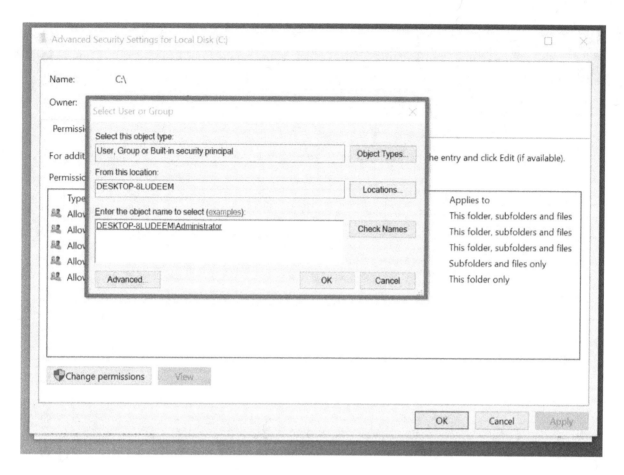

- Beside **Owner,** the new user you selected will be displayed. Then beneath the user, check the **Replace owner on subcontainers and object** box and click OK.

It will take a while for the operation to complete.

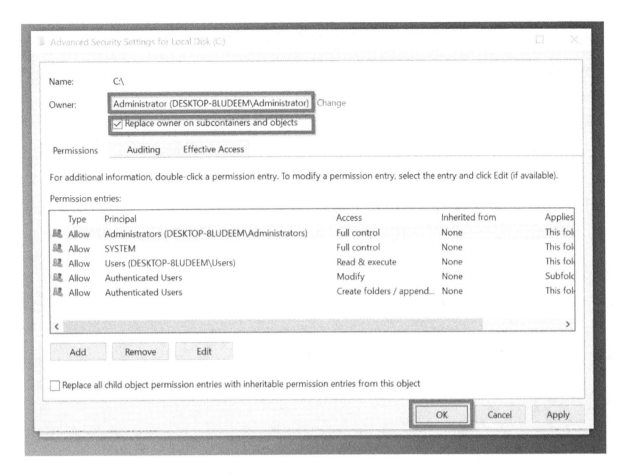

You should now be able to perform the task you wanted to perform without receiving "The requested operation requires elevation" message.

How to Fix "Remote Desktop Connection an Internal Error Has Occurred"

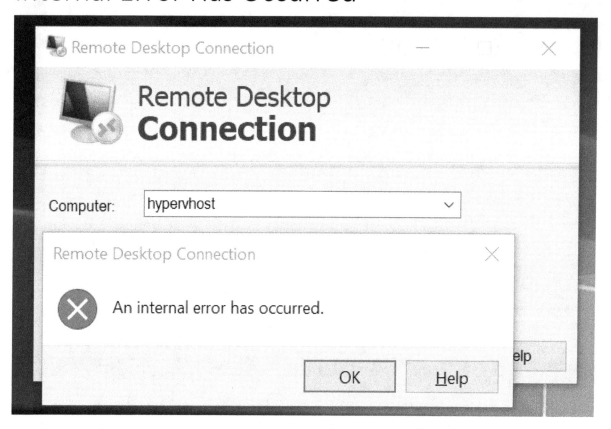

There are two steps to fix the problem:

1. **Step1**: Check that you can ping the computer by its IP address and telnet to port 3389
2. **Step2**: Adjust RDP experience settings, then RDP to the computer using its IP address.

Tip
If you are in a domain environment, ask your administrator to check that the computer you are connecting to is properly configured in the DNS server. That is, it has the proper records in the DNS server.

Here are the details of each step.

Step 1: Check that You Can Ping the Computer By IP Address and Telnet to Port 3389

- If you have access to the computer, logon to it locally, search for *cmd*. Then open *Command Prompt*. When it opens, run the command below:

`IPCONFIG`

Note the *IPv4 address*. See the highlighted portion of the image above.

- Back to your computer (where you maDe the RDP connection from), run the command below:

`PING   <IP address>`

Tip

Replace <IP address> with the computer's IP address.

- If the computer is reachable via it's IP address, you should receive replies. See the image below.

```
C:\>ping 192.168.0.101

Pinging 192.168.0.101 with 32 bytes of data:
Reply from 192.168.0.101: bytes=32 time=8ms TTL=128
Reply from 192.168.0.101: bytes=32 time=5ms TTL=128
Reply from 192.168.0.101: bytes=32 time=4ms TTL=128
Reply from 192.168.0.101: bytes=32 time=8ms TTL=128

Ping statistics for 192.168.0.101:
    Packets: Sent = 4, Received = 4, Lost = 0 (0% loss),
Approximate round trip times in milli-seconds:
    Minimum = 4ms, Maximum = 8ms, Average = 6ms

C:\>
```

If you received a reply, it confirms that the computer is online and reachable.

Tip

If you do not receive a reply, check that the computer's network cable is connected. You could also check the firewall on the computer.

Next, you need to confirm that you can telnet to the computer's IP on port 3389 (Remote desktop port number). On your computer, open command prompt. Then enter the command below and press the *Enter* key on your keyboard.

```
telnet <IP address> 3389
```

Tip

Change <IP address> to the IP address of the computer.

If the telnet is successful, you should see a blank screen as shown in the image below.

Step 2: Adjust RDP Experience Settings, then RDP to the Computer Using its IP Address.

The next step to fix "Remote Desktop Connection an Internal Error Has Occurred" is to RDP using its IP address. But first, you need to modify your Remote Desktop settings.

- Open **Remote Desktop Connection** and click **Show options**.

- Then click the **Experience** tab. On the **Experience** tab, uncheck **Reconnect if the connection is dropped.**

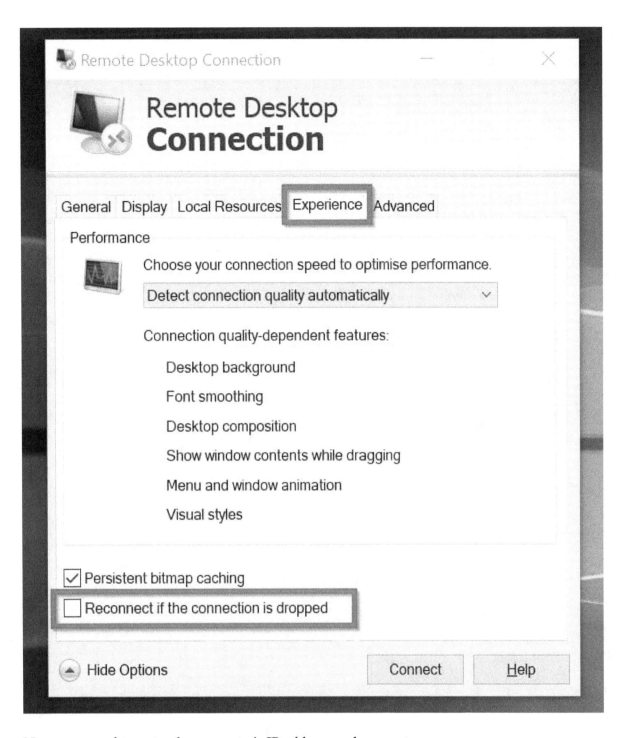

Now, you need to enter the computer's IP address and connect.

- Click the **General** tab. Then on the **Computer** field, enter the IP address of the remote computer you want to RDP to.
- Finally, click **Connect**. If you receive a certificate warning (second image below), check **Don't ask me again for connections to this computer** box. Then click **Yes**.

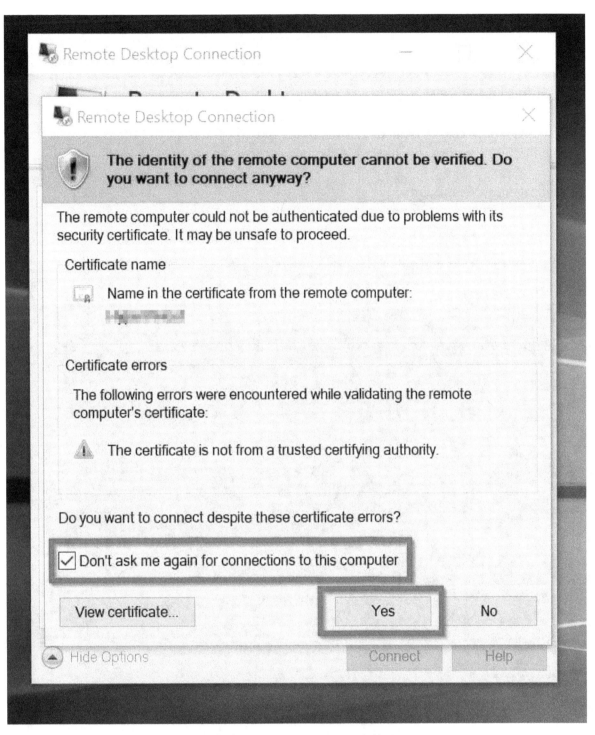

You should now be able to RDP to the computer successfully.

How to Fix "BootRec /FixBoot Access is Denied" Error in Windows 10

"BootRec /FixBoot Access is Denied" error is likely caused by corrupt EFI directory. The fix is to recreate the EFI directory structure.

Here are the steps to fix this error:

Step1: Boot to Windows 10 Recovery Environment - Command Prompt

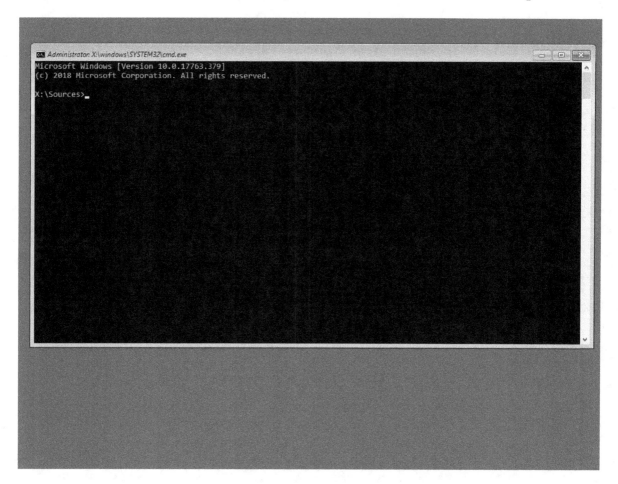

- Insert a Windows 10 boot media into your computer (DVD or USB)
- Configure BIOS boot sequence to boot from the above media first
- When you receive the prompt to boot from CD or DVD, press any key to continue

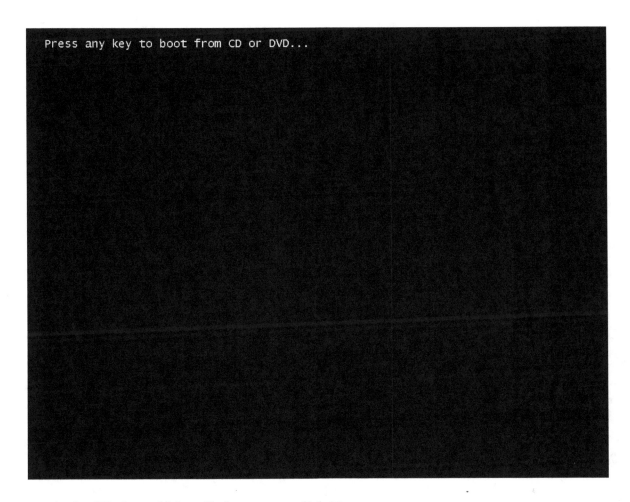

```
Press any key to boot from CD or DVD...
```

- At the Windows 10 installation screen, click Next.

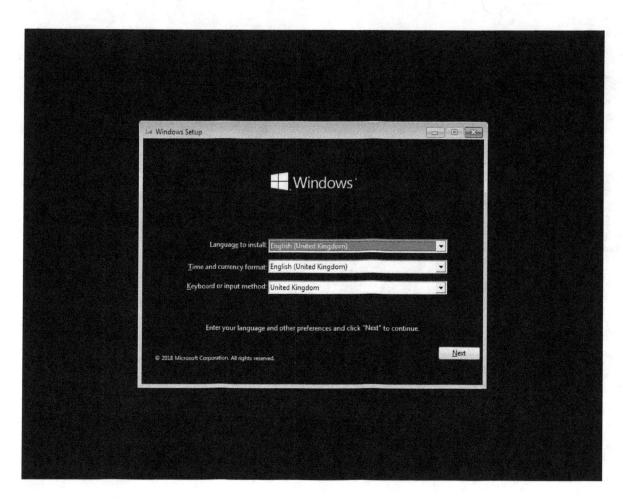

- Then click **Repair your computer**.

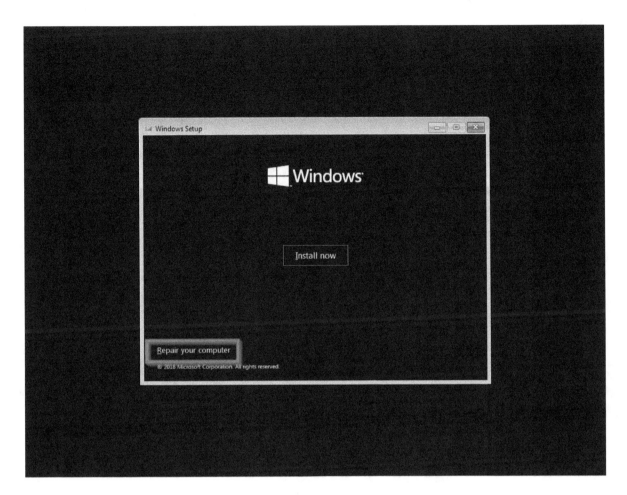

- When Windows boots to recovery environment, click **Troubleshoot**.

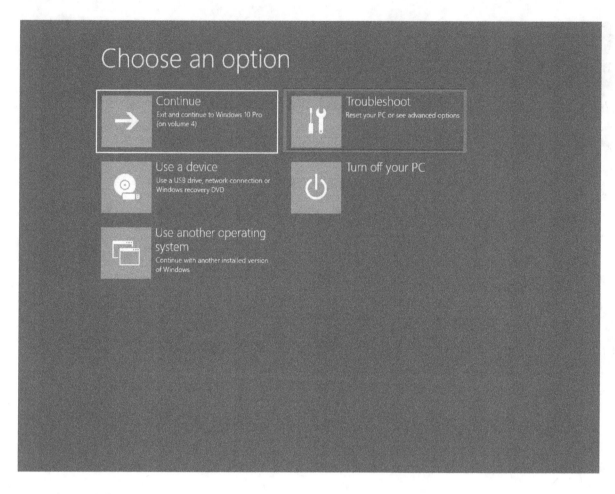

- Then, at the **Advanced options** screen loads, click **Command Prompt**. The Command Prompt will display. Proceed to step 2.

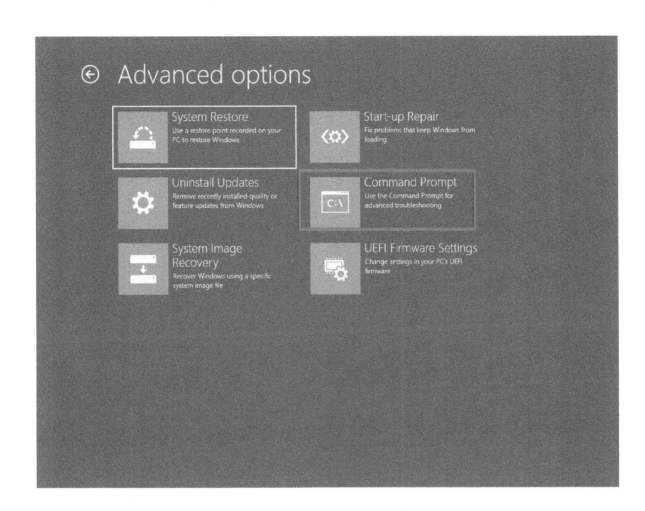

Step 2: Assign the EFI Volume a Drive Letter

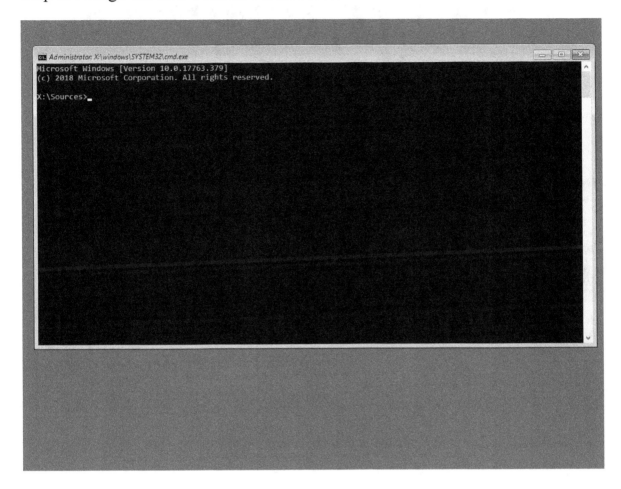

The next step to fix bootrec /fixboot access is denied error in Windows 10 is to assign the EFI volume a drive letter.

- At the Windows 10 recovery environment, command prompt type the command below. Then press enter

DISKPART

DISKPART prompt will open

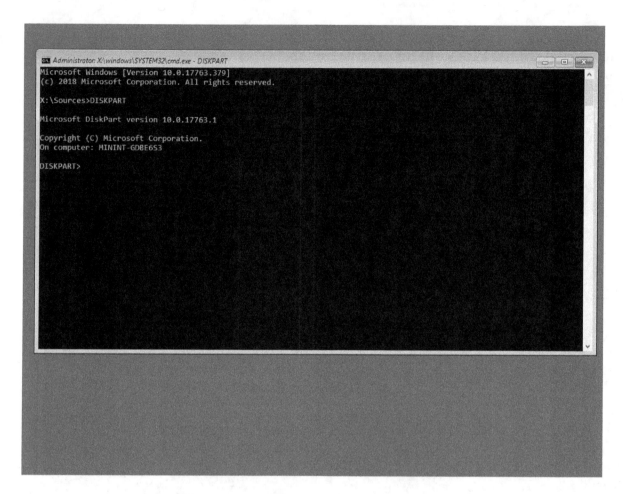

- At the DISKPART prompt, type this command and press enter

`list disk`

All available disks on your computer will be listed (displayed).

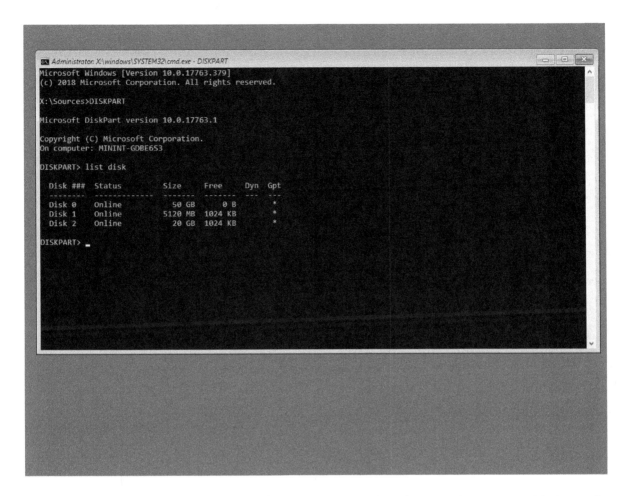

- Next, to select the disk with your Windows 10 installation, type the command below. Then press enter.

```
Select disk 0
```

My Operating system is installed in Drive 0. So, I used "disk 0". However, if yours is installed in a disk with a different number, in the previous command change 0 to that number.

The command will return the result below:

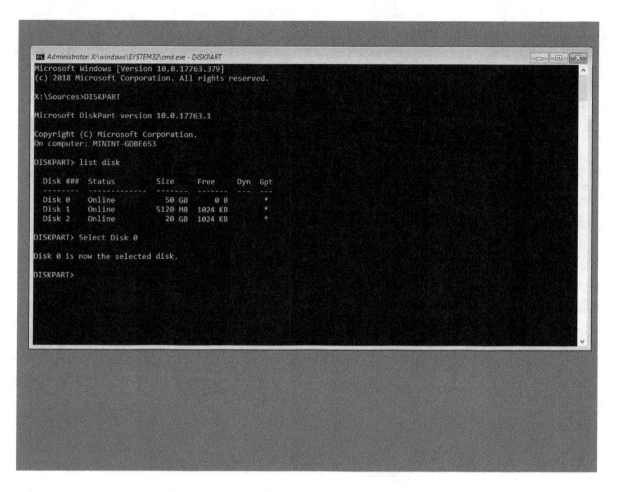

- To display volumes in the selected disk, type the command below. Then press enter.

`list volume`

The result of the command is shown below:

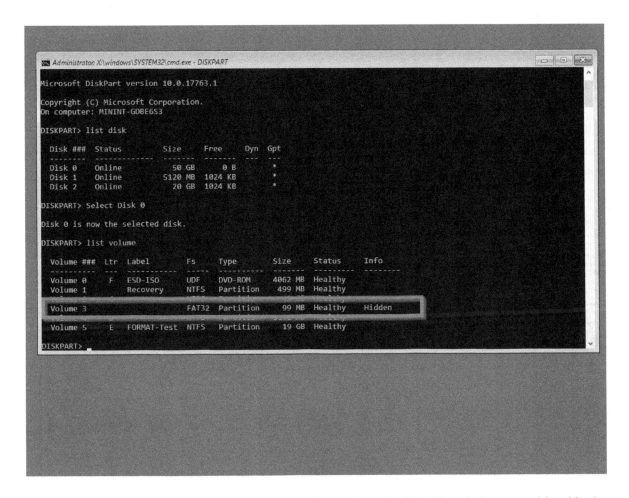

At this point, you need to identify your EFI volume from the list. Here is how you identify the EFI volume:

1. It should be formatted with FAT32
2. The size is likely to be about 100mb (shown as 99mb in this example)
3. The **Info** column is likely to show the volume as "Hidden"

To select your EFI volume, type this command and press enter.

```
select volume 3
```

Change 3 to your EFI volume number. Here is the result:

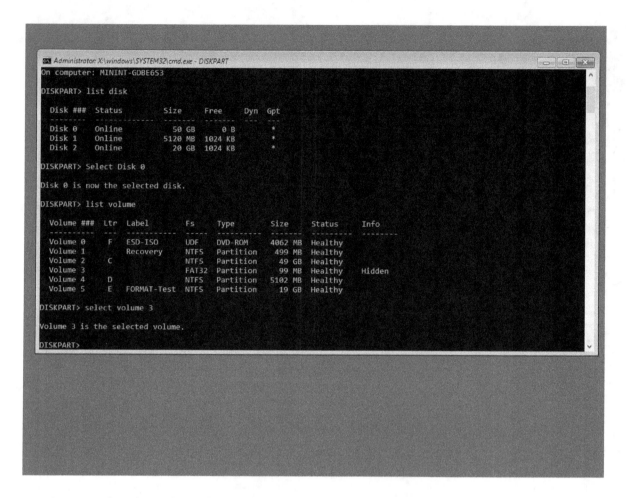

- Next, assign the volume a drive letter with this command.

```
assign letter P:
```

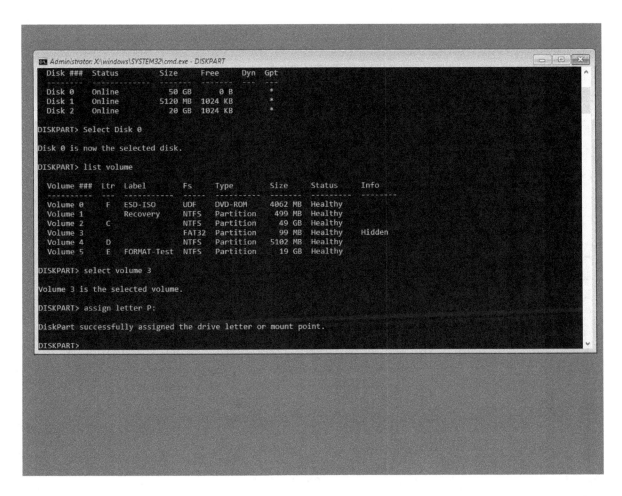

The last step to fix "bootrec /fixboot access is denied" error is to format the EFI volume. Then recreate the corrupt EFI directory structure.

Step3: Format the EFI Volume and Recreate the EFI Directory Structure

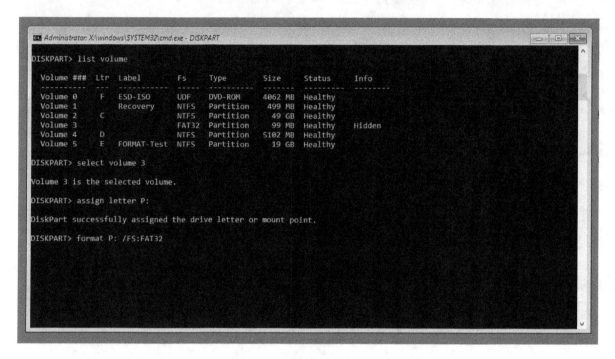

- To format the partition, type the command below. Then press enter.

```
format P: /FS:FAT32
```

If you assigned a different drive letter to the volume, change P to the drive letter.

Finally, the fix for bootrec /fixboot access is denied error...

- Recreate the EFI directory with this command:

```
bcdboot C:\windows /s P: /f UEFI
```

How to Fix "Windows Update Cannot Currently Check for Updates" Error

This guide covers 3 methods to fix the "Windows Update Cannot Currently Check for Updates" error.

Method 1: Check that Windows Update Service is Started

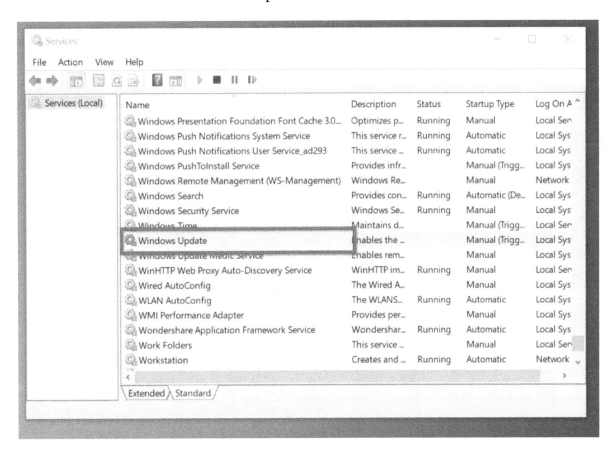

- Press **Windows + R** (Windows logo presses simultaneously with the R keys). The Run command will open.
- At the RUN command type *Services.msc*. Then click OK.

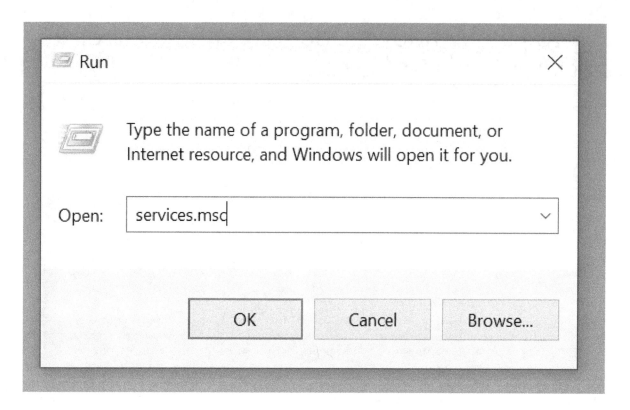

- When Services MMC opens, locate **Windows Update**. Then double-click it. Confirm that the *Startup Type* is set to *Manual* and the Service Status is *Running*. If you made any changes, click **Apply**.

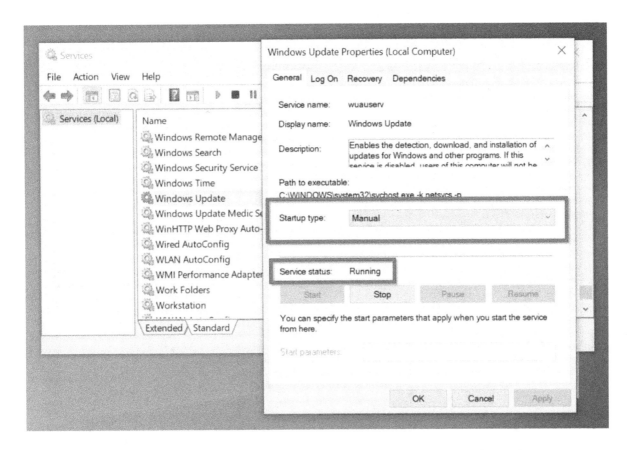

- Go back to Windows update and click "Check for updates". If you still receive an error, try the next fix.

Method 2: Recreate SoftwareDistribution Folder

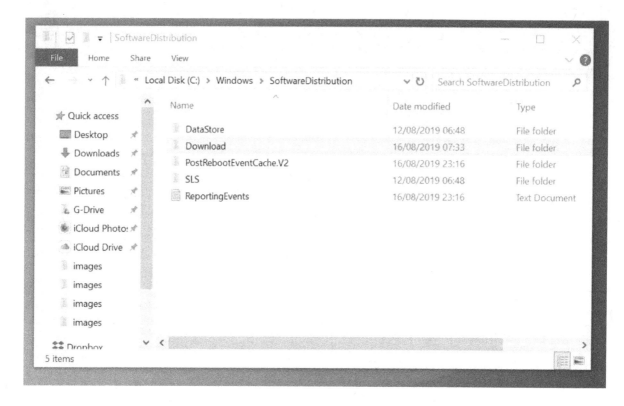

Sometimes the **SoftwareDistribution** folder may be corrupt. Simply renaming or deleting it may fix this problem. Here are the steps to recreate the **SoftwareDistribution** folder.

- Type *%Windir%* in the search bar. Then click **%Windir%**.

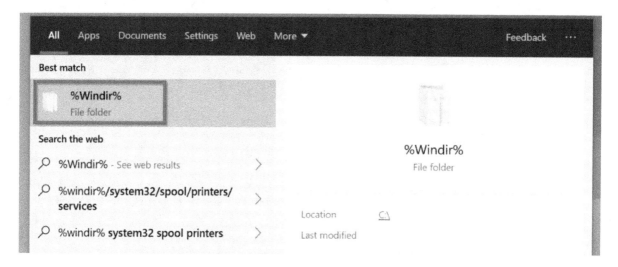

- When your Windows folder opens, locate the **SoftwareDistribution** folder and rename it – right-click the folder, select Rename, then add **_old** at the end of the folder.

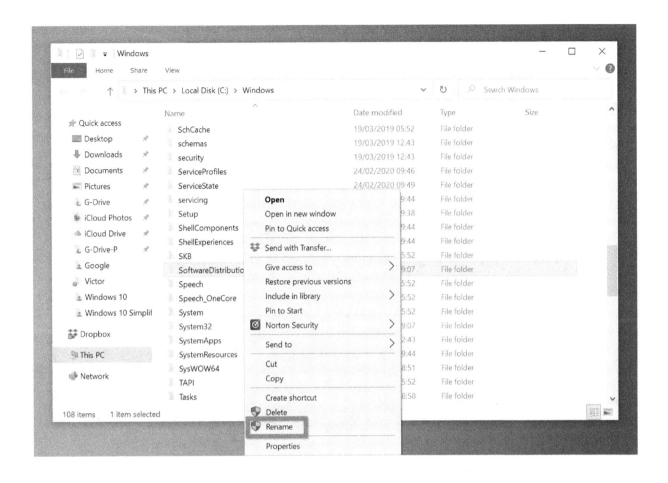

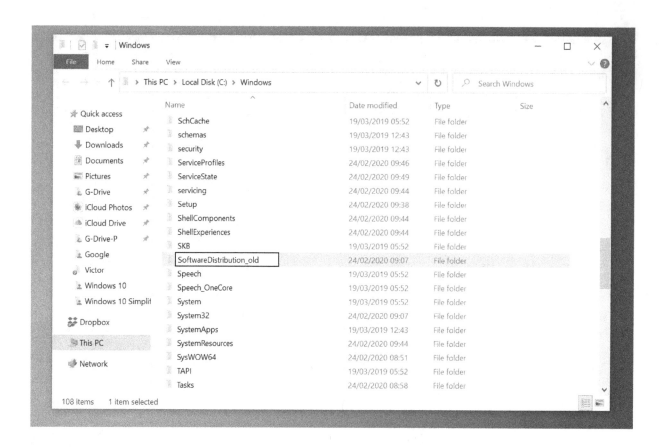

After renaming the **SoftwareDistribution** folder, the next step is to restart the Windows Update Service.

- To restart the Windows Update service, type *PowerShell* in the search bar. Then right-click **Windows Powershell** and select **Run as administrator**.
- When the User Account Control prompts you to allow the program, click **Yes**.

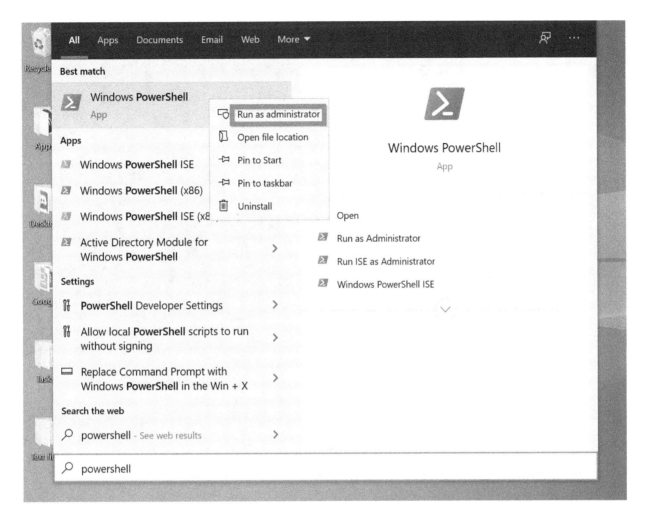

- Then, at PowerShell command prompt, type this command and press enter

```
Restart-Service -Name wuauserv
```

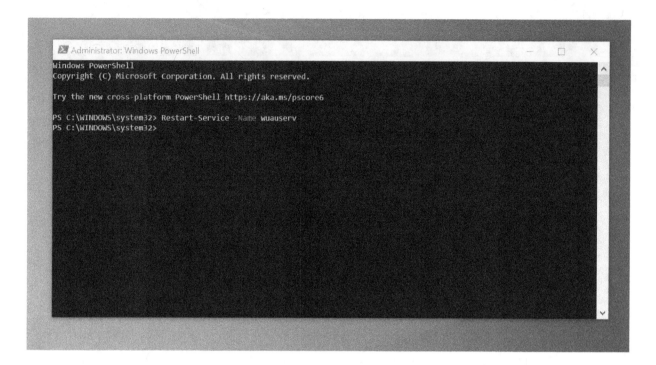

- Now go back to the **SoftwareDistribution** folder should be recreated.

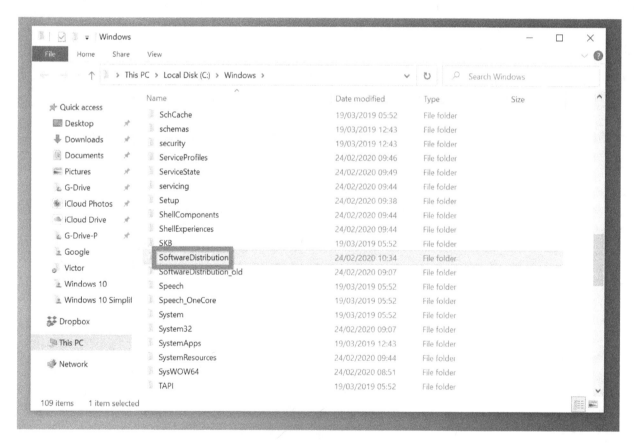

How to Fix "Windows Modules Installer Worker High CPU"

If *Windows Modules Installer Worker* has high CPU usage, it may slow your computer down. *Windows Modules Installer Worker* allows the installation, modification, and removal of Windows updates.

Ideally, it should not use high CPU but if it does use the steps in this guide to fix the problem. There are 2 steps to fix this problem:

Step 1: Change the Startup Type of Necessary Services

In this section, you will modify the *Startup type* of *Windows Modules Installer* and *Windows Update*. Here are the steps:

- Press (Windows + R) - Windows logo and R key simultaneously. This will open the *RUN* command window.

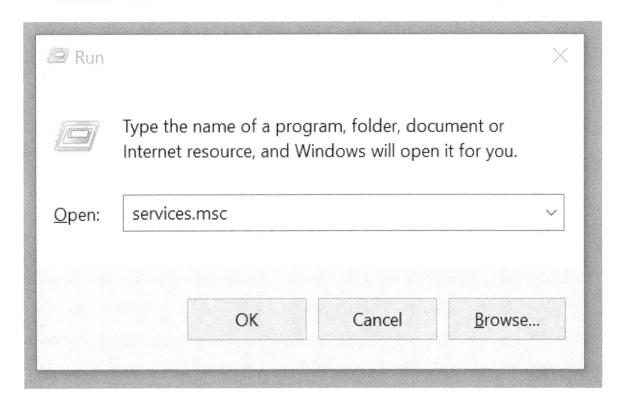

- On the *Run* window, type *services.msc* and click OK. *Services* MMC will open.

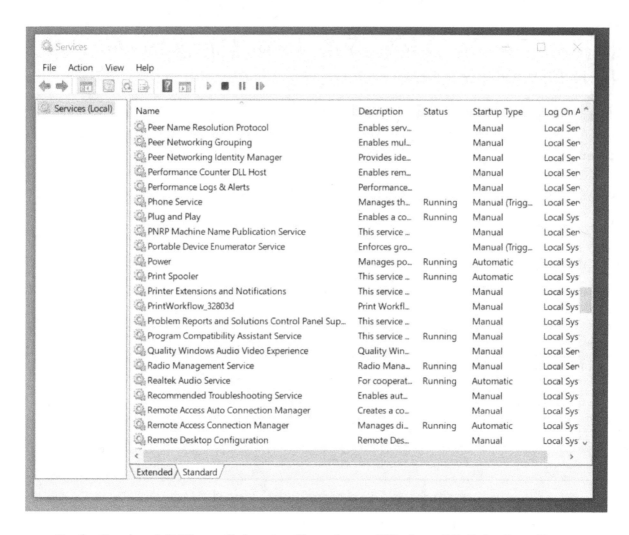

- On the Services MMC, scroll down until you locate **Windows Modules Installer**.
- Look at the **Startup Type** column (the 3rd column from the left). If it is set to *Automatic*, double-click the service to open its properties.

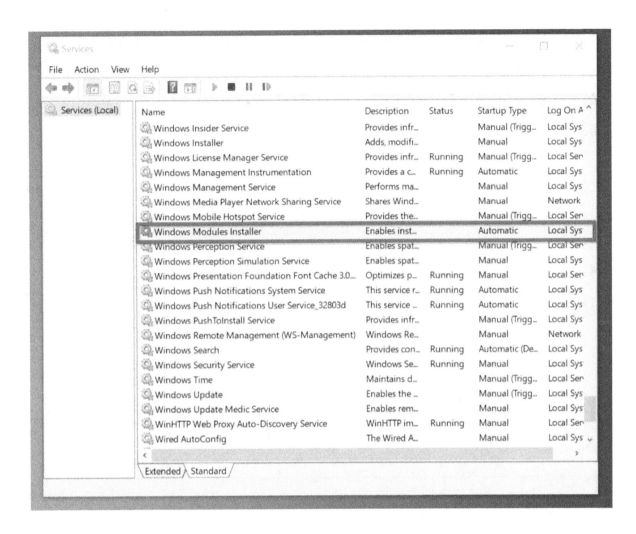

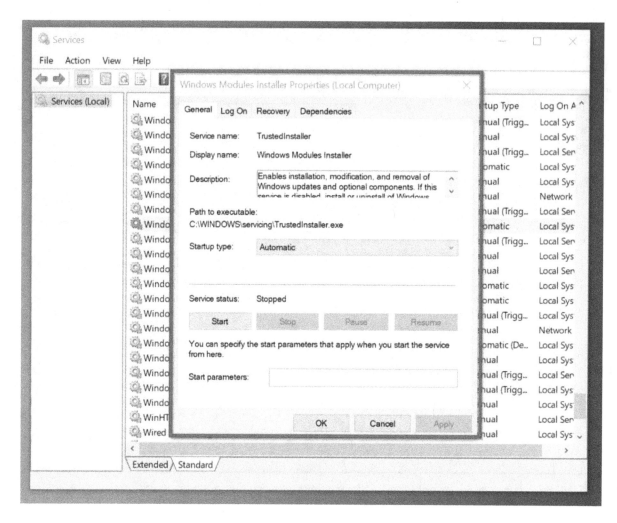

- Then click the drop-down beside **Startup type**. Select **Manual** and click OK.

260

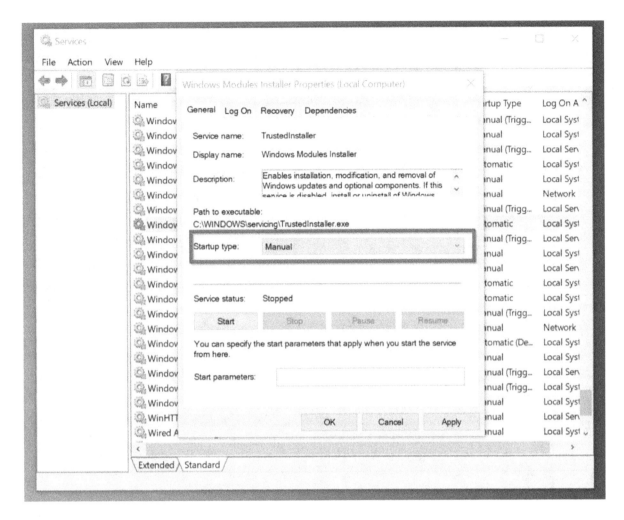

- Next, locate the **Windows Update** service.

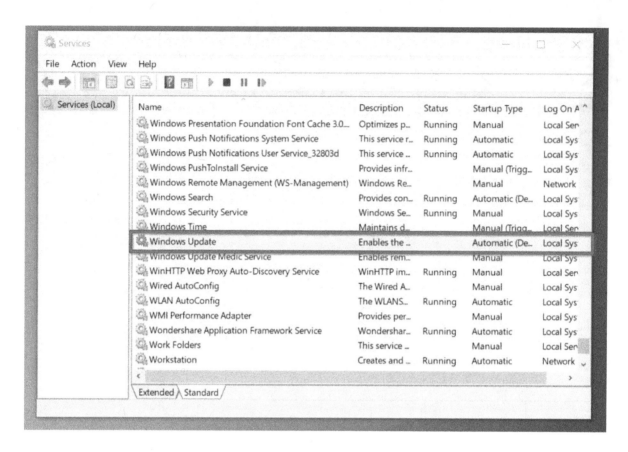

- Double-click it and change the **Startup Type** to *Manual*. Click OK to save your changes.

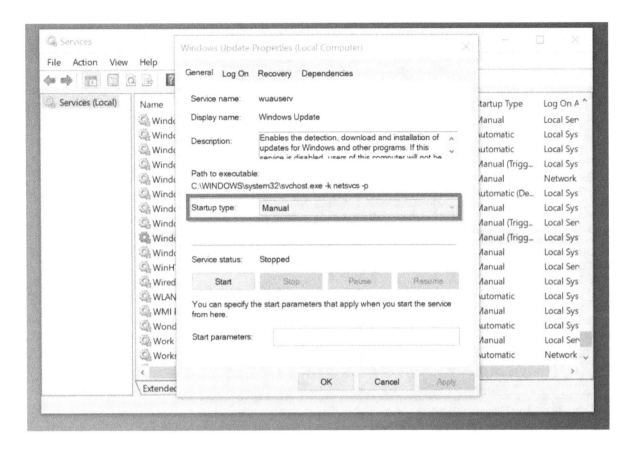

Step 2: Enable *Metered Connection* Settings

If you enable your network connection as "Metered" Windows update will not update automatically. This gives you control over when to download and install Windows updates.

This is one tricks to resolve **Windows Modules Installer Worker High CPU** problem. If you are able to control when updates download and install, you can prepare for it. You can stop other tasks, download and install Windows updates, then resume your normal tasks.

Here are the steps to set your connection as "Metered":

- Right-click the Windows logo and click **Settings**.

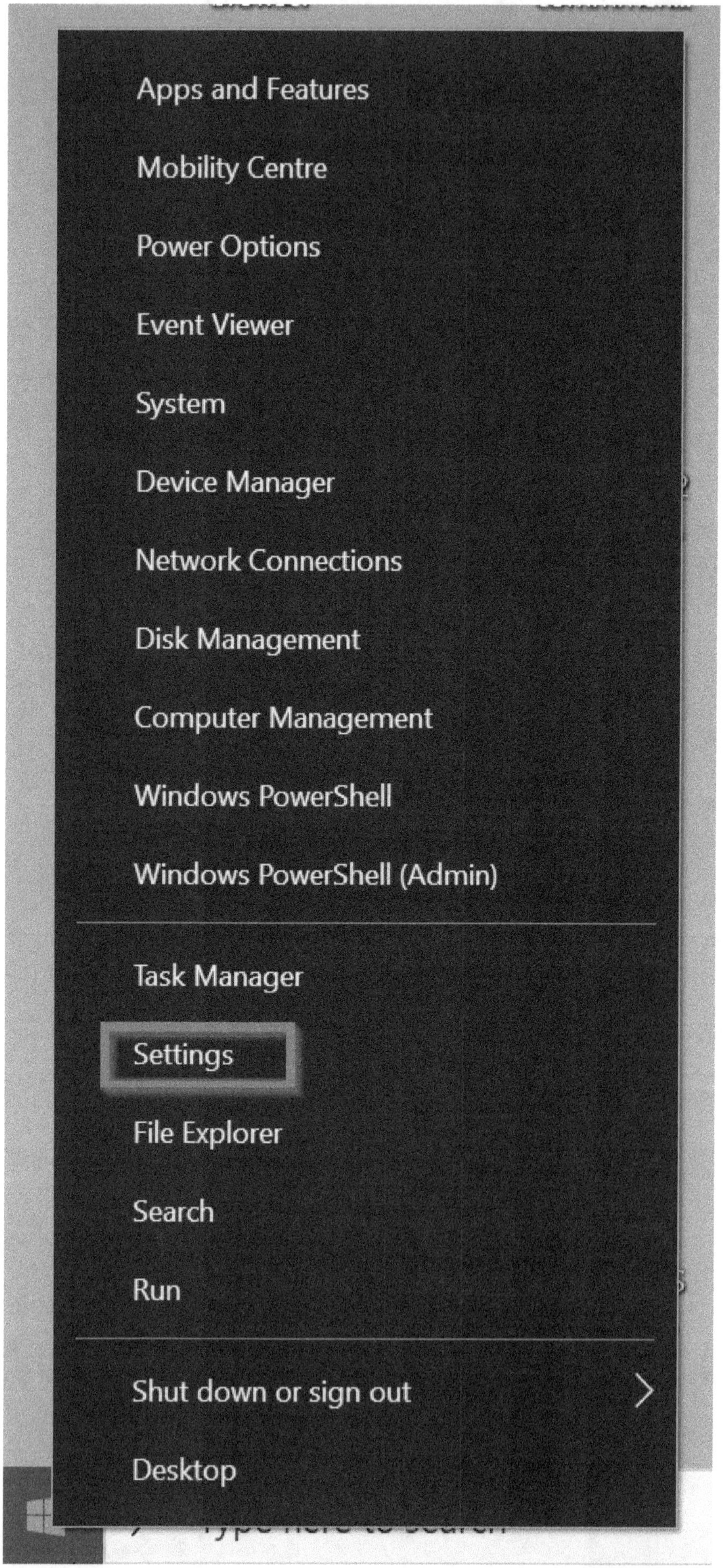

Apps and Features

Mobility Centre

Power Options

Event Viewer

System

Device Manager

Network Connections

Disk Management

Computer Management

Windows PowerShell

Windows PowerShell (Admin)

Task Manager

Settings

File Explorer

Search

Run

Shut down or sign out   >

Desktop

- On **Windows Settings**, locate **Network & Internet** and click it. This opens the network you use to connect to the internet. The second image below shows that I connect to the internet via Wifi.

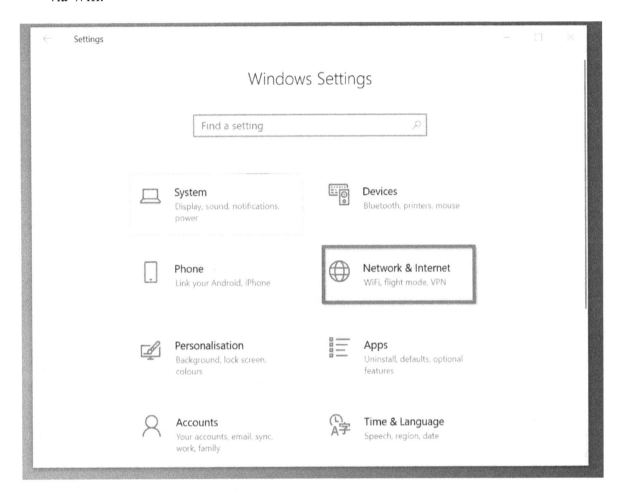

- When **Network status** opens, click **Change connection properties**.
- Then scroll down until you find *Metered connection*. Finally, flip the switch below *Set as metered connection* ON.

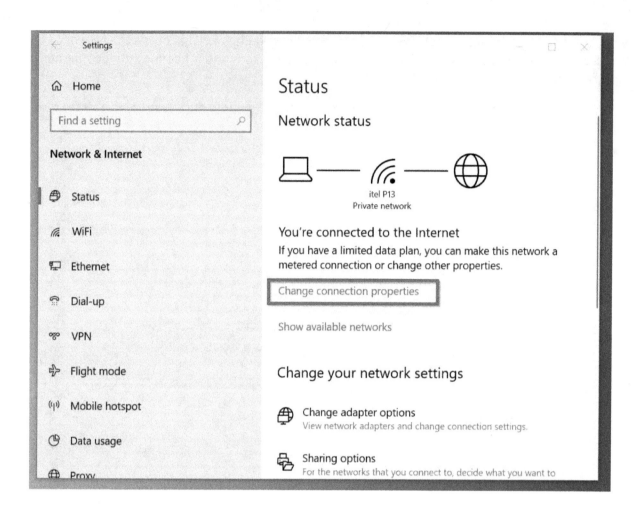

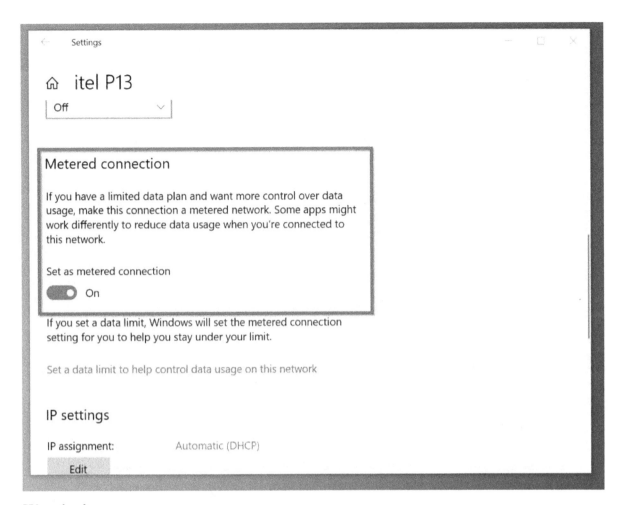

Warning!

Setting your connection as "Metered" effectively means that Windows update will not download automatically. Though this will solve your high CPU problem, you have to ensure that you check for Windows updates manually at least once a month.

How to Fix "Hard Drive not Detected" Problem in Windows 10

If you receive "Hard drive not detected" error, it could be caused by one of the following:

- Your BIOS Settings
- Physical Hard drive connection settings
- Hard drive drivers

Based on my experience and how several other users have fixed the "hard drive not detected" issue, I have recommended 4 fixes in this guide.

Method 1: Check that the Disk is Online

Before we get to the tough bits, let's do the basic stuff. Check that your disk is not offline. If the disk is offline, the hard drive will be not detected. Here is how to check:

- Press **Windows logo + R** keys on your keyboard. This will open Run command.
- At the Run command, type *diskmgmt.msc* then click OK.

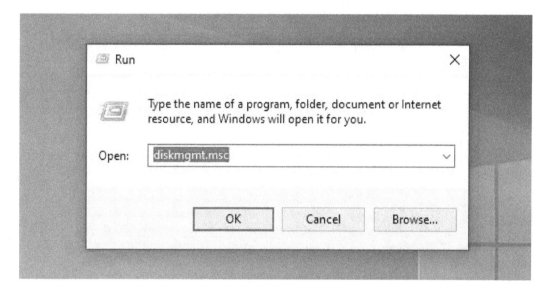

- When Disk Management opens, look at the disks on the left pane of the Disk Management tool. If the disk has a red circle, it may mean that it is offline. See the highlighted portion of the image below.

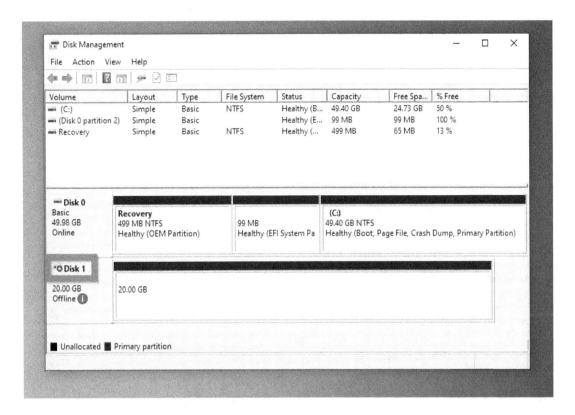

- To bring the disk online, right-click it. Then select **Online**. The disk will come online, and the red circle will no longer be there.

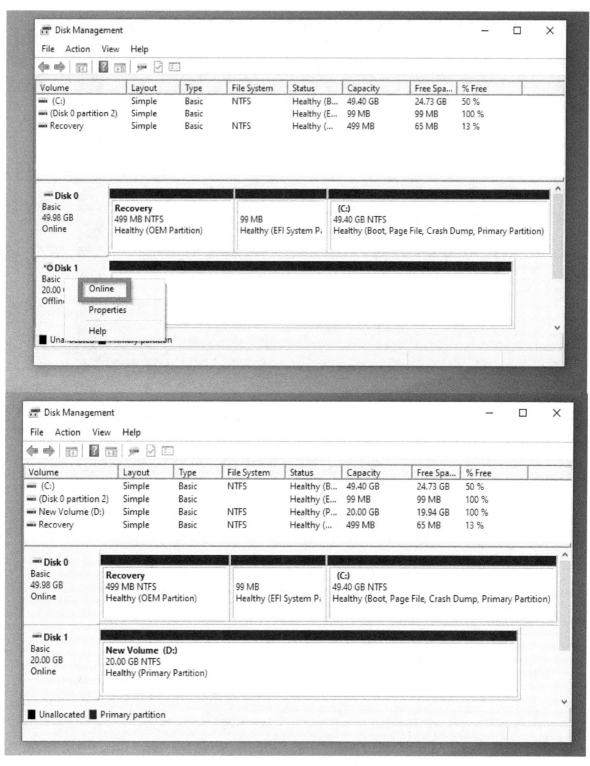

The hard drive will now be detected by the computer and becomes available in "This PC".

If at this point, the hard drive is not detected, then try the next fix.

Method 2: Convert the Drive to GPT, Change BIOS to UEFI Boot

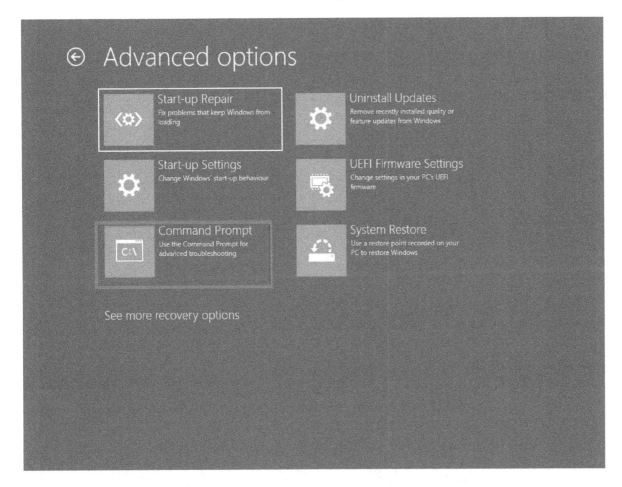

If you have two drives on your computer, one GPT and the second MBR, the second drive may not be detected. Converting both drives to GPT may fix the "Hard drive not detected" problem.

Warning!
Before you proceed with the next steps, connect your drive to another computer and BACK IT UP! When you convert from MBR to GPT, you are likely to lose your data.

There are 2 steps to apply this fix:

1. Convert the second hard drive from MBR to GPT
2. Change your computer from Legacy to UEFI boot

Here are the steps to complete this task in Windows 10:

- Start your Windows 10 computer. When it gets to the point where it is displaying the circles, press and hold the power button until the PC goes off

- Press the power button again and power it off at the point where the circle displays.
- When you power the PC again, it will boot to **Automatic Recovery**.
- Then, at the **Choose an option** screen, click **Troubleshoot**.

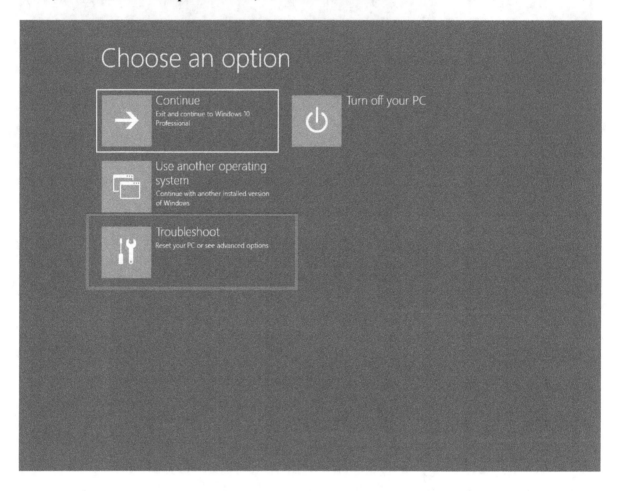

- When **Troubleshoot** opens, click **Advanced options**.

- At **Advanced options**, click **Command Prompt**.

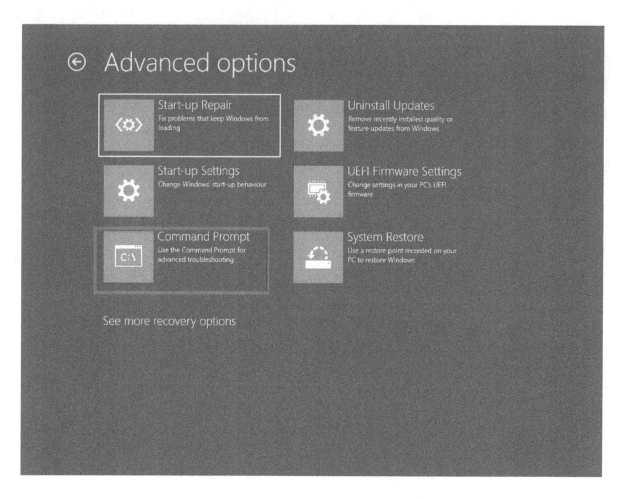

- At Command Prompt, to confirm that the drives meet the requirement, type this command and press Enter.

```
mbr2gpt/disk:1/validate
```

- To convert the drive, type this command and press enter.

```
mbr2gpt /convert
```

You can also convert MBR disk to GPT using DISKPART. To use this method, execute these commands in order.

```
DISKPART
LIST DISK
SELECT DISK 1
```

Change 1 to the disk number of the drive you are converting.

```
CONVERT GPT
```

274

After converting the drive to GPT, boot to BIOS and change to UEFI boot. The steps to change from BIOS to UEFI boot is not included in this guide because it may vary from one computer manufacturer to another.

If you do not change your boot to UEFI in BIOS, your computer may not boot!

When you boot your computer, the "hard drive not detected" issue should be resolved. But if your hard drive is still not detected, try the next fix.

Method 3: Install the Vendor's Driver for the Hard Drive

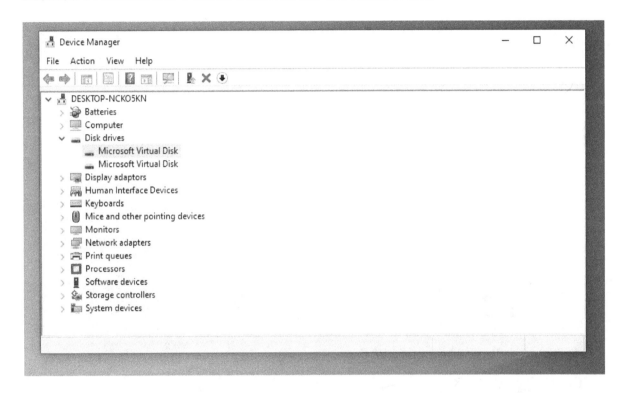

If you have tried the first 2 fixes covered above but your computer is still not detecting your hard drive, download the driver for the hard drive and install it.

How to Fix "Remote Desktop Can't Connect to the Remote Computer"

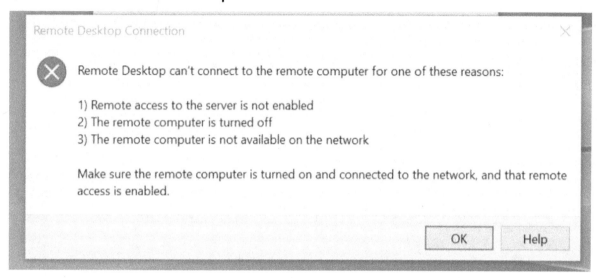

The fixes discussed in this guide should be performed from the remote computer.

Method 1: Check that the computer is on and connected to the Network

The first step to fix this error is to perform some physical inspections.

- Check that the remote computer is powered up

- Confirm that the network cables are connected. If connects to the network via Wireless, check that the Wifi is enabled and connected to the network

Once you have completed physical checks of the computer proceed to step 2 below.

Method 2: Check that Remote Desktop is Enabled

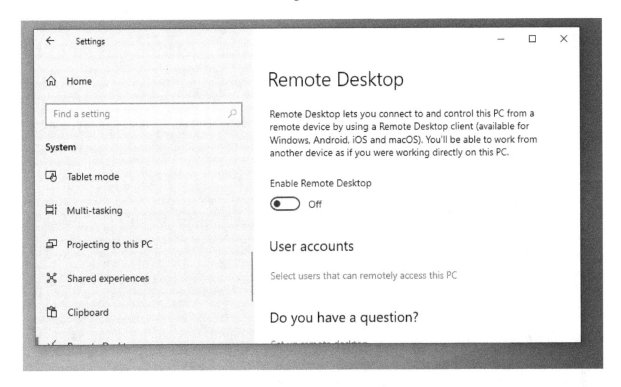

The next step to try to fix "remote desktop can't connect to the remote computer" is to confirm that **Remote Desktop** is enabled on the remote computer.

- Log in to the remote computer. Then, right-click Windows 10 start and click **Settings**.

- When Windows Settings opens, click **System**.

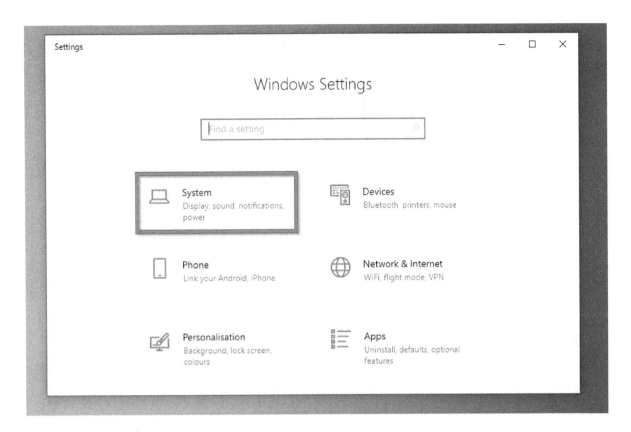

- Then scroll down the left pane of the Settings screen and click **Remote Desktop**.

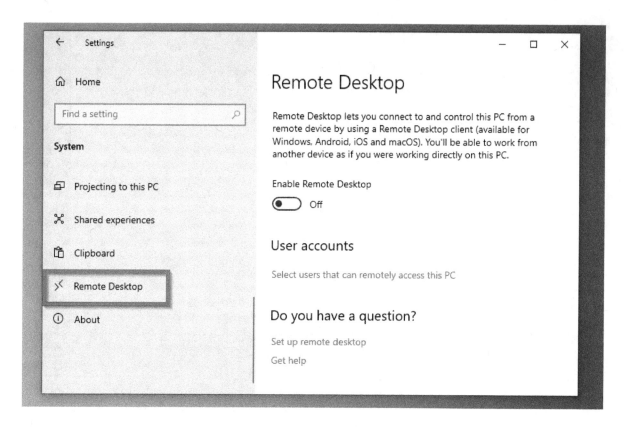

- If *Enable Remote Desktop* switch is Off, flip the button to turn it On. To confirm that you want to turn on Remote Desktop, at the prompt, click **Confirm**.

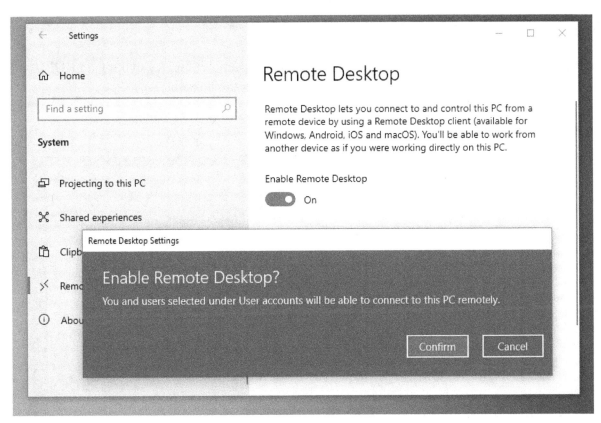

If Remote Desktop was not enabled, enabling it will likely fix "remote desktop can't connect to the remote computer". However, if it was enabled or after enabling it you still cannot RDP to the computer, try the next fix.

Method 3: Restart Computer

If at this point the problem is not fixed, restart the remote computer and try making an RDP connection. If RDP connection error is still not resolved, try the next fix.

Method 4: Check Windows Defender Firewall

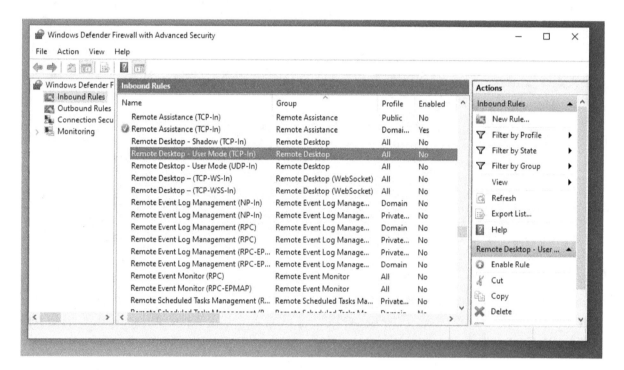

If "remote desktop can't connect to the remote computer" is still not resolved, it is likely that Windows Defender Firewall is blocking the RDP port. Here is how to check and fix this problem:

- Press the **Windows logo + R** key on your computer. The *run* command will open.
- At the Run command, type *control panel*. Then click OK.

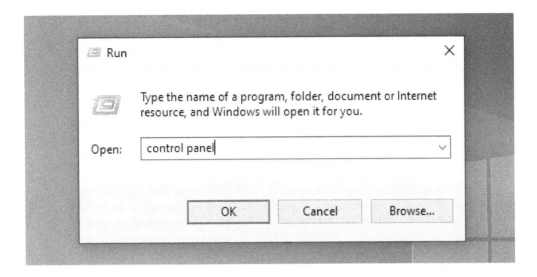

- When **Control Panel** opens, click **System and Security**.

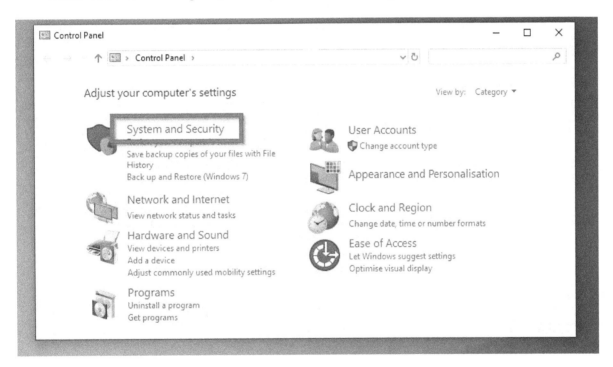

- Then click **Windows Defender Firewall**.

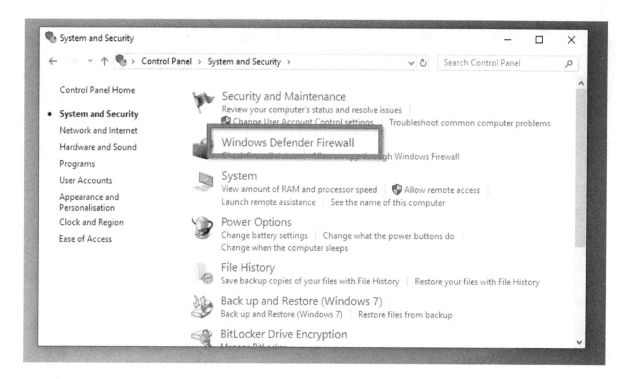

- Next, click **Advanced settings**.

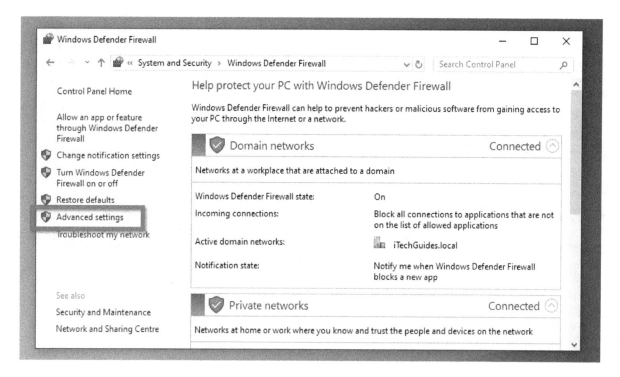

- When **Advanced settings** open, locate the *Remote Desktop - User Mode (TCP-In)* rule. Double-click the rule to open it for editing.

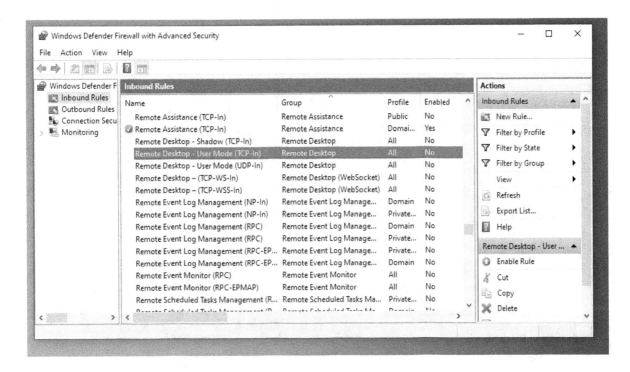

- Check the *Enabled* box. Then select *Allow the connection* and click OK.

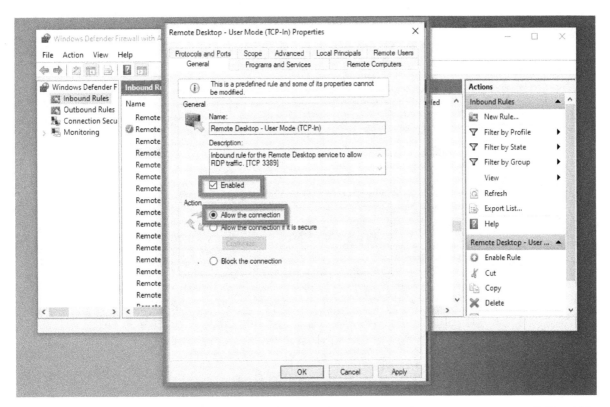

9 out of 10 times this will fix "remote desktop can't connect to the remote computer". But if in the rare instance that you are still having RDP connection error, try the next fix.

Run DISM and SFC

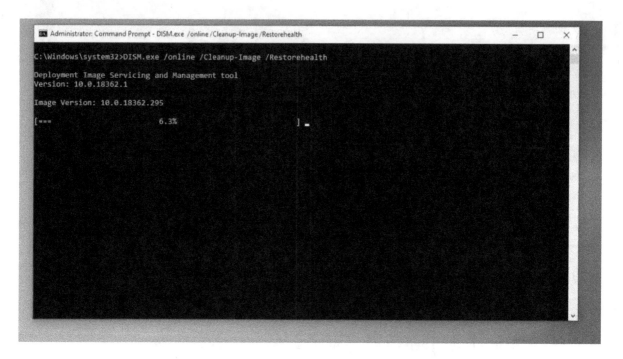

- Type *Command* in the search bar. Then right-click **Command Prompt** and select *Run as administrator*.

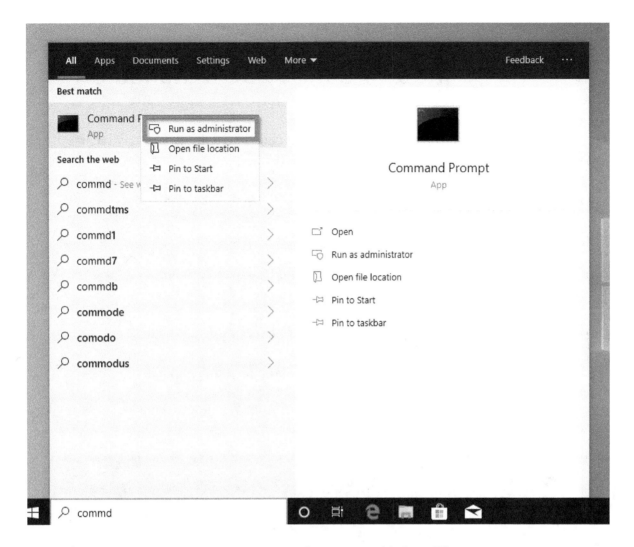

- When **Command Prompt** opens, type the command below. Then press enter.

```
DISM.exe /Online /Cleanup-Image /Restorehealth
```

- Wait for the command to complete. Then type this command and press enter.

```
SFC /scannow
```

When both commands complete successfully, restart your computer. Then try connecting to the remote computer using RDP.

How to Fix "Windows Cannot Be Installed on this Disk" Error

If you try to install Windows 10 on a non-Windows formatted hard drive, you may receive "Windows cannot be installed on this disk" error message.

The steps in this guide will help you resolve this error and install Windows 10 successfully.

The fix discussed in this guide is a 2-step process:

1. Step 1: Boot to Windows 10 to Automatic Recovery, Command Prompt
2. Step 2: Use DISKPART to fix "Windows cannot be installed on this disk"

Step 1: Boot Windows 10 to Automatic Recovery

- Insert Windows 10 installation media (DVD or USB) into your computer
- Then change the boot sequence to boot from the device above
- Restart your computer then, when prompted to boot from Windows 10 media, press any key to continue.

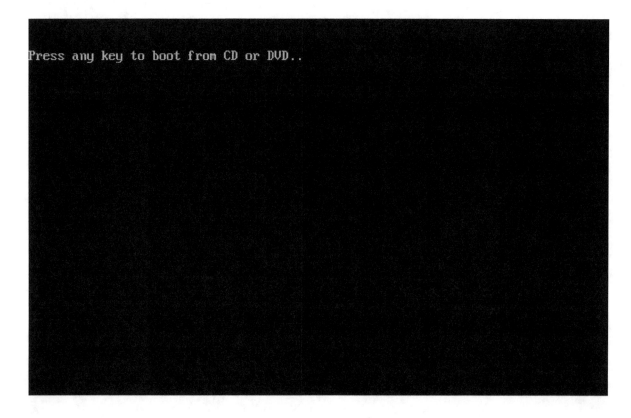

- Wait for Windows 10 installation screen to display, then click **Next**.

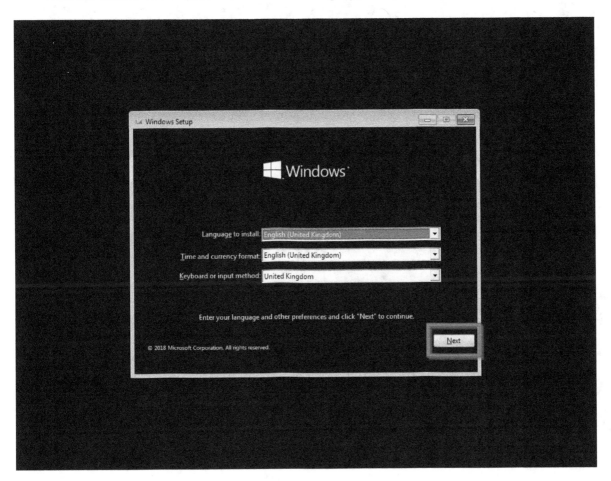

- When this screen displays, click **Repair your computer**.

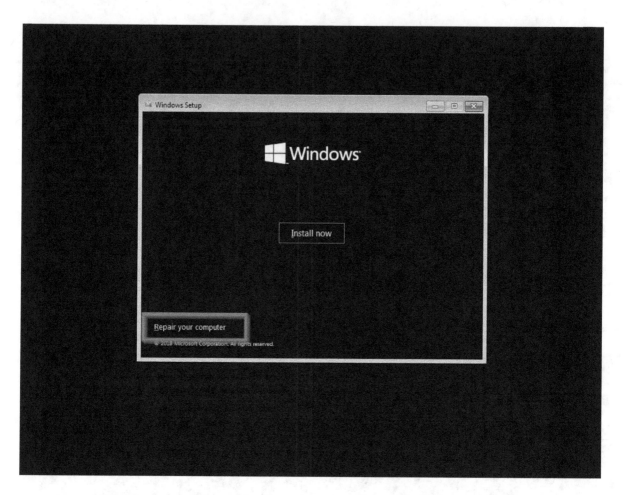

- Then at the **Chose an option** screen, click **Troubleshoot**.

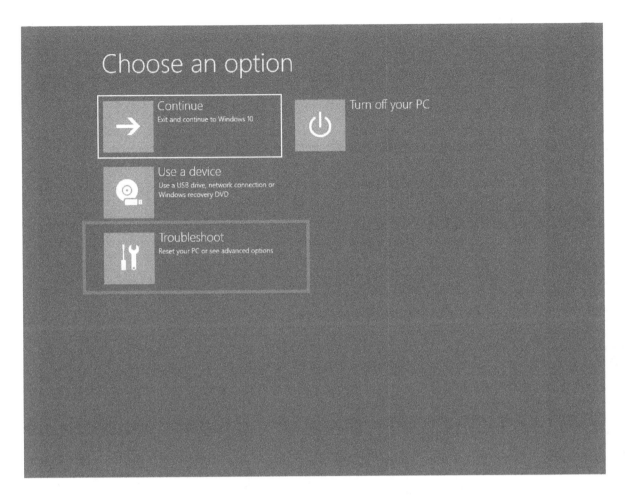

- Finally, when **Advanced options** open, click **Command Prompt**.

← Advanced options

 System Restore
Use a restore point recorded on your PC to restore Windows

 Start-up Repair
Fix problems that keep Windows from loading

 Uninstall Updates
Remove recently installed quality or feature updates from Windows

 Command Prompt
Use the Command Prompt for advanced troubleshooting

 System Image Recovery
Recover Windows using a specific system image file

 UEFI Firmware Settings
Change settings in your PC's UEFI firmware

See more recovery options

Step 2: Use DiskPart to Fix Problems with the Disk

Warning!

Before you perform any of the steps in this section be sure to BACKUP your data to another drive. When you go through the steps here, you will lose your DATA! Backup before you proceed!

Once your Windows 10 PC is in Automatic Recovery, Command Prompt, there are 3 methods you can use to fix the "Windows Cannot Be Installed on this Disk" Error.

Method 1: Use DISKPART to Convert the Drive to MBR

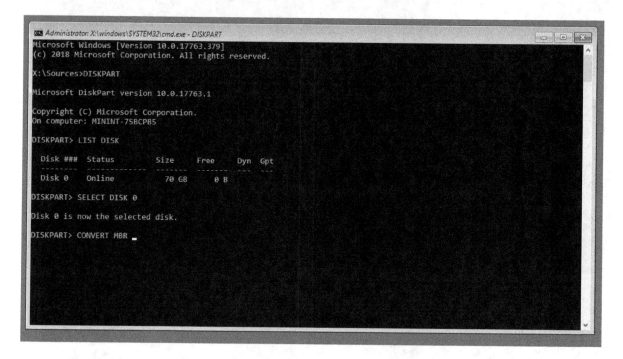

Here are the steps:

- From Command Prompt in Windows 10 Automatic Recovery environment, type the command below and press Enter key.

```
DISKPART
```

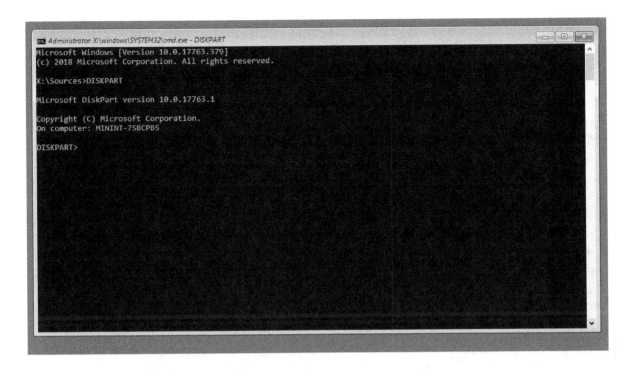

- Then, at the DISKPART prompt, type this command and press Enter.

```
LIST DISK
```

All disks on your computer will be displayed.

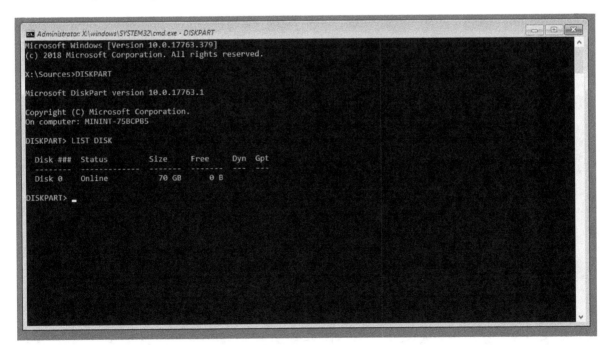

- Then type the command below and press enter.

```
SELECT DISK 0
```

If you have more than one disk, determine the disk you want to install Windows. Then replace 0 in the last command with the disk # from the LIST DISK command.

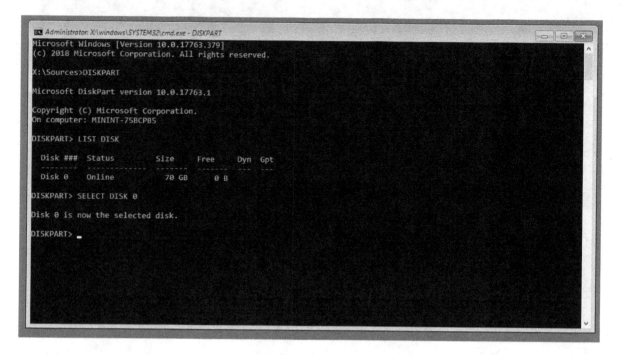

- Once your disk is selected, use this command to convert the disk to MBR.

```
CONVERT MBR
```

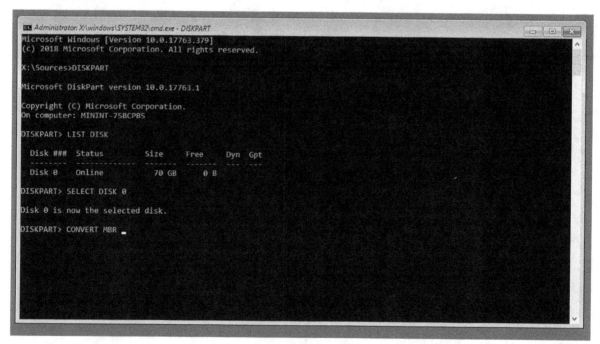

- To exit DISKPART, type *EXIT*. Then press enter.

```
EXIT
```

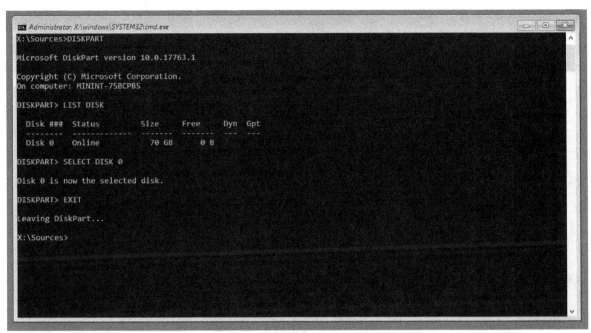

- Finally, to exit Command Prompt, type *EXIT* and press enter. Then click **Turn off your PC**.

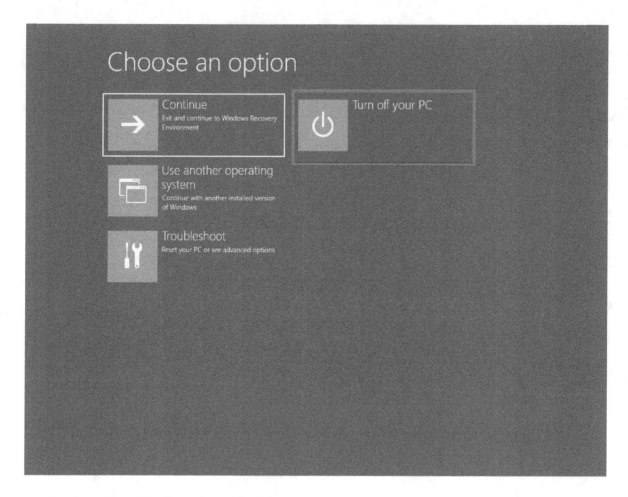

- Try installing Windows into this disk.

If you still receive "Windows cannot be installed on this disk" error, try the next fix.

Method 2: "Clean" the Disk with DISKPART

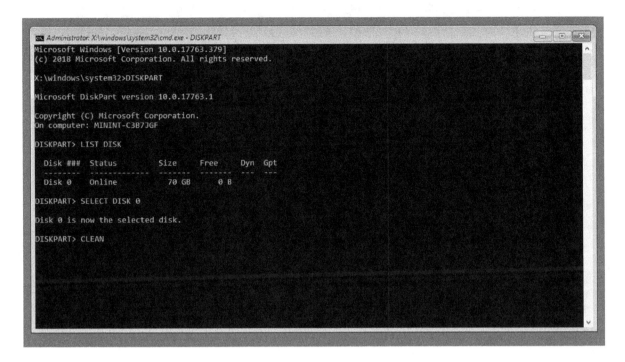

This method is very similar to the last one except for the DISKPART commands.

Here are the steps:

- From Command Prompt in Windows 10 Automatic Recovery environment, type the command below and press Enter key.

```
DISKPART
```

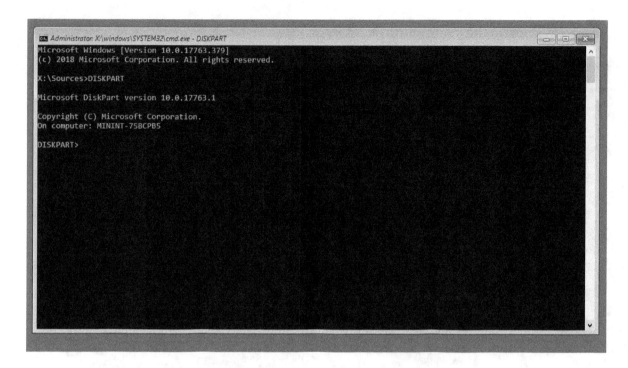

- Then, at the DISKPART prompt, type this command and press Enter.

```
LIST DISK
```

All disks on your computer will be displayed.

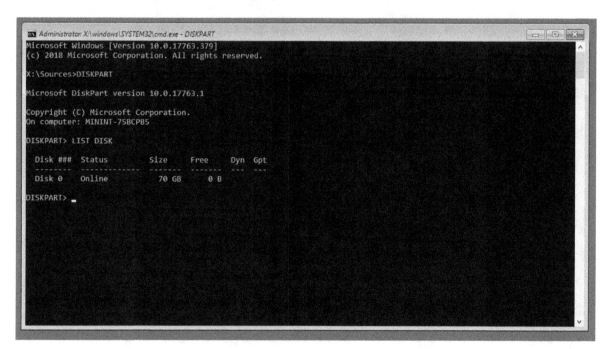

- Then type the command below and press enter.

`SELECT DISK 0`

If you have more than one disk, determine the disk you want to install Windows. Then replace 0 in the last command with the disk # from the LIST DISK command.

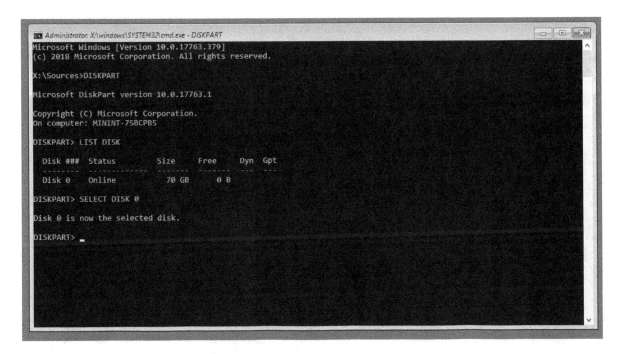

- To "Clean" the disk, type the command below and press Enter.

`CLEAN`

The CLEAN command may take up to an hour to complete

- When the command is done, to exit DISKPART, type *EXIT*. Then press enter.

```
EXIT
```

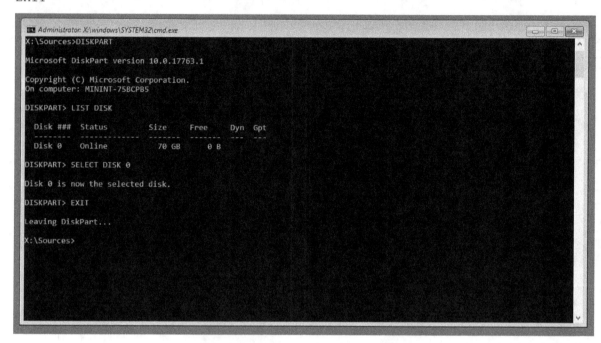

- Finally, to exit Command Prompt, type *EXIT* and press enter. Then click **Turn off your PC**.

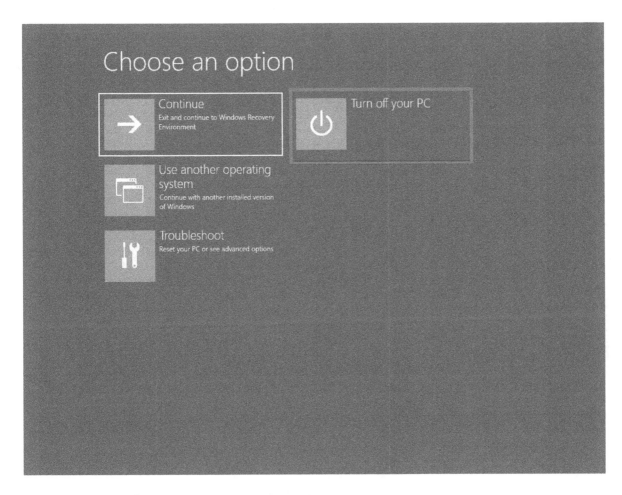

Boot the computer and try installing Windows 10 again. If "Windows cannot be installed on this disk" error is still not fixed, you need to format the disk. See the next fix for details.

Method 3: Format the Disk with DISKPART

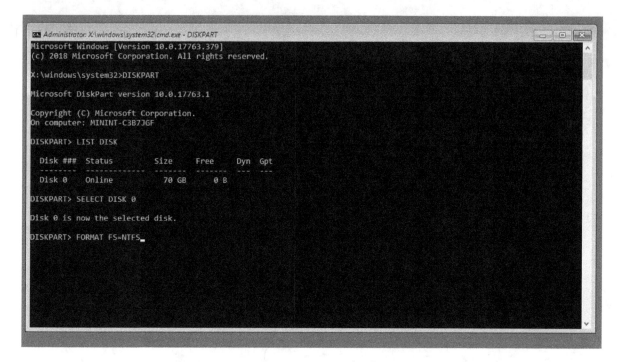

- From Command Prompt in Windows 10 Automatic Recovery environment, type the command below and press Enter key.

```
DISKPART
```

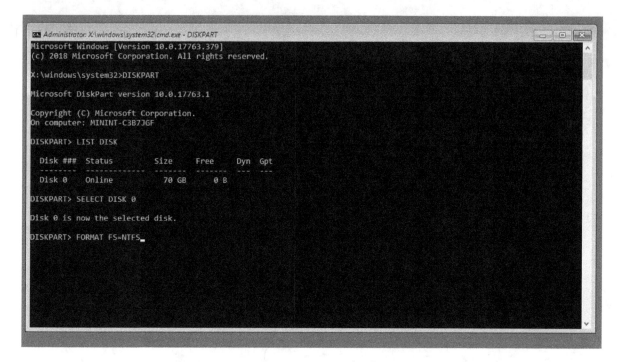

- Then, at the DISKPART prompt, type this command and press Enter.

LIST DISK

All disks on your computer will be displayed.

```
Administrator: X:\windows\SYSTEM32\cmd.exe - DISKPART
Microsoft Windows [Version 10.0.17763.379]
(c) 2018 Microsoft Corporation. All rights reserved.

X:\Sources>DISKPART

Microsoft DiskPart version 10.0.17763.1

Copyright (C) Microsoft Corporation.
On computer: MININT-75BCPB5

DISKPART> LIST DISK

  Disk ###  Status         Size     Free     Dyn  Gpt
  --------  -------------  -------  -------   ---  ---
  Disk 0    Online          70 GB      0 B

DISKPART> _
```

- Then type the command below and press enter.

SELECT DISK 0

If you have more than one disk, determine the disk you want to install Windows. Then replace 0 in the last command with the disk # from the LIST DISK command.

- Once you have selected a disk with the last command, to list all available volumes (partitions), type this command and click Enter.

LIST VOLUME

Note the volume number of the volume you want to install Windows. Mine is Volume 2.

- Then type this command and press enter.

```
SELECT VOLUME 1
```

Replace 1 above with the volume number for the drive you want to install Windows 10.

- Finally, format the volume with this command.

```
FORMAT FS=NTFS
```

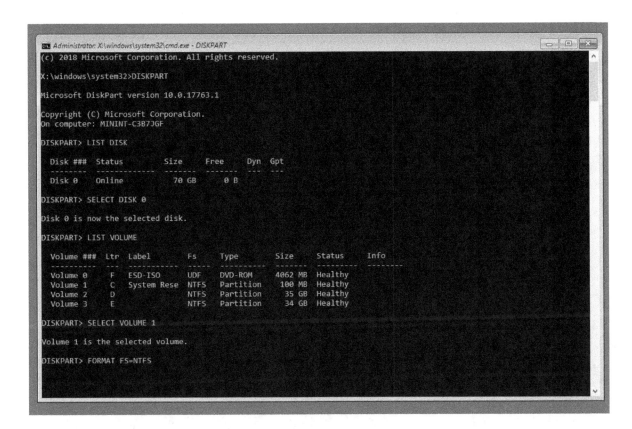

- When the drive is formatted, to exit DISKPART, type *EXIT*. Then press enter.

```
EXIT
```

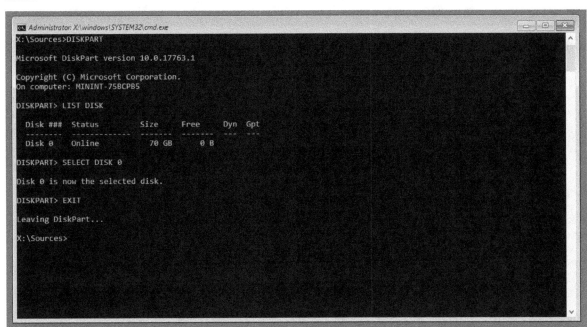

- Finally, to exit Command Prompt, type *EXIT* and press enter. Then click **Turn off your PC**.

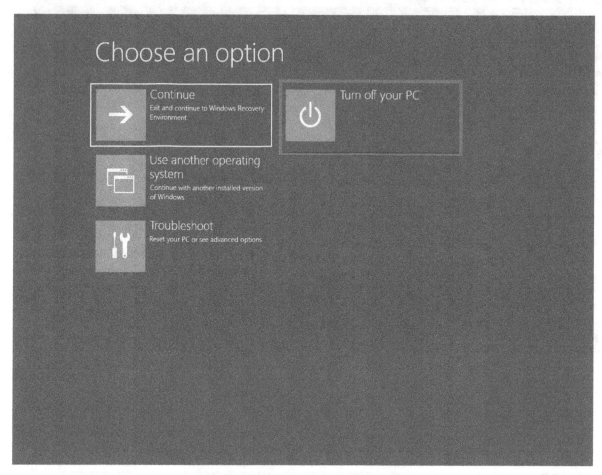

You should be able to install Windows 10 without any errors.

How to Get Windows 10 Wifi to Work if it Won't Turn on

If after upgrading to Windows 10, Wifi won't turn on, use the steps in this guide to fix the problem.

4 Methods are discussed in this guide. After each method, check whether your Wifi is fixed before trying the next method.

Method 1: Modify Your Wireless Adapter's "Channel Width for 2.4GHz" Property

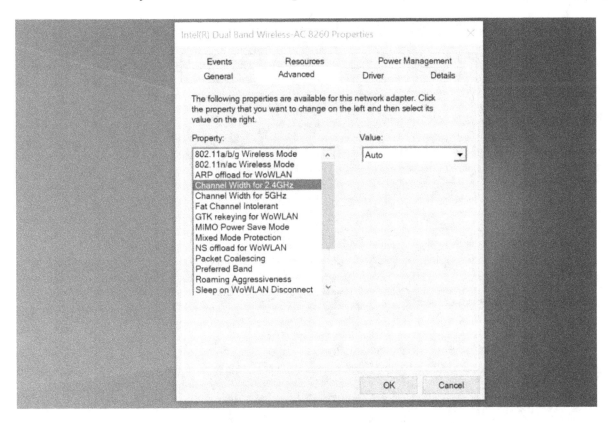

This method fixes this problem 90% of the time. Follow these steps to apply this fix:

- Right-click Windows 10 start menu. Then click **Device Manager**.

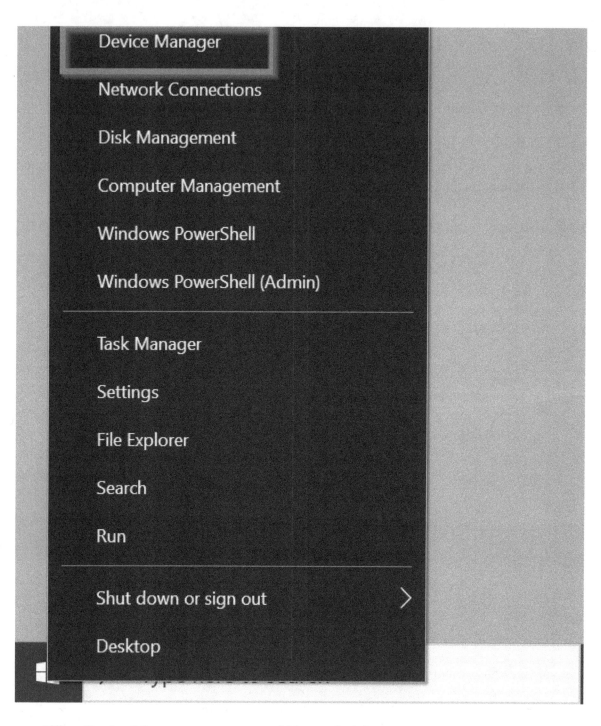

- When **Device Manager** opens, expand **Network Adapters**.

- Then locate the adapter that has "Wireless" in its name.

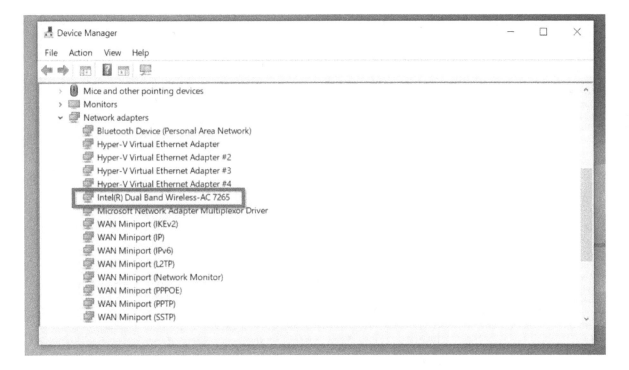

- Right-click the Wireless network adapter and select **Properties**.

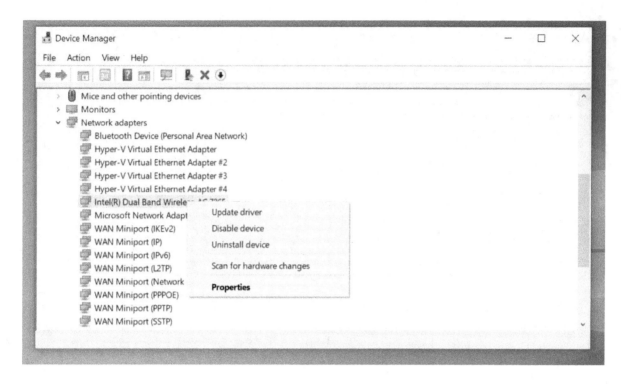

- On the Properties page of the adapter, click the **Advanced** tab.

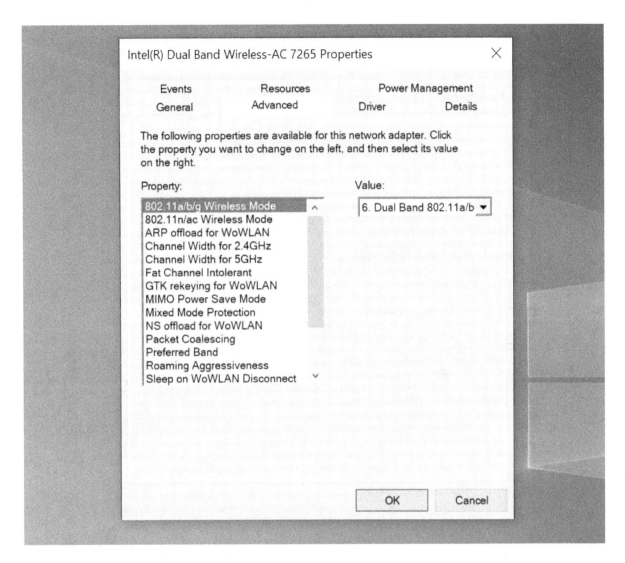

- Then, locate "Channel Width for 2.4GHz" and click on it. If the value is set to Auto, change it to **20 MHz Only**. See the image below. When you finish, click OK.

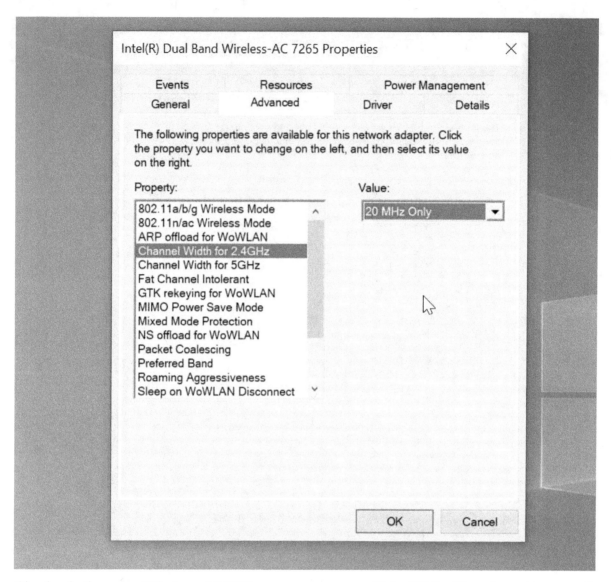

Check whether your Windows 10 Wifi can come on now. If the Wifi still can't come on, try the next fix...

Method 2: Roll Back to Previous OS, Turn off Wifi Device, Upgrade Again

Here are the steps for this fix:

1. Unplug your Wifi device from your computer (if it is an external device). For a built-in Wifi device, boot to BIOS and turn it off.
2. Rollback to the previous Operating System (Windows 7 or Windows 8.1)
3. Repeat the upgrade to Windows 10
4. When the upgrade is completed turn your Wifi via BIOS on or plug it back in.
5. Windows 10 should automatically detect the device and install the driver

After going through these steps, check your Wifi. If your Windows 10 Wifi still won't turn on, try the next fix.

Method 2: Restore BIOS Settings to System Defaults

Here are the steps for this fix:

1. Shut down the PC
2. Unplug the power from the wall outlet. If it is a laptop, remove the battery as well
3. Wait for about 5 minutes
4. Fit your battery (for laptops) back. Then plug your power back on
5. Boot your computer to BIOS.
6. *On the BIOS, locate a place to reset BIOS settings to system defaults. Save your changes. Then boot to Windows.

*For some systems, F9 will restore your BIOS settings to system defaults. F10 will save the changes.

When your computer boots and you log in, check your Wifi. If your Windows 10 Wifi still won't turn on, try my last recommended fix...

Method 3: Disable "Allow the computer to turn off this Device to Save Power"

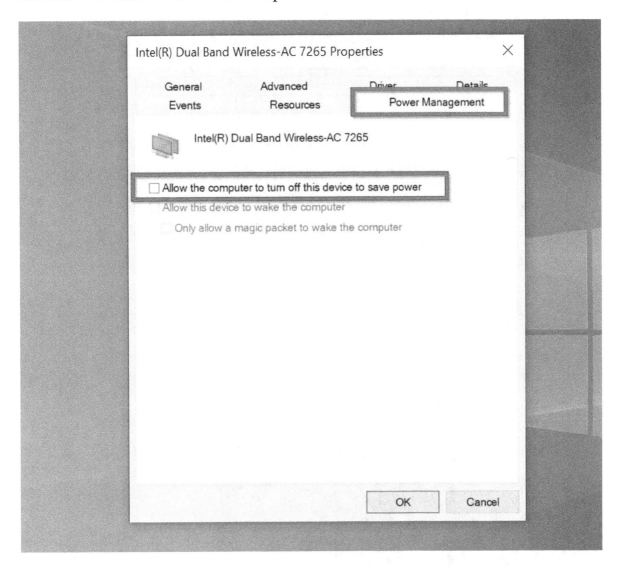

Modifying this setting have resolved Wifi problem for a number of users as well. Here are the steps:

- Right-click the Start menu and select **Device Manager**.

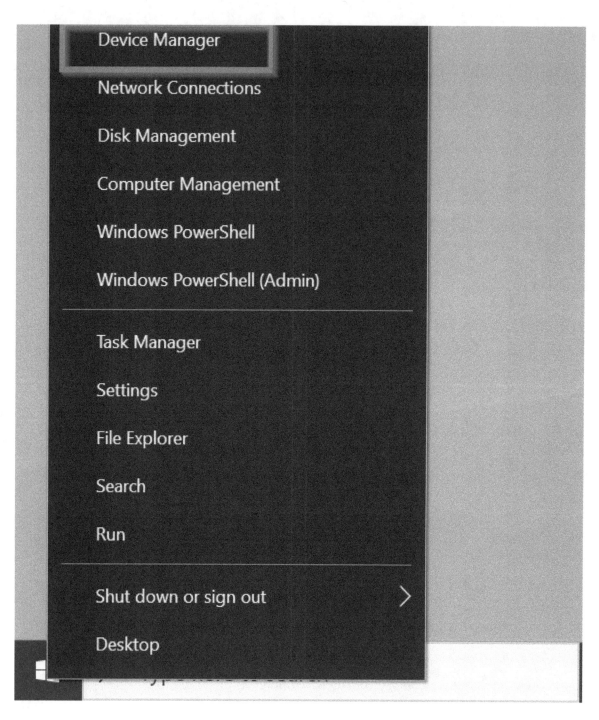

- When **Device Manager** opens, expand **Network Adapters**.

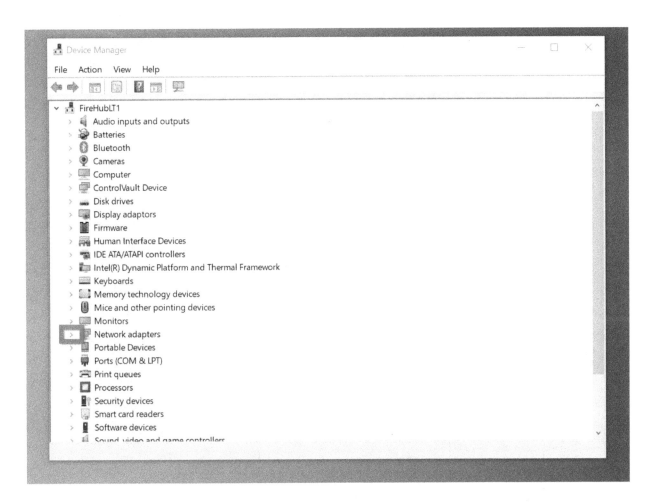

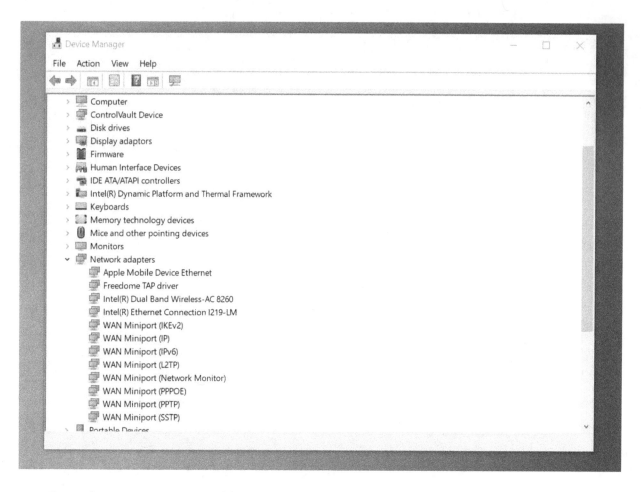

- Beneath **Network adapter**, locate the adapter that has "Wireless" in its name.

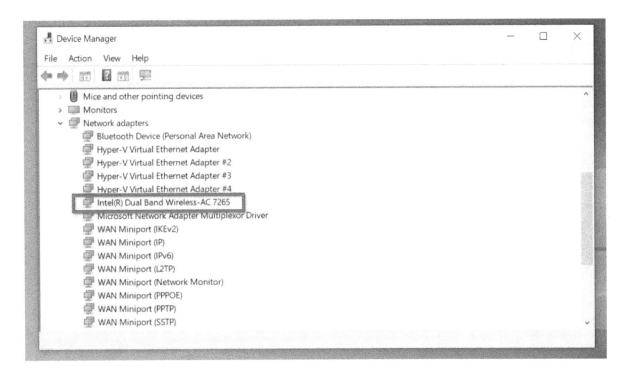

- Then, right-click the Wireless network adapter and click **Properties**.

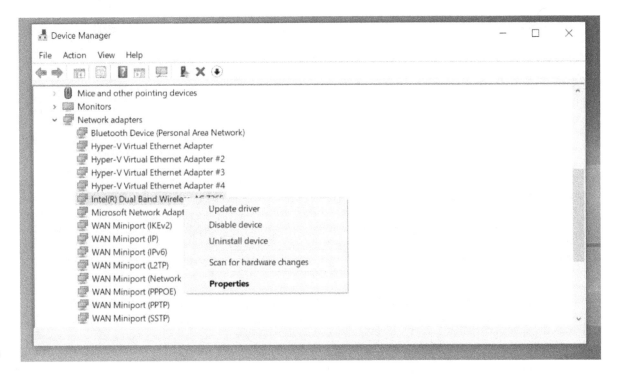

- When the Properties of your Wireless network adapter opens, click the **Power Management** tab.

- Then **uncheck** "Allow the computer to turn off this Device to Save Power". When you finish, click OK.

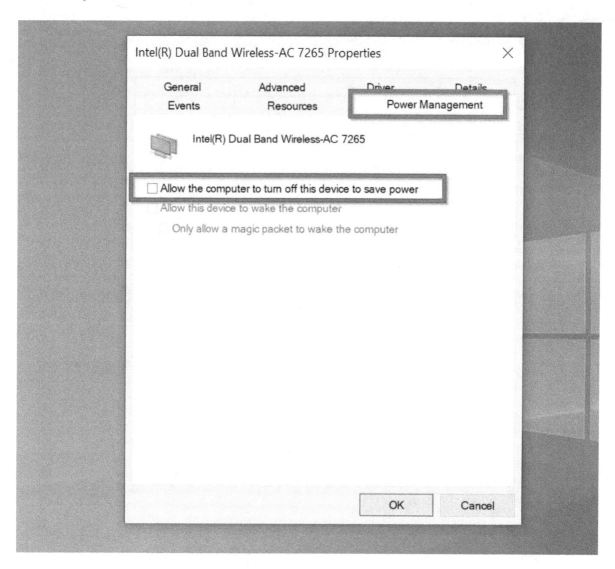

How to Fix "DISM Error 50" in Windows 10

If received DISM error 50: "*DISM doesn't support servicing Windows PE with the /online option*", this is because you tried to run DISM command with the */online* switch from Windows PE or Windows recovery environment.

DISM /online only works when you are logged on to Windows. If you use it in a WinPE environment or in Windows recovery mode, you will receive a DISM error 50. Here are the steps resolve DISM error 50:

1. Determine the Drive for Your Windows Installation
2. Run the Correct DISM Commands, then SFC

Step 1: Determine the Drive for Your Windows Installation

While in the Windows recovery environment or WinPE, the next step is to determine the drive that Windows is installed. This step is critical to resolving DISM error 50.

Here is how to determine the drive for your Windows installation:

- At command prompt, type the command below. Then press Enter.

```
DIR c:
```

If the drive has a **Windows** folder, it is likely where your Operating System is installed.

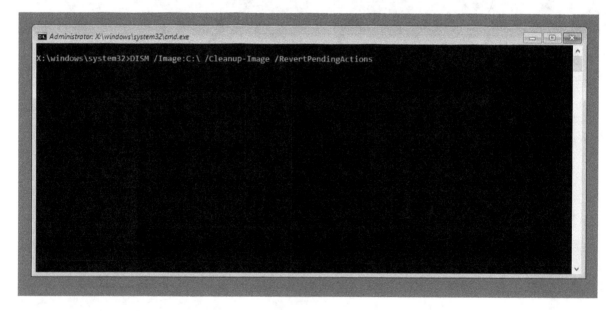

- If drive C: does not have a **Windows** folder, try **DIR d:**, then **DIR E:** until you determine where your OS is installed.

Once you have identified the drive your Operating System is installed, proceed to step 2 below....

Step 2: Run the DISM Commands with the Correct Switch

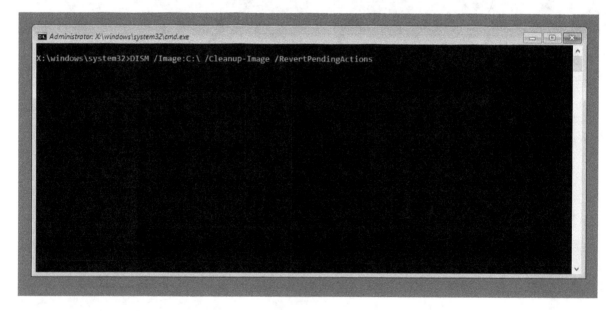

- When you have determined the drive your Operating System is installed, to fix DISM error 50, type the command below. Then press enter.

```
DISM /Image:C:\ /Cleanup-Image /RevertPendingActions
```

Replace **C** with the drive letter for your Windows installation.

The secret is to replace */online* with */Image* switch. But when you specify the */Image* switch, you have to specify the path to your Windows installation.

If you have other Windows 10 or Windows Server 2016 boot problems, use this command next. Wait for the last command to complete. Then type the command below and press enter.

```
DISM.exe /Image:C:\ /Cleanup-Image /RestoreHealth
```

Replace **C** with the drive letter for your Windows installation. Your DISM command will run successfully without any errors.

How to Fix "Bad Pool Header Blue Screen" Error in Windows 10

Bad Pool Header error is related to memory allocation issues in Windows 10. Bad Pool Header error usually triggers the Blue Screen of Death (BSOD) error. The following are likely to cause Bad Pool Header blue screen error in Windows 10:

1. Device driver issues
2. Existence of bad sectors on your hard drive
3. Disk write issues may also trigger this error message

Available Options to Fix Bad Pool Header Blue Screen Error in Windows 10

1. Disconnect All Attached Devices
2. Uninstalled Recently Installed Drivers or Software

Here are the details for each Fix

Method 1: Disconnect All Attached Devices

Follow the steps below to try this fix:

1. Shutdown your computer
2. Then, disconnect the mouse, keyboard, modem and any external device connected to your computer.
3. Then start the computer.
4. If the computer starts without errors, connect the devices one at a time and start the computer. I suggest you start by connecting your mouse. Then keyboard (for desktops)
5. When you discover the device that is causing the error, you may disconnect it permanently or try restarting the device. You could also try changing the cable connecting the device to your computer.

If this fix does not resolve bad pool header error, try the next fix.

Method 2: Uninstalled Recently Installed Drivers or Software

I mentioned in the introduction of this guide that bad pool header error is most likely caused by a device driver.

My next recommended fix is to uninstall any device driver or software you installed recently. To be able to uninstall recently installed drivers or software, you have to start your Windows 10 in Safe mode.

Here are the steps to apply this fix:

- Press the power button on your computer to start Windows 10 boot. Then wait for the Windows 10 logo to pop up. Once the dots (highlighted in the image below) start circling, press the power button to power off your computer.

- Press the power button again to start Windows 10. Then power off the PC when the circling begins.

- When you power your computer again (for the third time), it will boot and display the screen below. After some time, it will display the **Automatic Repair** screen.

- To boot to recovery mode, click **Advanced options**.

- Then on the **Choose an option** menu, click **Troubleshoot**.

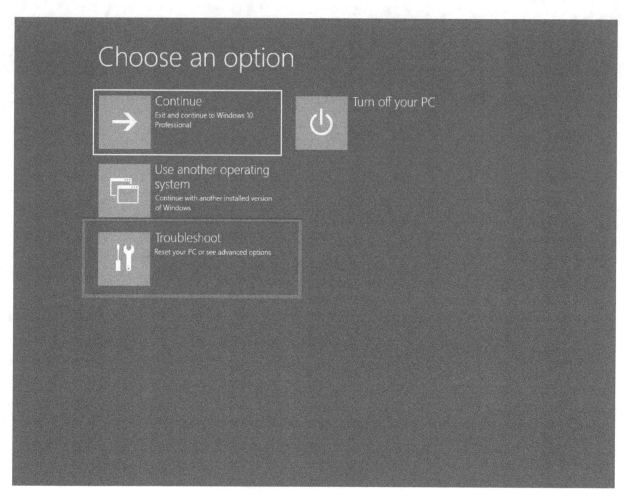

- On the **Troubleshoot** menu, click **Advanced options**.

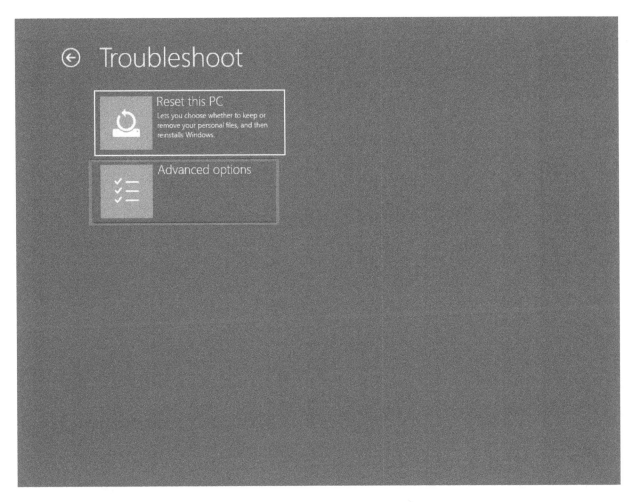

- When **Advanced options** open, click **Start-up Settings**.

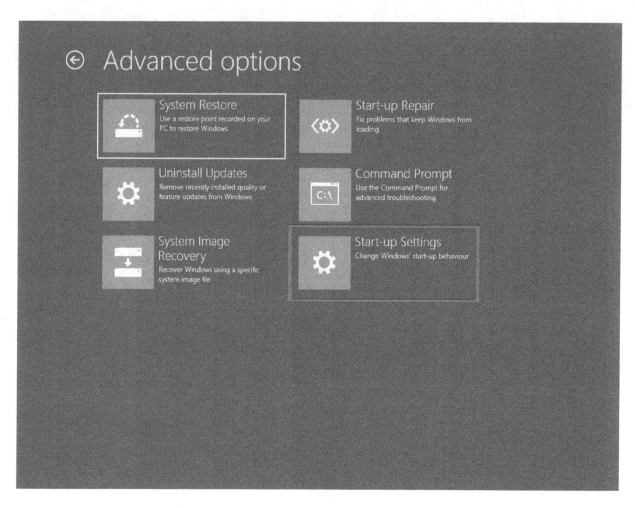

- Finally, on the *Start-up Settings* screen click **Restart**.

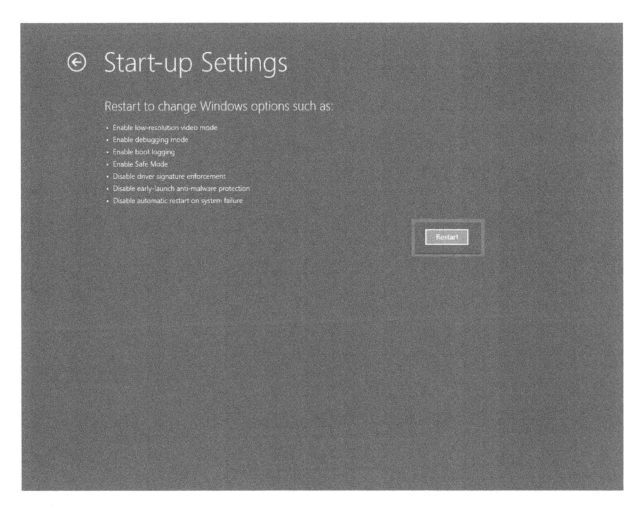

- Your computer will boot to *Start-up Settings*. Press key 4 or function F4 to start safe mode.

- Log in to your computer with your usual username and password. Then open Device Manager and uninstall any recently installed device driver.

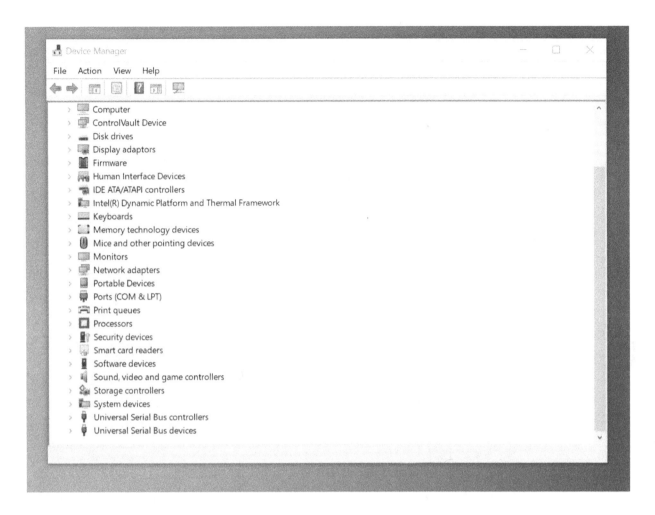

- Open Apps & features and uninstall any recently installed software.
- Restart your PC normally.

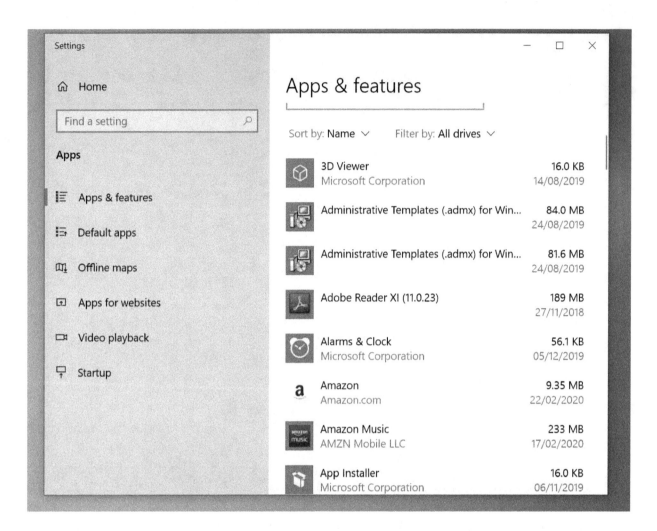

How to Fix "Windows has Detected an IP Address Conflict"

In a computer network, every computer must have a unique IP. If two computers or devices have the same IP address, you will receive "Windows has Detected an IP Address Conflict".

IP address conflict is most likely to occur in a network where IP addresses are issued manually instead of with DHCP.

If you receive this error, use the steps below to determine which computers have the conflicting IPs and resolve it.

Step 1: Get More Information from Systems Event Log

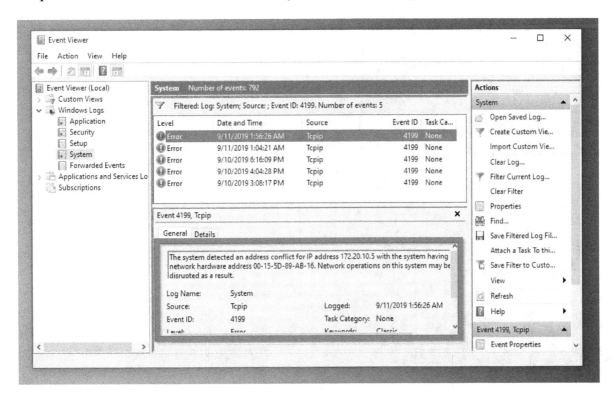

When you receive "Windows has Detected an IP Address Conflict" error, the first step is to determine the other device with the same IP address. The best place to get this information is the System Event log.

Here are the steps to get more information about this error from the event log:

- From the computer you received the IP conflict error, right-click Start menu. Then select **Event Viewer**.

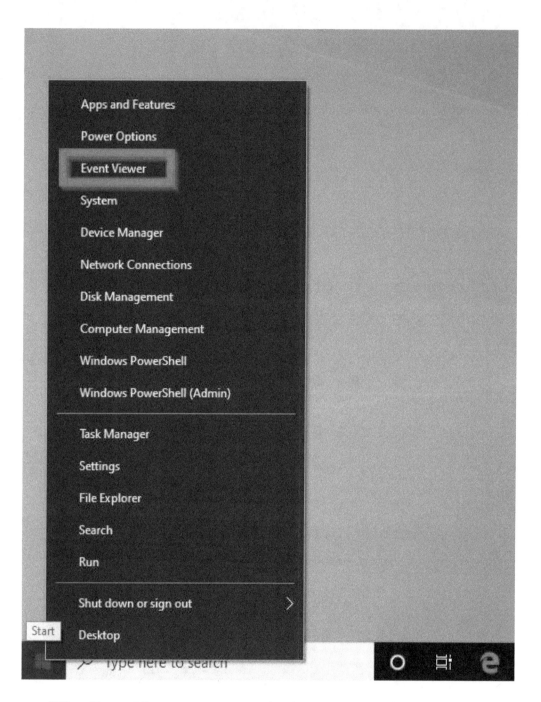

- When **Event Viewer** opens, expand **Windows Logs**. Then click **System**.

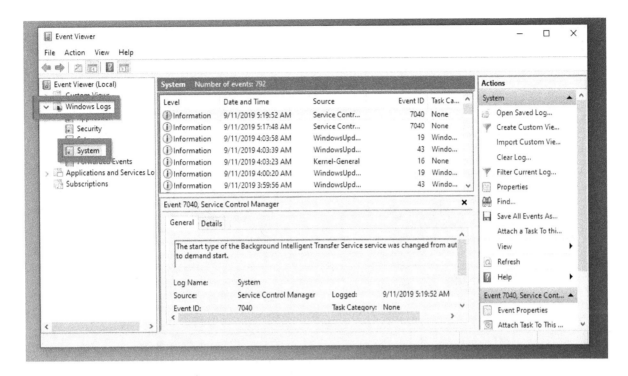

- Right-click **System**. Then click **Filter Current Log**...

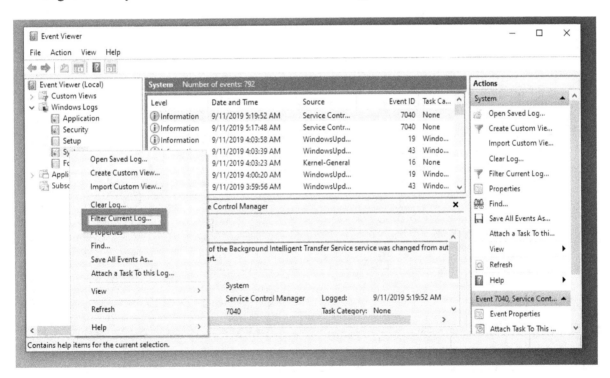

- When **Filter Current Log** opens, click on **<All Event IDs>**. Then type 4199 and click OK.

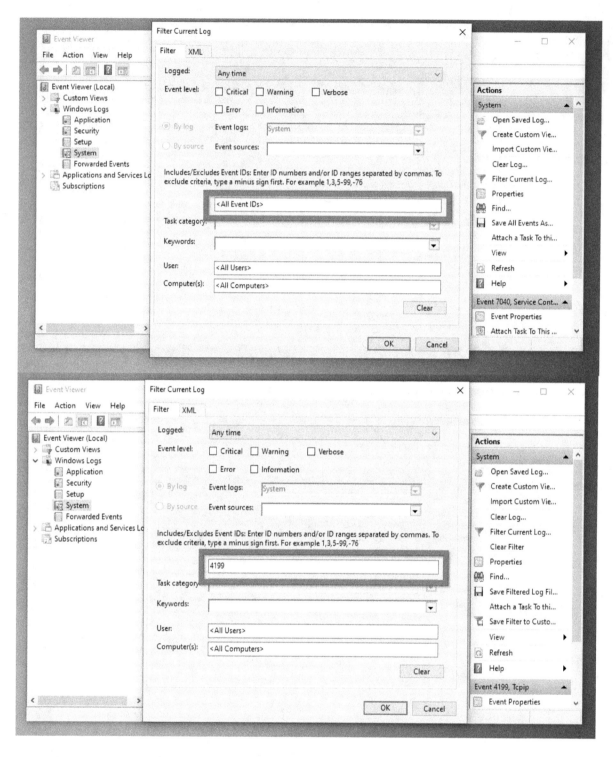

- The System event log will now display events with ID 4199 - *the system detected an address conflict for IP address...*
- Click on one of the errors. Note the MAC address and IP address of the other device.

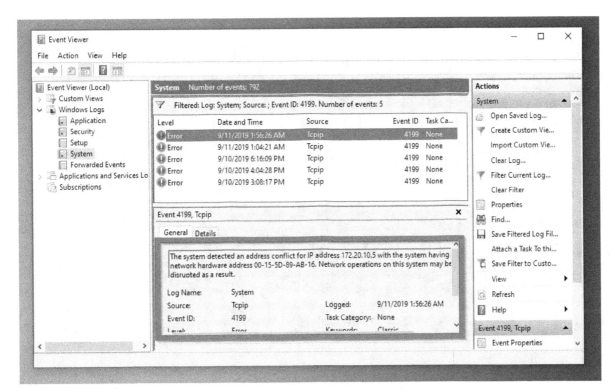

Now that you have the IP address of the other conflicting device, the next step is to compare that IP with the IP of the device where you received the error message.

In my example, from the last image, the event viewer reported the IP of the other device as 172.20.10.5.

To compare this IP with the IP of the current device, get the IP of the device you are troubleshooting from. Here is how:

- Open command prompt. Then type the command below and press enter.

```
IPConfig
```

Here is the result. In my example, the IPv4 address is 172.20.10.4. They do not have the same IP address. So, there must be other reasons for the "Windows has detected an IP address conflict" error.

Before you proceed to the next step to fix this error, if this last check confirmed that both devices have the same IP, change the IP address of the current device.

Step 2: Disable IPv6

Disabling IPv6 may fix "Windows has detected an IP address conflict" error message.

Here are the steps to disable IPv6:

- Press **Windows logo + R** keys to open Run command.

- At the RUN command, type *control panel*. Then click OK.

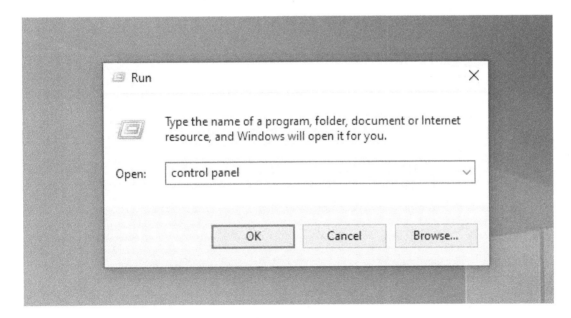

- When Control Panel opens, navigate to **Network and Internet** > **Network and Sharing Centre** > **Change Adapter Settings**. See the images below.

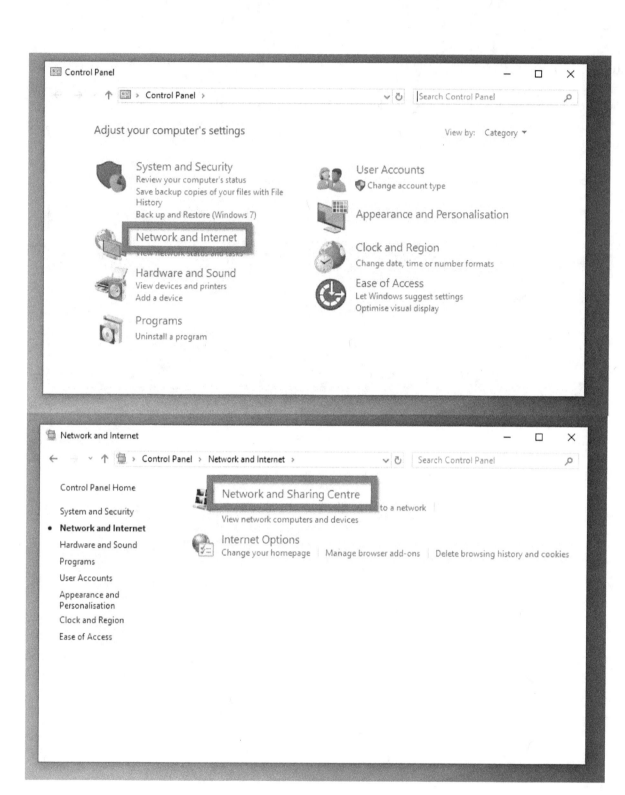

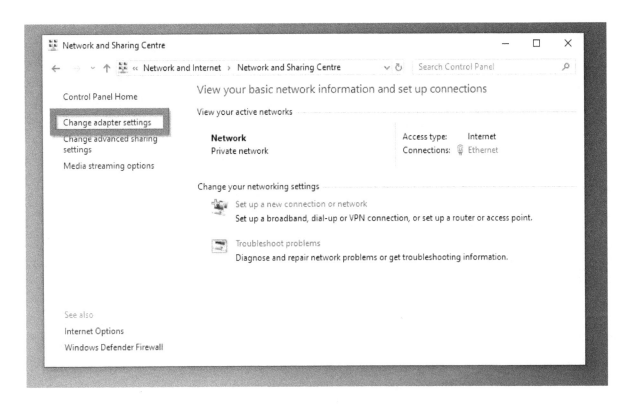

- At **Network Connections**, double-click the network adapter.

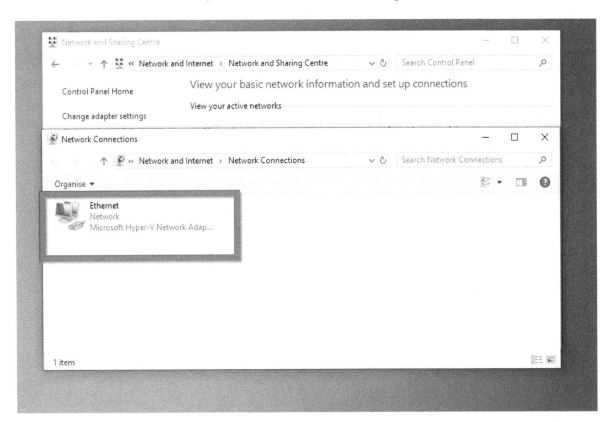

- Then click **Properties**.

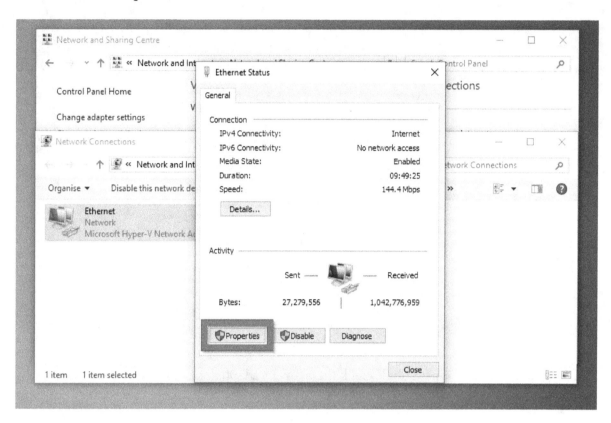

- Finally, to disable IPv6, **uncheck** the box beside **Internet Protocol Version 6 (TCP/IPv6)**. Then click OK.

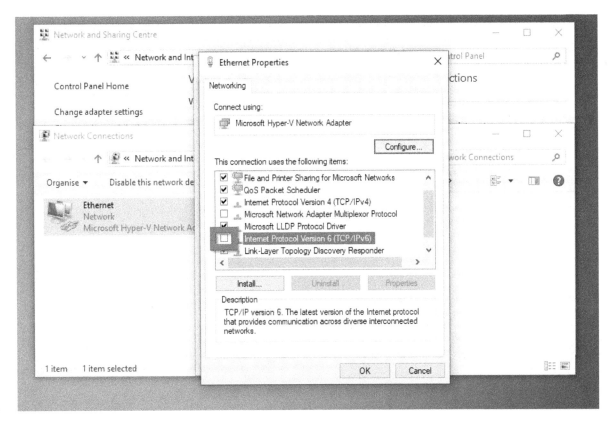

Restart your computer to see whether "Windows has detected an IP address conflict" error is fixed. If not try the next fix.

Method 3: Reset the Network Card

- Type *Network Reset* in the search box. Then click **Network Reset** from the result.

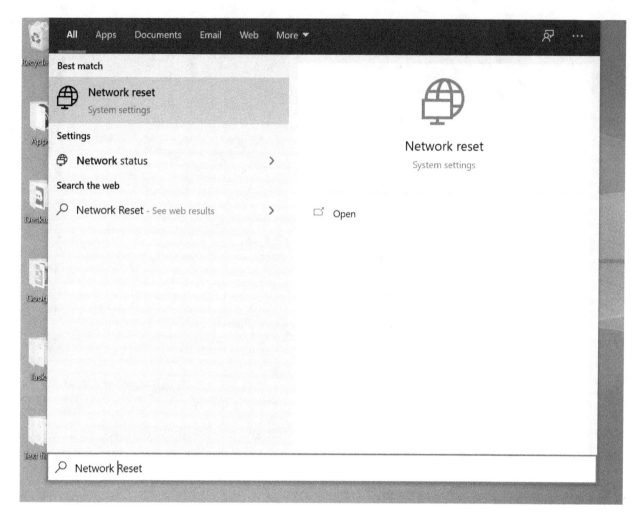

- When **Network Reset** opens, click **Reset now**. Then confirm that you want to reset your network.
- Your PC will restart.

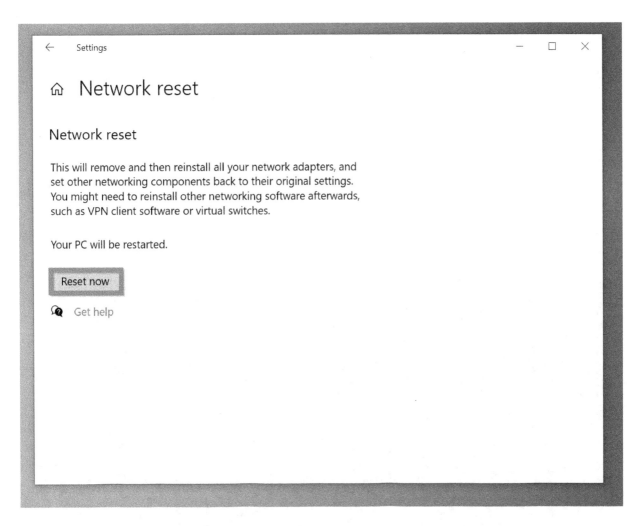

Check whether the IP address conflict error is fixed. If not, try the next method…

Method 4: Release and Renew IP, Flush DNS

The following commands may fix IP address conflict error:

- Open Command prompt. Then type the following commands and press enter. Run the commands one at a time.

```
IPConfig /Release
IPConfig /FlushDNS
IPConfig /RegisterDNS
IPConfig /Renew
```

How to Fix "We Couldn't Format the Selected Partition" Error During Windows 10 Installation

Here are the steps fix "We Couldn't Format the Selected Partition" error.

Step 1: Boot to Repair Mode Command Prompt

- On the "We Couldn't Format the Selected Partition. [Error: 0x80070057]" error message, click OK.

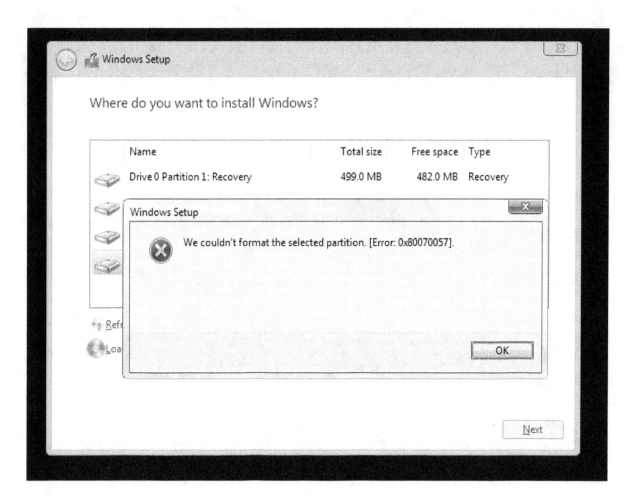

- Then click the cancel button to exit the Windows 10 installation wizard.

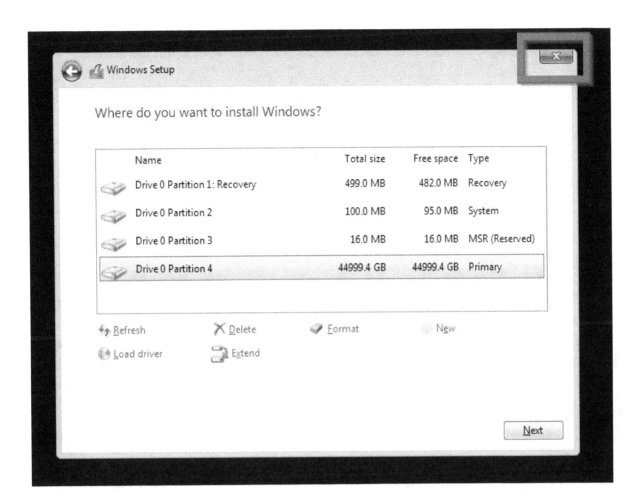

- To confirm that you wish to exit setup, click **Yes**.

- You will be returned to the original installation window. Click **Repair your computer**.

- When the **Choose an option** screen is displayed, click **Troubleshoot**.

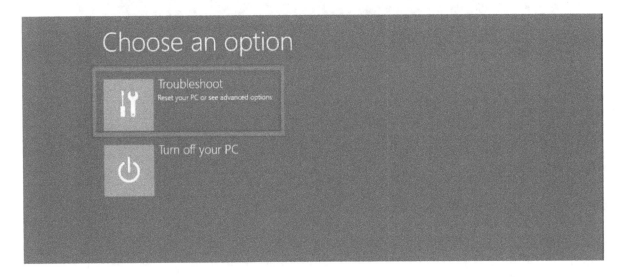

- Then, at **Advanced options**, click **Command Prompt**. When Command Prompt opens, proceed to step 2.

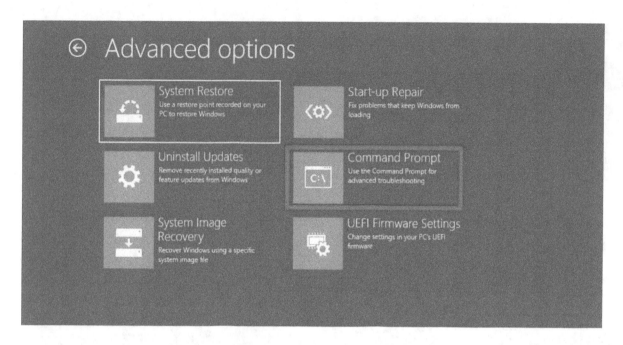

Step 2: Format Partition with DISKPART

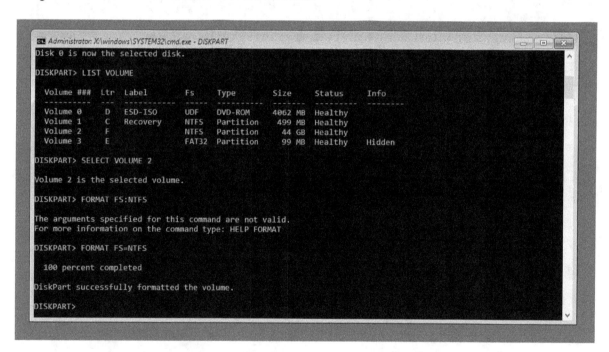

Once you are in Command Prompt, the final step to fix "We Couldn't Format the Selected Partition. [Error: 0x80070057]" error message is to format the drive with DISKPART.

Here are the steps

- When Command Prompt opens, type this command. Then press enter.

DISKPART

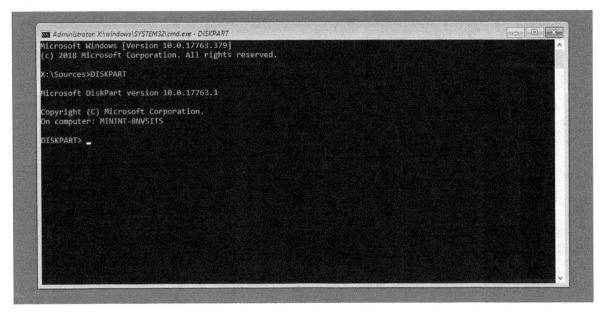

- At the DISKPART prompt, type the command below and press enter.

LIST DISK

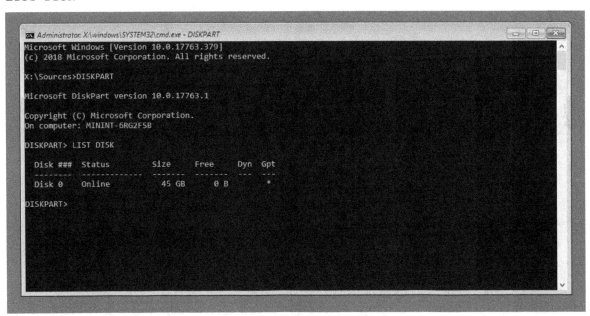

- Then type this command and press the enter key.

SELECT DISK 0

Replace 0 with your disk #.

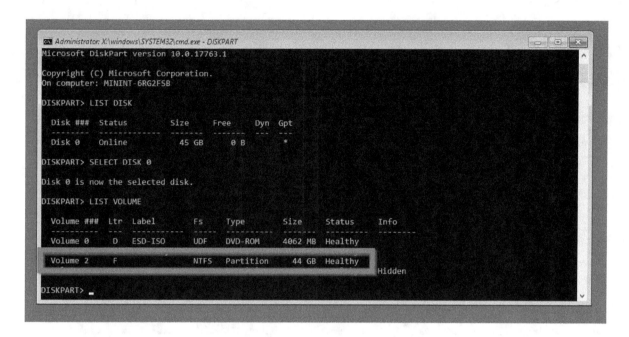

- To list available volumes (partitions) in the selected disk, type the command below and press Enter.

```
LIST VOLUME
```

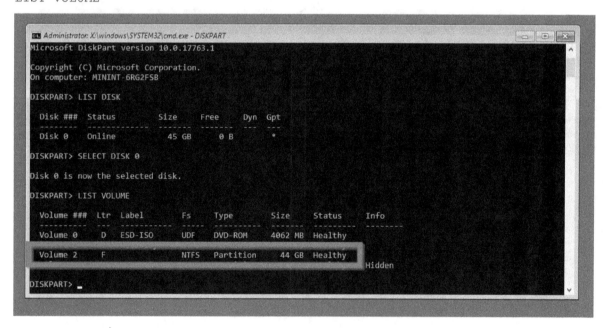

- The next step is to select the volume (partition) you tried to format that gave you "We Couldn't Format the Selected Partition. [Error: 0x80070057]" error. Here is the command:

```
SELECT VOLUME 2
```

Change *2* to the volume # for your partition.

- Once the volume is selected, format it with this command:

`FORMAT FS=NTFS`

Here are the results of the last 2 commands

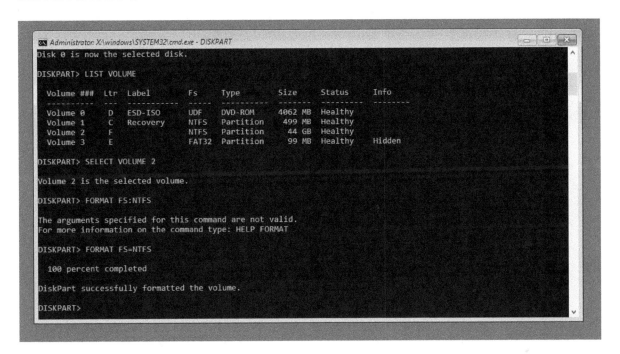

- Now that you have successfully formatted the drive, you can restart your installation.
- To exit DISKPART, type **exit** and press enter. To exit command prompt, type **exit** again and press enter.
- When you return to **Choose an option**, click **Turn off your PC**.

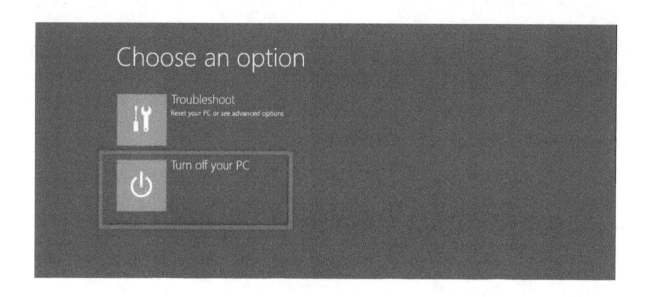

How to Fix "Not recognized as an internal or external command" in Windows 10

Sometimes when you run a command in Windows, you may receive the error message "the program is not recognized as an internal or external command. This guide details steps to fix this error.

Here are the high-level steps I took to resolve "not recognized as an internal or external command" error:

- Confirm that the command is in %systemroot%\system32 Directory
- Configure Path Environment Variable
- Run DISM and SFC Commands

Step 1: Confirm that the Command is in *%systemroot%\system32* Directory

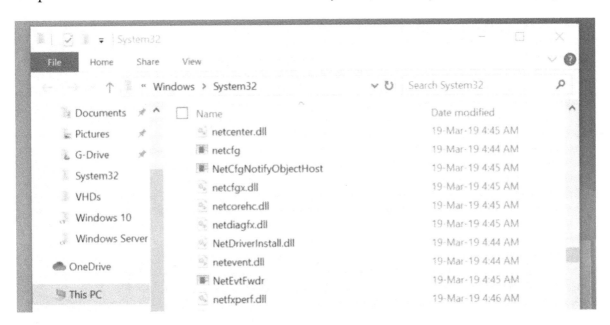

Most Windows commands are in the **system32** folder. If you receive *command not recognized* error, the first thing to do is to confirm that command is in this folder.

If it is not, it may be that the program is not installed on your computer. Otherwise, if it is a Windows built-in program, it may mean that some of your Windows installation files are corrupt.

Here are the detailed steps to check that the program that returned this error message is available in the **system32** folder:

- Type **%systemroot%\system32** in the search bar. Then click the folder in the search results.

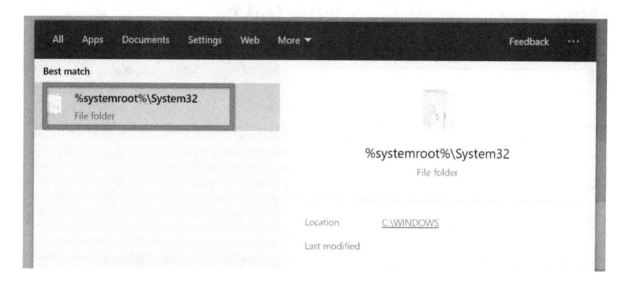

- Check if the command exists in this folder.

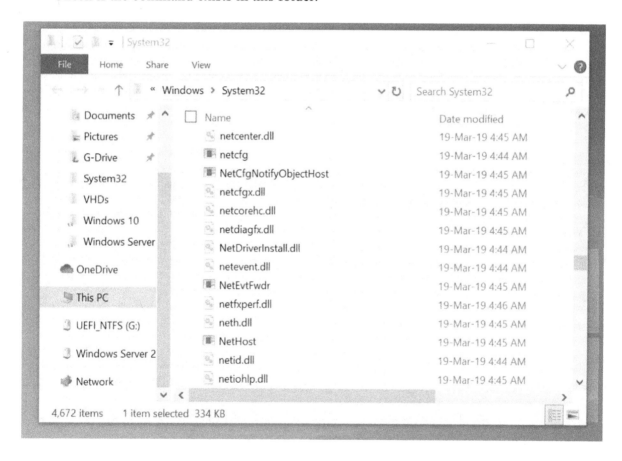

If the command exists in **%systemroot%\system32**, then the problem is an environmental variable issue. Proceed to step 2. Otherwise, if it is a Windows program, some Windows files may be missing or corrupt. In that case, proceed to step 3.

Step 2: Configure Environment Variable

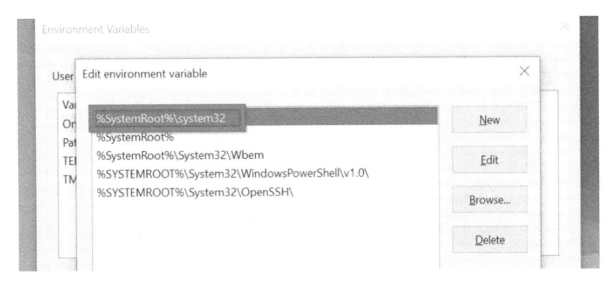

Perform this task only if the program that returned "not recognized as an internal or external command" error is in the **system32** folder. Here are the steps:

- Right-click Windows 10 start menu. Then select **File Explorer.**

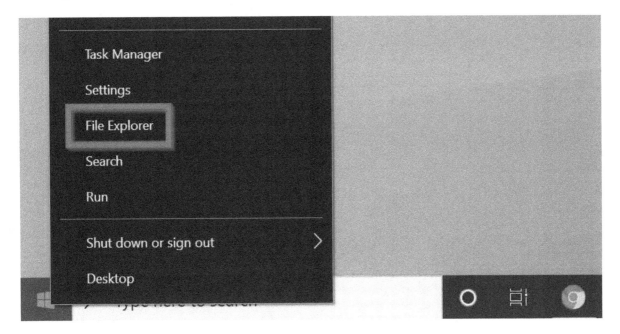

- When **File Explorer** opens, right-click **This PC** and select **Properties**.

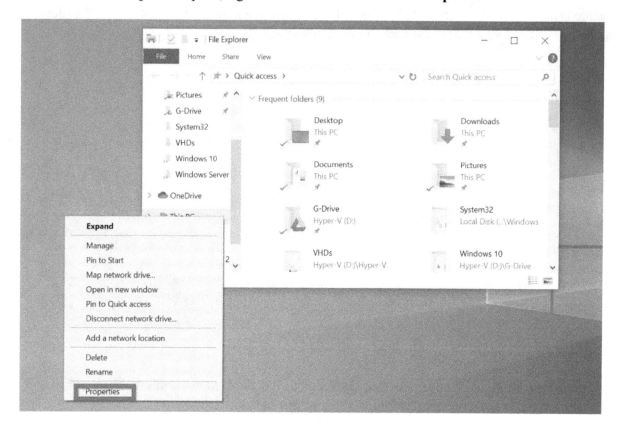

- When **System** settings open, click **Advanced system settings**.

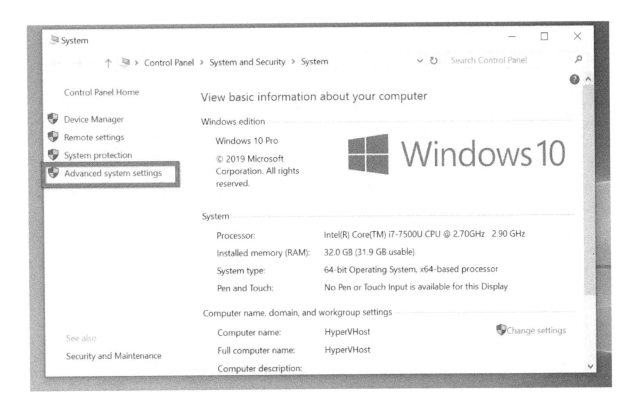

- When **Advanced System** Properties opens, click **Environment Variables**.

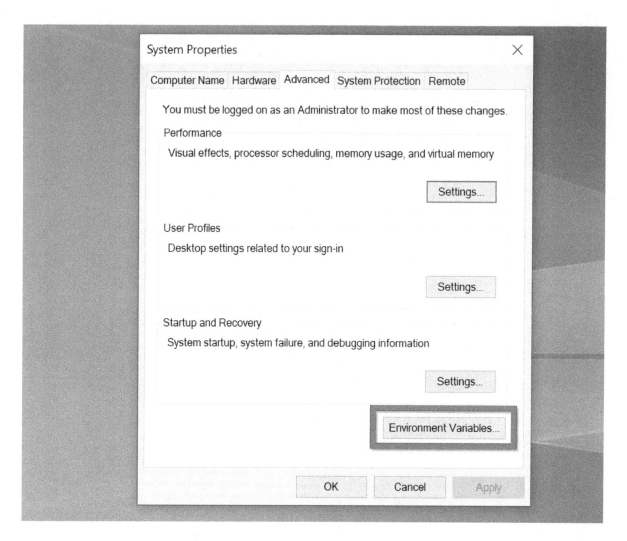

- Then, at **Environment Variables** settings, select **Path**. Then click **Edit**.

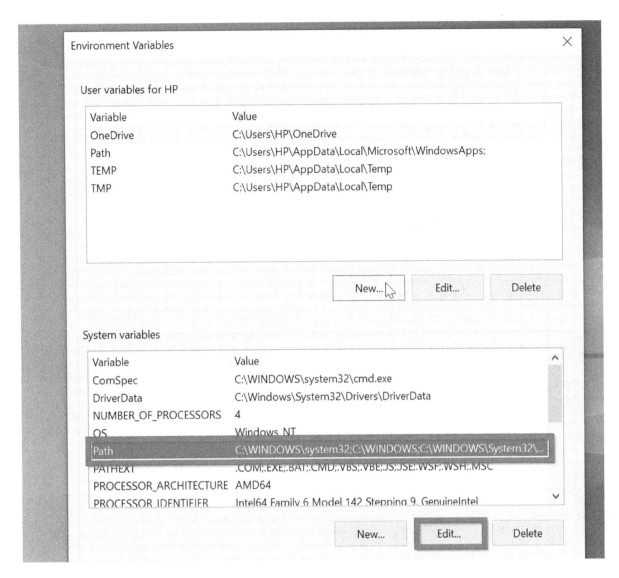

- Finally, confirm that **%systemroot%\system32** is on the list. If it is not, click **New** and add it to the list.

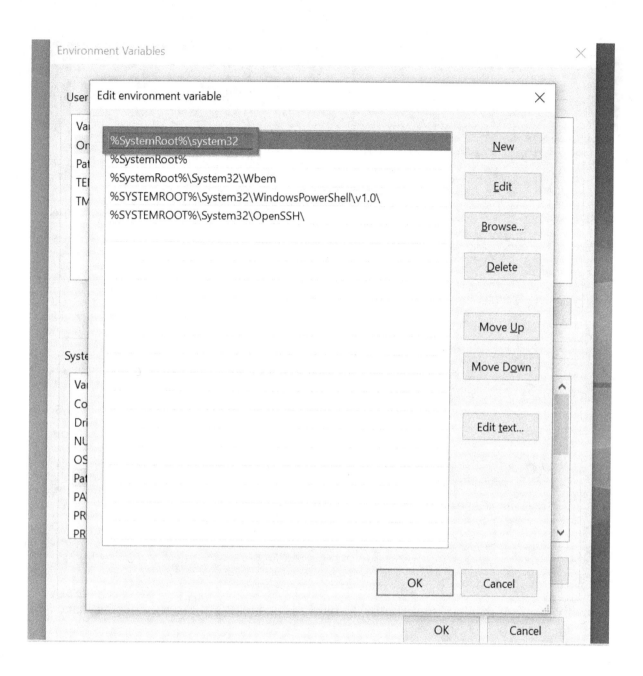

Step 3: Run DISM and SFC Commands

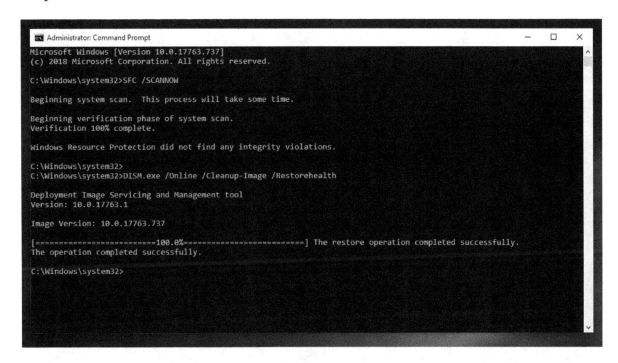

Perform the task in this section if the program that returned "not recognized as an internal or external command" is not in **%systemroot%\system32** and the program is a Windows program.

- Type **cmd** into the search bar. Then click **Run as administrator**.

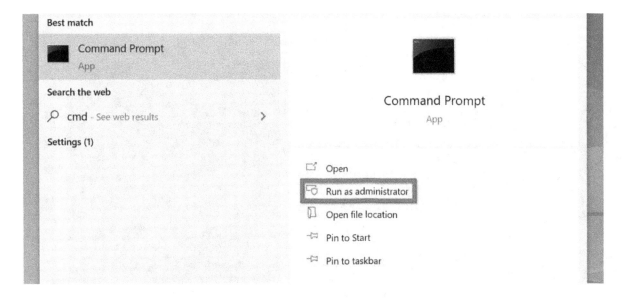

- At the **User Account Control** confirmation, click **Yes**.

369

- At command prompt, type this command and press enter. Wait for SFC to finish and report back...

SFC /SCANNOW

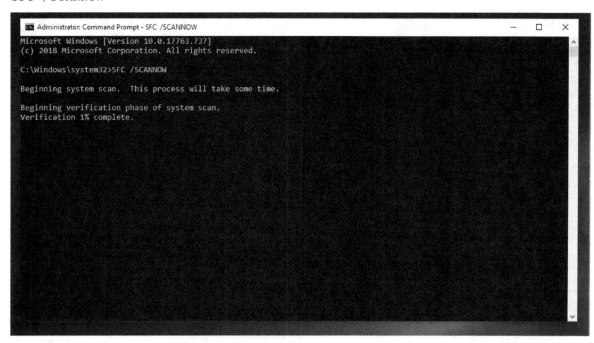

- When the SFC command completes, it may report that "Windows Resource Protection did not find any integrity violation".
- Or that it found and replaced corrupt file. It may also report that it found corrupt files but could not fix the problem.

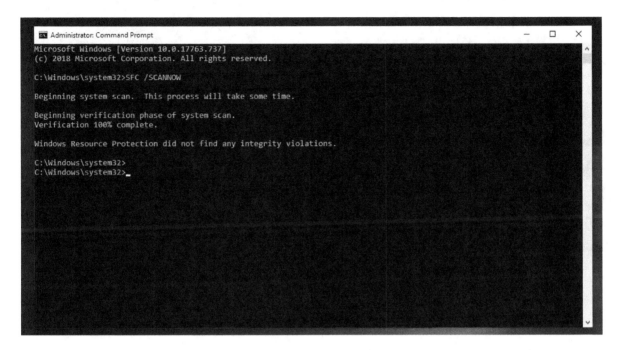

- If SFC reports that it did not find integrity violations or that it found but could not fix it, type the command below. Then press enter.

```
DISM.exe /Online /Cleanup-Image /Restorehealth
```

Wait for the command to finish then restart your computer.

- When the command completes successfully (gets to 100%), restart your PC and check.

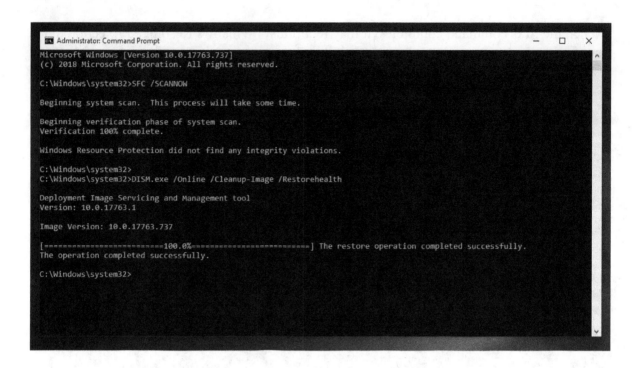

How to Fix Black Screen in Windows 10

Sometimes, when you log in to Windows 10 your desktop will display a black screen. This guide offers 4 methods to fix black screen problem in Windows 10.

Here are the 4 methods discussed in this guide:

1. Kill the Windows Audio Service
2. Add "NT AUTHORITY\INTERACTIVE" Account to the Local "Users" Group
3. Turn UAC (User Account Control) Off
4. Disable the 'AppReadiness' Service

Due to the unique problem presented by the issue this guide is set to fix, the steps use keyboard shortcuts.

Method 1: Kill the Windows Audio Service

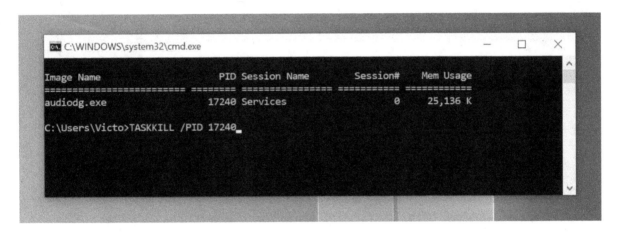

To fix black screen problem in Windows 10 with this method follow the steps below:

- Login to Windows 10 and press the **Windows logo + R** on your keyboard. The *run* command will open.

- At the RUN command, Type *CMD* and click OK.

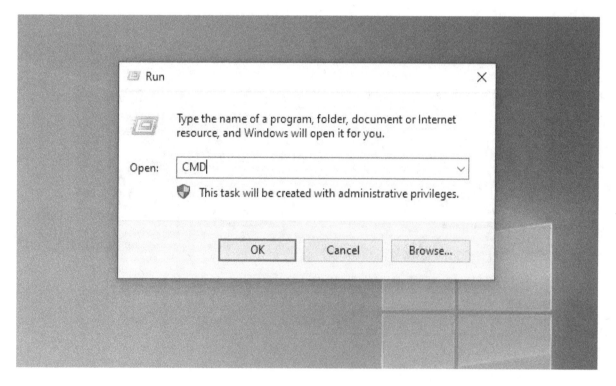

- Then on the command prompt, type the command below and press Enter.

```
TASKLIST /FI "ImageName eq audiodg.exe"
```

The command returns the task details of the **Windows Audio** Service on your PC. Note the PID. In this example, the PID of the **Windows Audio** Service on my PC is 17240.

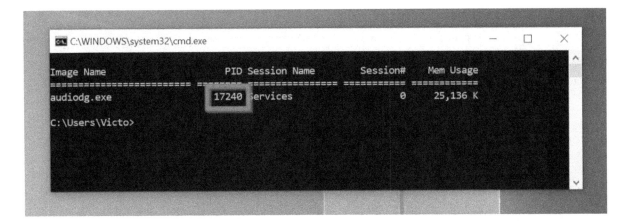

The command may return "INFO: No tasks are running which match the specified criteria.". This means that audio service is NOT running on the PC.

If this is your situation proceed to the second method to fix black screen in Windows 10.

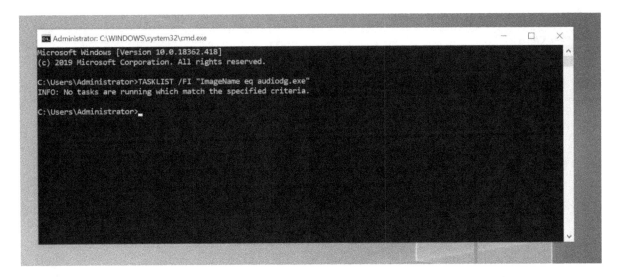

- But, if on the other hand, the command returned a result, to kill the audio service, type the command below. Then press enter key on your keyboard...

```
TASKKILL /PID <audiodg.ex-PID>
```

Replace <audiodg.ex-PID> with the PID from the last command. In my example I used the command below:

```
TASKKILL /PID 17240
```

- Sometimes the above command may return "access denied" error. This may indicate that the logged-in user does not have permission to stop the audio service. In this situation, type a command like this sample command...

```
TASKKILL /PID <audiodg.ex-PID> /U <username> /P <password>
```

Replace **<audiodg.ex-PID>** with the PID from the **TASKLIST /FI "ImageName eq audiodg.exe"** command.

<username> is the user name of a user with administrative privilege.

<password> with the password for the user specified with **<username>**.

If the steps in this first solution do not fix black screen in Windows 10 try the second recommended solution...

Method 2: Add "NT AUTHORITY\INTERACTIVE" Account to the Local "Users" Group

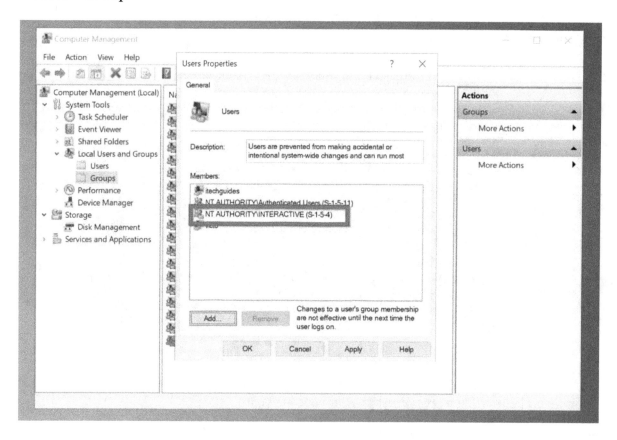

Adding the "NT AUTHORITY\INTERACTIVE" account to the Local "Users" Group may also fix black screen in Windows 10. Here are the steps to try this fix...

- While logged in to Windows 10, press **Windows logo + R** on your keyboard. The *RUN* command will open.

- At Run command, type **compmgmt.msc** and click OK. **Computer Management** MMC will open.

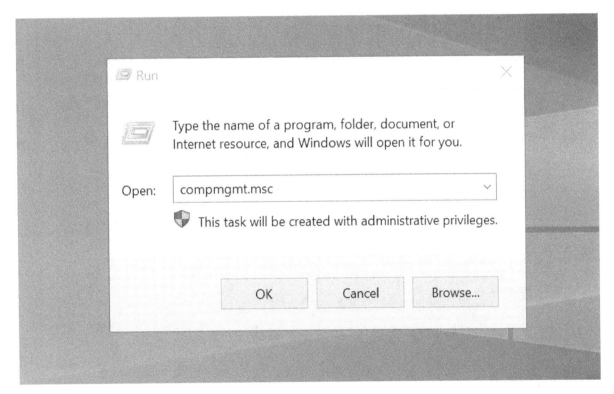

- When **Computer Management** opens, expand **Local Users and Groups** (click the right-pointing arrow).
- Then click on the **Groups** node. Finally, on the details pane, double-click **Users** group.

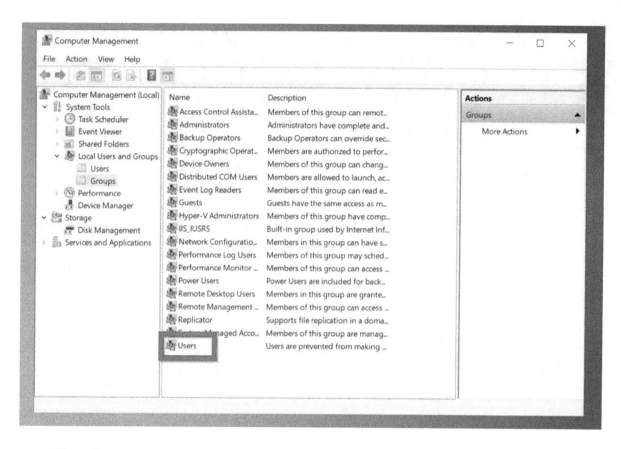

- When **Users** group properties open, click **Add**.

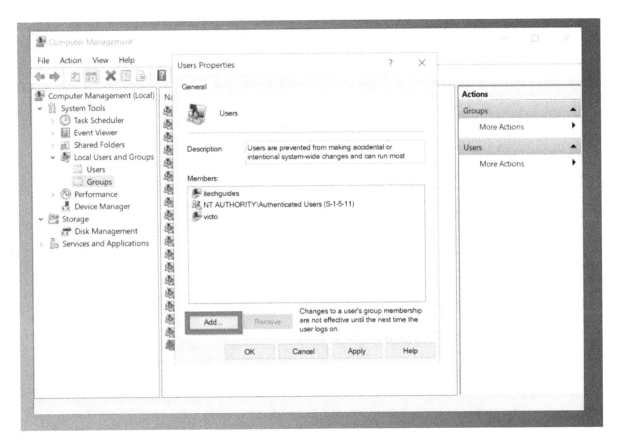

- Then, at the **Select Users** screen, type **INTERACTIVE**. Then click **Check Names**. **INTERACTIVE** should now be underlined. Click OK.

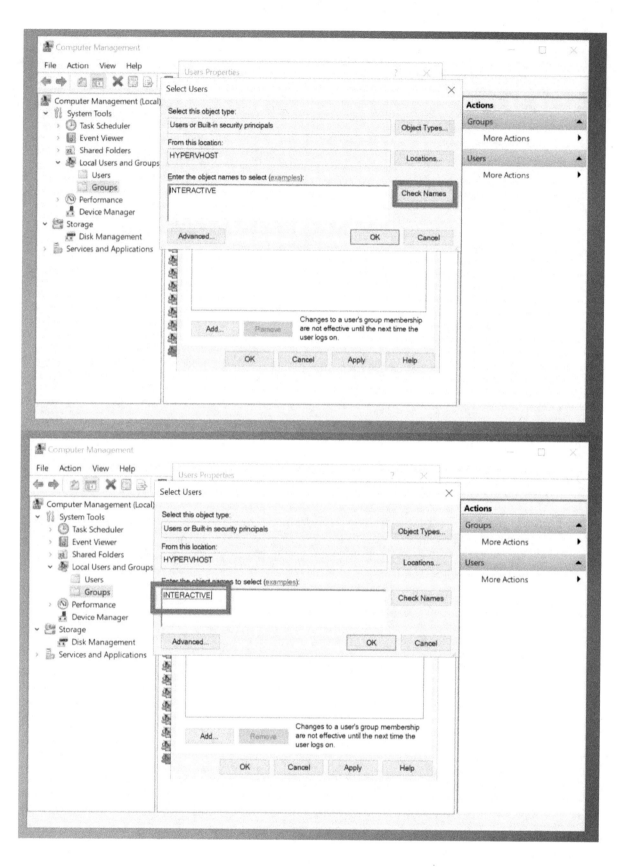

- **NT AUTHORITY\INTERACTIVE** will now be listed as a member of the **Users** group. To save your changes click OK.

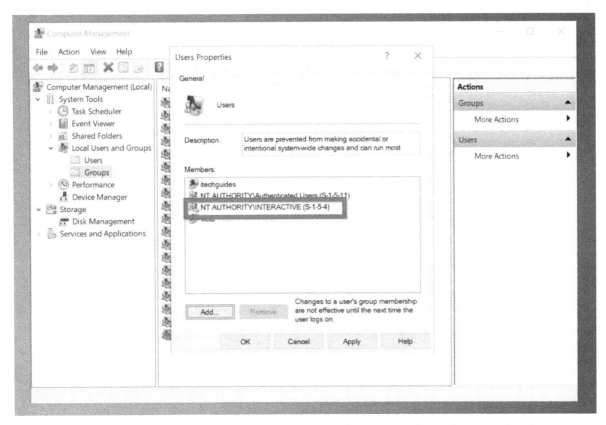

Before you proceed to the next method, restart your computer. Then when you log in to your PC, check whether the black screen problem is resolved. If not, try the fix in method 3.

Method 3: Turn UAC (User Account Control) Off

- Type *user account control* in the search bar. Then, click **Change User Account Control settings.**

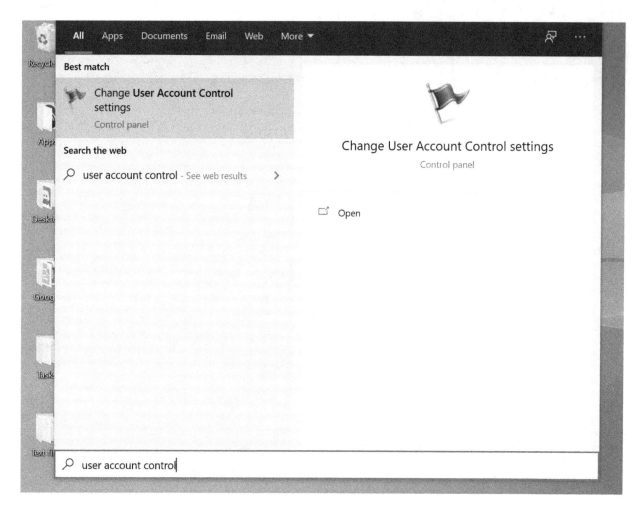

- Move the slider down to **Never notify**.

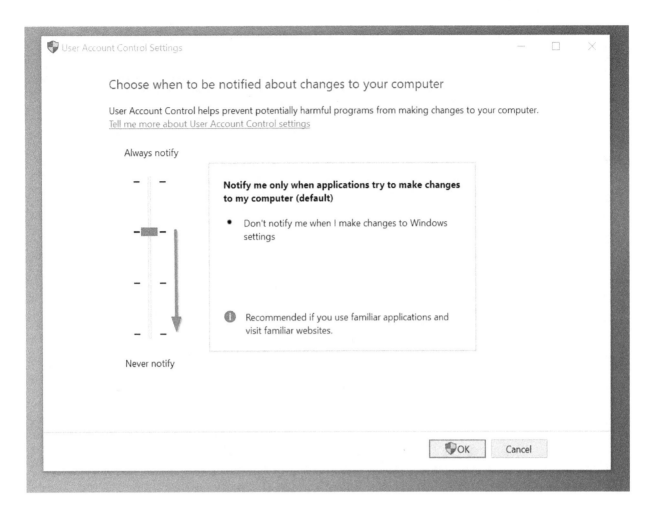

- To save your changes, click OK.

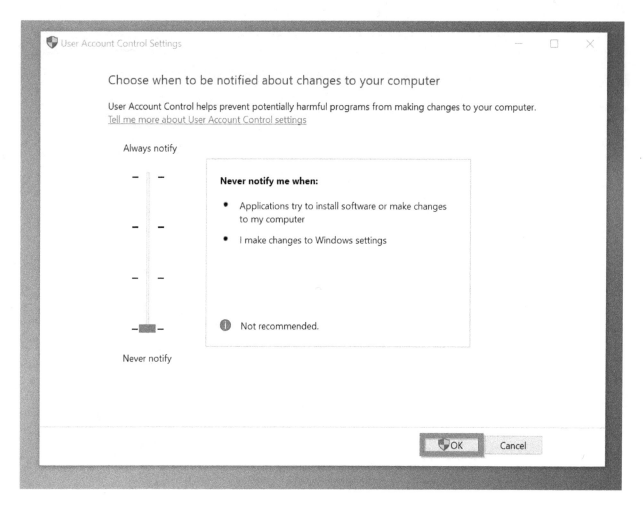

If this does not fix the black screen Windows 10 problem for you, try this...

Method 4: Disable the 'AppReadiness' Service

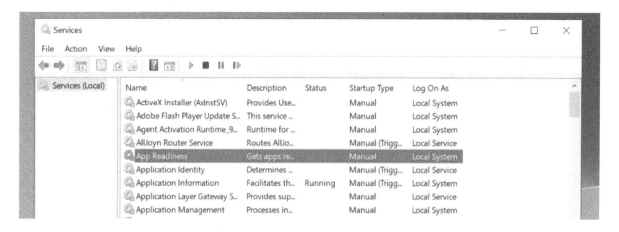

Disabling the 'AppReadiness' Service can also resolve black screen problems. Here are the detailed steps to apply this fix...

- Press the **Windows logo + R** on your keyboard to open RUN command.

- At Run command type **services.msc**. Then click OK.

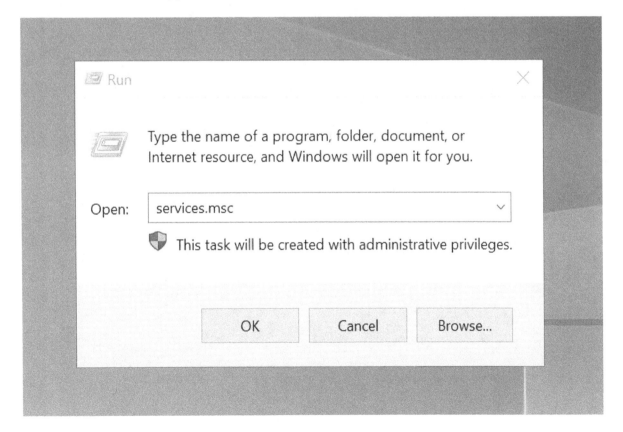

- When Services console opens, double-click **App Readiness** service.

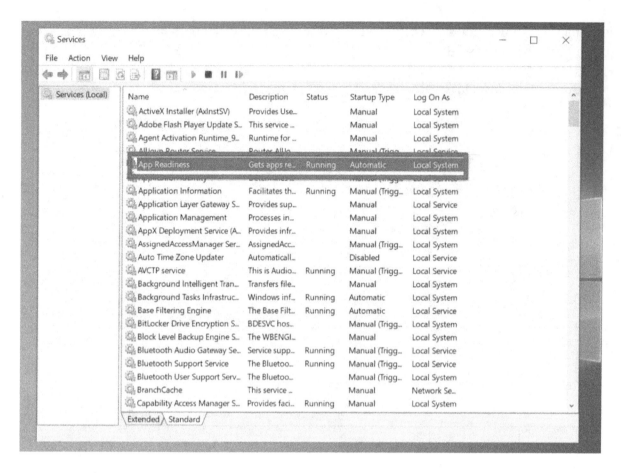

- Then change the **Startup type** to *Manual* and stop the service. Finally, click OK.

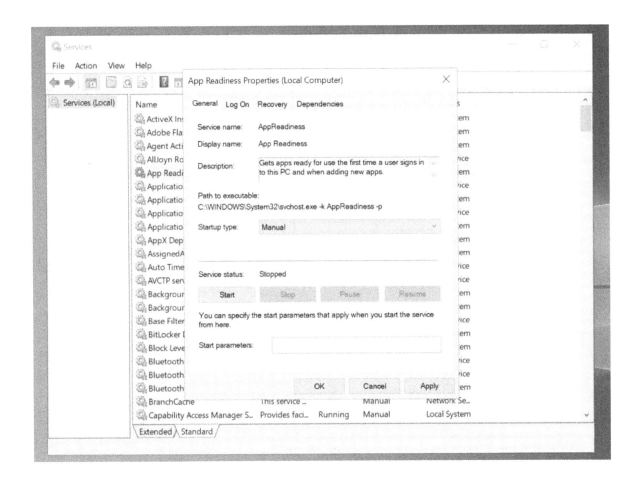

Sign up to my Windows 10 mailing list

Want more useful Windows 10 guides? Visit this link to sign up to Itechguides' Windows 10 mailing list:

Itechguides.com/subscribe-windows-10/